GOOD PARENTS
for HARD TIMES

raising responsible kids in the age of drug use and early sexual activity

*joanne barbara koch &
linda nancy freeman, m.d.*

A Fireside Book
Published by Simon & Schuster
New York London Toronto Sydney Tokyo Singapore

FIRESIDE
Simon & Schuster Building
Rockefeller Center
1230 Avenue of the Americas
New York, New York 10020

FIRESIDE and colophon are registered trademarks
of Simon & Schuster Inc.

Designed by Pei Loi Koay
Manufactured in the United States of America

10 9 8 7 6 5 4 3 2

Library of Congress Cataloging in Publication Data

Koch, Joanne.
  Good parents for hard times / Joanne Barbara Koch & Linda Nancy
Freeman.
      p.   cm.
  "A Fireside book."
  Includes index.
  1. Child rearing—United States. 2. Parenting—United States.
3. Self-respect in children.   I. Freeman, Linda Nancy.   II. Title.
HQ769.K556   1992
649'.1—dc20   92–3331
                                                          CIP

ISBN: 0-671-68800-6

To Ceil Schapiro, mother, grandmother, friend and shining example, and to my wonderful partner in parenting, Lewis Koch, and my children Lisa, Rachel and Josh who taught me volumes about the value of love.

To my parents, Myrtis and James Freeman, and my remarkable grandmother, the late Mrs. Mary D. Andrews, whose encouragement, wisdom, and high expectations have inspired all my achievements.

CONTENTS

THE CHALLENGE OF PARENTING

"**W**hy is the sky blue?"
"Why do dogs bark?"
"Why do people die of AIDS?"

Childhood has changed. Between the ages of five and twelve, most children will (1) be encouraged by peers to try alcohol, (2) hear and see explicit descriptions of sexual intercourse in movies, song lyrics or on cable TV, (3) know at least one person who has died of AIDS, committed suicide or become addicted to either alcohol or drugs.

childhood isn't what it used to be

Childhood is beginning to seem downright grim. In the back of every parent's mind is the realization that one mistake made by their children can be fatal. By the time they have completed their twelfth year, most girls will experience at least the first signs of puberty. For boys, the process of sexual maturation begins a brief two years later. One impulsive sexual encounter with a person with AIDS can lead to death. One "experiment" with highly addictive crack can suddenly pull a young person into committing desperate crimes—a way of life that is a living death. One vehicle accident under the influence of alcohol . . .

Yet childhood, even in these difficult times, is not without hope, especially for the children of caring, informed parents.

a crucial time for building self-esteem

While there is no vaccine to protect children from AIDS, no magic pill to prevent them from trying alcohol and other drugs, there are steps parents can take to protect their children from the risk of premature and unprotected sexual activity, from the risk of anxiously seeking acceptance in the drug culture, from the risk of feeling such little self-worth that life does not seem worth living.

Over the past ten years researchers have been finding certain patterns, certain connections between early sex activity, teenage drug and alcohol use, accidental deaths, suicide and other high risk behavior. These patterns shed new light on parenting.

The dangerous behaviors seem to cluster together. The young person who experiments with alcohol and other drugs also tends to engage in early and unprotected sexual activity. The young person who becomes involved in heavy use of alcohol and other drugs is more likely to take other risks and more likely to attempt suicide.

Behind all these dangerous behaviors lurks something that presents the real, long-term threat to children: low self-esteem. Beginning at birth and throughout infancy and childhood, children develop feelings about their own behavior, beliefs, ideas and decisions. These feelings become more clearly defined during childhood, moving in either a positive or negative direction toward either high self-esteem or low self-esteem.

On any given day a child may feel good or bad, proud or ashamed, confident or uncertain. But gradually during the school years children develop a notion of whether they are valuable, worthy, capable of making a good decision, deserving of love.

Children with high self-esteem are less likely to drink alcohol and use other drugs, less likely to become sexually active in their early teen years and continue sexual activity with many partners. They are less likely to feel hopeless and unloved, less likely to attempt or actually commit suicide. And, since children with high self-esteem are less likely to become involved with drugs and early unprotected sexual activity, they are also less likely to be exposed to AIDS and other sexually transmitted diseases.

Children who have high self-esteem will make mistakes, but they are more likely to learn from their mistakes. They are less likely to be hurt by or even killed by their mistakes. High self-esteem is related to other social skills, including the ability to feel relaxed with oneself and others, knowing how to talk to others and express feelings and thoughts effectively, self-reliance, self-confidence and the ability to handle stress.

High self-esteem and positive social skills do not magically appear as a child grows up. They must be taught. This is not the kind of teaching that can occur in school, though teachers can reinforce, or diminish, a student's self-esteem.

This is the kind of teaching that occurs over time, through the everyday interaction of parents and children. It occurs through gesture and word, through verbal and nonverbal communication, through the arm around the shoulder, the kind word, the rules and limits set firmly but with love.

The roots of self-esteem are "love and limits." Touching, gazing and smiling, satisfying physical and emotional needs—these constitute the language of love. You have already begun to teach your children this language. You have already begun to build their self-esteem.

your golden opportunity

But during the five- through twelve-year-old period, you as a parent have a unique "window of opportunity." Though this age of childhood is no longer the protected, totally innocent era it once was for many children, this period remains a time of unique possibilities and, yes, hope for families seeking to build self-esteem.

The years between five and twelve are prime time for learning, a time when a child can try a new skill without excessive embarrassment. At six any child may try to get the ball in the basket, float and swim, glide out on the ice, toot on a tuba, pull a bow across a violin string, venture a ballet step or jazz dance. At thirteen the same child might be hesitant, worried what his or her friends might think, less willing to risk looking foolish or uncool.

Between the ages of five and twelve a person's capacity for learning expands at a remarkable pace. Children of this age have much improved language mastery and the ability to conceptualize. They can express a good or bad feeling. They can understand why six ounces of milk in a fat glass is still six ounces when it's poured into a tall thin glass. They are beginning to understand and be able to think about not only what is before their eyes but what happened yesterday or last week. Past and present mean something to them. And they are developing that strange, bedeviling, uniquely human feature—a conscience. They are beginning to have a sense of what is right and what is wrong. They are beginning to understand that "intentions" play a part in actions, that the child who intends to hit someone is more in the wrong than the child who accidentally bumps into someone.

new challenges of childhood

Childhood, especially as it is lived in the 1990s, is a period of spending more time away from home. Many children of five have already been at day care, nursery school or prekindergarten, but when they are five or six they spend this time away with a greater capacity for learning. They will be exposed to new values, behaviors and beliefs. They will see other adults who may be quite different from the ones in their own families. If their mothers have not been working outside the home until then, this is a time when the shift is likely to occur. As of 1989, 57 percent of preschool children had mothers working outside the home. For school-age children, the figure jumped to 72 percent.

That means the majority of school-age children cannot expect to find a parent at home when they return from school. They may be returning home to a baby sitter or housekeeper. They may be going to a special after-school program. The traditional type of family, with father working and mother at home, which many of us may have been raised in, is fast disappearing. Only one in ten families follow this pattern. Families in which both parents work or single-parent families are more likely to be the norm. These arrangements accelerate children's involvement with other adults and with other children, and give them less time with parents.

Most parents don't realize how radically their school-age children are changing. Unless they are alerted to the internal development taking place in school-age children, adults may overlook the profound mental, emotional, and moral changes going on just beneath the surface. Though the interior transformation of this period is dramatic, it is more subtle than the transformation of infant into toddler or the sudden growth spurt of the adolescent. In fact the period between six and twelve has often been referred to as "the latency years," the time when few significant changes are occurring, when, in Sigmund Freud's view, sexual energy or libido is under wraps, latent, lying fallow.

Though Freud was writing until his death in 1939, he formulated his most influential theories in turn-of-the-century Vienna. In the interim years, profound shifts have occurred in our views of sex roles and our attitudes toward children. As the twentieth century draws to a close, the world is changing in the direction of foreshortening childhood. Perhaps more importantly, male and female are now being given equal attention. The timetable of girls and women is beginning to get equal consideration with the later maturing pattern of men. Between the ages of nine and thirteen and a half, girls show at least one sign of puberty. (Males show signs of puberty approximately two years later.)

This places most girls beginning puberty, the most profound biological changes of their lives, before the so-called "latency years" are over. In the United States the onset of menstruation, or menarche, ranges from age nine to age twenty, though it is most likely to occur between eleven and fifteen years of age. There is some evidence to show that the onset of adolescence is now somewhat earlier than it was one hundred years ago.

Sex education, if it is going to be helpful and have the effect of preventing unsafe sex, needs to occur well before the first signs of puberty. It needs to come from parents, the only people who can transmit the information in the context of helping a child to feel confident in his or her decisions about sexual behavior.

A schoolteacher or textbook can teach a nine-year-old about menstruation, but only a parent can help a boy or girl to understand that he or she doesn't have to engage in sexual behavior in order to be accepted. A schoolteacher or textbook can teach a child the facts about AIDS and other sexually transmitted diseases. Only a parent can guide a child to feel enough self-worth to say no to unwanted sexual advances from a peer or stranger.

Once upon a time, children were not exposed to alcohol and other drugs until they were well into high school. A 1987 National Survey on Drugs and Drinking conducted by the *Weekly Reader* school publication found that more than one third (36 percent) of all fourth-grade students report having experienced peer pressure to try alcohol.

In today's world, many children of ages nine and ten are actually offered alcohol and other drugs. So by the time they finish fifth grade, many children have to make crucial decisions about drinking and drug use. Though marijuana use among high school students has declined, alcohol use has not. Alcohol is the drug of choice for teenagers, with approximately half of all junior high school students and three out of four high school seniors drinking occasionally. One out of four of these occasional drinkers turns into a problem drinker. Derek Miller, director of a program for adolescents at Chicago's Northwestern Memorial Hospital, estimates that one out of three adolescents uses alcohol and/or other drugs every weekend. A good deal of this drug use begins with experimentation at ages eleven and twelve.

If childhood is a dangerous time, it's also a time rich with possibilities for positive learning. It's a time when a child who has never stood before a group can learn to give a brief talk, take a role in a play, acquire the social skills necessary for making friends and functioning independently. This is a time when children can learn to play on a team. They can understand rules and follow them. They can realize when they have broken the rules and what the penalties will be. Their recently developed ability to understand rules and social conventions makes them ripe for joining the basketball team—or joining a gang. What they do in the coming years with their new social skills will depend to a great extent on what you do during this period.

Your willingness to do things with them—not only to send them off to soccer or skating lessons but to throw the ball in the backyard with them, rehearse the part in the school play with them, talk to them about why they didn't make the team—your involvement and encouragement of their budding skills are essential in the all-important effort of building their self-esteem.

There is one more reason why children of ages five through twelve need your special attention and guidance. Childhood is the last stop before adolescence. For parents who have made some mistakes in the past—and which parent hasn't?—it's another chance to adjust and improve on what we've done as the parents of infants and toddlers. It's a major building block in the series of crucial stages that form a person's sense of identity.

At one time in the past, children were thought of as miniature adults. Have you ever seen one of those eighteenth-century paintings where the little girls at court are wearing décolleté gowns exactly like their mothers'? People living in the 1700s believed that children just had to get larger to become adults. But a group of great thinkers and a new attitude about the importance of the individual changed our way of looking at childhood.

We now have a so-called developmental or "epigenetic" model defined by Erik Erikson, who built on the works of Freud and others. Development is believed to occur in a series of stages, each built upon the previous successfully mastered stage, or stages, and in its own time. So what parents do now prepares a child for success, or failure, in meeting the challenges of adolescence.

Parents do not have a *tabula rasa* or blank slate on which to inscribe their lessons. Each child has already had a certain type of nurturance in infancy and preschool. In most cases, when children reach the age of five or six, they are already primed for successful learning.

the importance of a parent's personal history

Parents also have their personal history, their past experiences, which will influence how they interact with their children. A parent who was sexually abused as a child and has never dealt with that violation may try not to discuss sexual decision making with his or her children. If one considers that as many as one in three women may have had such an experience in childhood, we have a large number of parents feeling conflicted about a subject that is vital to their children's future.

Being able to talk to children about sex may require some type of support system—counseling, guidance and at the very least supportive information. By supportive information, we mean facts presented in a human context.

But it is not only the individuals who were molested as children who have inhibitions about discussing sex with their children. Everyone has a psycho-sexual history. That history harks back to the behavior of one's own parents, the way they taught about sex and how they behaved, as well as the history of one's experiences with sex. Is there any parent alive who has not made at least one mistake in this area?

Taking into account the whole arena—from violations such as incest, sexual abuse, date rape and stranger rape to unwanted pregnancies, divorces, infidelities and just plain stupidity—it's no wonder that parents feel a bit uneasy when they try to transmit "healthy and correct" attitudes about sex. Sex education needs to include accurate facts, but it also needs to be sensitive and supportive. It needs to recognize that sex is a human activity and human beings make mistakes.

Parents also have a history with alcohol and other drugs. If they have not had personal problems with drinking or drugs, including pills and cigarettes, chances are someone in the family has had such a problem. If the problem of alcoholism or other drug addiction is kept in the closet, the child is more likely to develop a similar dependency.

Yet, it's not easy to talk to children about alcohol and other drugs, especially if members of the family have a history of problems in this area. To start this vital process of communication about substance abuse, parents require supportive information, at the very least, and possibly counseling and guidance. Parents who come from families that have successfully advocated abstinence need to be aware of the new pressures that exist for children to drink and try drugs, pressures that may not have existed in their generation.

don't wait to get involved

Too often, parents get involved when problems have reached major proportions. Whether it's teenage alcoholism and drug abuse, teenage pregnancy or teenage suicide, most parents weren't aware and up-to-date when their children were young enough to have averted these tragic consequences. We urge you to weigh your reluctance to discuss problem areas against the vital need for your communication.

We wrote this book to make it as easy and comfortable as possible for you to maintain close contact with your school-age children. Linda Freeman, in her practice as a child psychiatrist, Joanne Koch, in her experiences as a mother of three and a specialist writing on human behavior, have both recognized this common dilemma of American parenting—too little too late.

We say this not to engender guilt. The last thing in the world a parent needs is more guilt. We say this to help you overcome the hurdle of overwork, the obstacle of your own anxieties about saying the right thing or doing the right thing. If you talk to your children with sensitivity, you are doing the right thing. If you need a bit more information and insight, we have tried our best to provide it.

What we offer you is not a textbook or scholarly treatise. It's a friendly guide, sprinkled with information and anecdotes concerning children like yours and people like yourselves. We know you love your children. That's a given. We know you want what's best for them. It may help you to know that everyone who takes parenting seriously worries about how well he or she is doing this most important of all jobs. The simple fact that you have these worries suggests that you've probably been a fine mom or dad up until this point. All we want is for you to hang in there. Continue the loving support, adapting your parenting style to the changing needs of your growing child, but never forgetting that these are still children and they continue to need you.

We also wrote this book because we believe that most parents want to do well by their children, that most parents aren't fully aware of the pressures that exist during childhood. They don't know how early their children will be offered drinks and drugs, how early children will become concerned about how they look and how acceptable they are to their friends. They don't know what an enormous difference a mother and father can make during the school-age years in a child's feelings of self-worth. They don't realize what a major role those feelings will play in making healthy choices during childhood and during adolescence.

We didn't know these things, either, until we started talking to children and parents, examining the research of the past decade and making personal contact with some of the people on the frontiers of investigations into children's self-esteem, childhood depression, AIDS, teenage suicide, family patterns of alcohol and drug use.

the authors' outlook on parenting

Our understanding of childhood emerges from two different perspectives.

joanne's perspective

I've been a working mother most of my life. My three children are grown now, so I've gained perspective on their childhoods. And I was fortunate to have a partner in parenting who shared this great challenge with loving commitment. But the extraordinary demands of meeting the family's needs while continuing to be a productive writer are still very vivid.

Most of my work has been devoted to understanding human behavior, especially in a family context. I've coauthored ten nonfiction books on human behavior, three of them college textbooks on child development and family relations. I wrote the six books in the *Families In Touch Series*, which deals with building self-esteem and preventing alcoholism and other drug abuse, premature sexual activity and sexually transmitted diseases including AIDS. Over one million of these InTouch books are now in use in homes, schools and prevention education programs throughout the country. I'm also the writer of an Emmy Award–winning six-part children's television series, "High Top Tower," which helps children cope with growing up in the nineties. I've written hundreds of newspaper and magazine articles, as well as plays and films, several of them on such family problems as domestic violence, child abuse, and teen pregnancy.

I've experienced my own joys and anxieties in parenting, and I've interviewed hundreds of parents across the country, as well as many therapists and other experts in the field of human behavior. (The experts also make mistakes in parenting, the excellence of their research notwithstanding.)

I've found that parents can provide children with a source of strength and hope that will nourish them through adolescence and throughout their adult lives. Parents can also cause deep scars that will prevent children from leading full and satisfying lives. It's an awesome responsibility. But each set of parents is uniquely capable of making this kind of difference for their children. By and large, I've found that when parents are offered practical suggestions as to what to do along the way, when they are made aware of both the problems their children face and what they can do to help their children, they will make the effort to help. And to the extent that they can overcome their own past family histories and the pressures of their own personal existence, they will succeed. It's a struggle to be sure. But in my opinion, there is no struggle more important.

linda's perspective

I'm a child psychiatrist, holding the Marion E. Kenworthy Chair of Psychiatry at the Columbia University School of Social Work in New York City. I'm recently married and not a parent myself, but I've nurtured many children in my professional capacity. I've treated a wide variety of children and their parents, from many racial, ethnic, and socioeconomic backgrounds, and I've learned about their experiences and the challenges these families confront. I've written several professional articles on childhood depression and led professional and parent seminars on childhood depression, children of alcoholics and the effects of violence on inner-city children. And, as many of you probably have, in adulthood I realized the profound self-affirming influence of my parents and grandmother on my feelings of self-esteem and ability to make good and healthy decisions. I was one of the first black children to integrate an all-white Boston grammar school. Ever since I faced that racial alienation and was able to bridge that cultural gap, I've felt that many other things were doable—including medical school, specializing in child psychiatry . . . and even deep sea diving.

I see children every day, both as a consulting child psychiatrist, and in my various research projects. I have often thought to myself, "If only I could have spoken to their parents a year or two ago. If they could have realized how their gestures of love and affection might have changed this child's state of mind, how sharing their time and telling this child honestly how they felt might have given that child an entirely new outlook . . ."

I'm the editor of the *Families In Touch Series*. After doing this prevention series, Joanne and I realized that we could collaborate on a book for parents and create the "what if" opportunity. The book would give me the chance to talk to parents before their children needed to come to my office. I could get those families to come for help before the children had gotten too far off the developmental track. Joanne and I realized that we could deliver some good news for parents, some advice that could come in time to prevent serious problems in the teenage years. Here was our opportunity. And we seized it.

you are the final authority

In the pages that follow, we will be offering information culled from our many years of research and experience. Occasionally, we will offer an anecdote or example from our personal or professional lives. But we do this with the utmost respect for the difficult job you have as a parent. And we urge you, always, to filter our advice and insights through your own knowledge and experience. For you are the best and last expert on your own child.

We feel strongly that every parent has what it takes to build his or her children's self-esteem. We also firmly believe that the education a parent can give about sex, drugs and sexually transmitted diseases, including AIDS, is more valuable to a child than any other form of sex or drug education. We have tried to open the door to parents, encouraging them to adapt this information to their own values, their own spiritual or specific religious beliefs.

We don't regard parenting and the vital job of building self-esteem as an easy job. We'll offer many suggestions along the way for additional resources that may help you with specific information or counseling.

We know these are not easy times in which to bring up children. Yet we also know that—with a little help—you can become a good parent for these hard times.

2
PARENTING: THE MIRROR AND THE LAMP

parents as reflectors and guides

An infant gazes at her parent. The parent gazes back at the child. But the parent is not just a mirror of the child. The parent is a mirror and a lamp.* The parent mirrors or reflects what the child has done, but then the parent adds something new to the child's repertory. As a parent you've done this a hundred times. Almost unconsciously, you've imitated your baby's face, gestures or mood—scrunching up your own face, changing your voice and your manner of speech to reflect what the baby has just done. And then, without giving it a thought, you've guided your child. You've flooded the child's world with light and shown that child a new word, a new thought, a new gesture.

As a parent, you may have gazed back and smiled, gazed back and vocalized, gazed back and touched. Research shows that either member of the pair gazing at the other increases the probability of the partner gazing back. So from the very beginning, parent and child are drawn to each other and drawn to this magnetic interaction designed to transmit to the child smiling, talking, touching and a myriad of social skills.

The mirror and lamp activity teach the child to regulate and

---

* M. H. Abrams applied this concept to literature in his book *The Mirror and the Lamp*, W. W. Norton, New York, 1958.

modulate behavior. The child cries. The parent comes, picks up the child, asks "Is my baby sad?" and even mirrors in his or her face some of the discomfort the child feels. But then the parent calms and soothes the child so that the discomfort dissipates. Hundreds of such interactions—along with the child's maturing mind and body—allow the child to learn a degree of self-control. The parent regulates the child's behavior but little by little the child internalizes these regulations.

This special reciprocity is the basis for later feelings of self-control, self-confidence and self-esteem. The person who learns to regulate or modulate his or her behavior to fit the social situation is more likely to feel good about himself or herself and more likely to gain social acceptance.

You may be surprised, as you look back, at how important you've been to your child up until this point. Here you have taught your child all the basic skills he or she needs to function in the world—you did it, not the experts, not your pediatrician, not your more experienced parents and in-laws. You were your child's first and best teacher.

the importance of continuing give and take between parent and child

While you may not have been aware of this back and forth, mirror and lamp reciprocity as it was happening, you knew when your children were born that you were essential to them. You continued to feel essential to your children as they became toddlers and on into the early preschool years of childhood. You may be surprised to find out that even during the school years of childhood, you continue to be their best and most significant teacher.

It's less obvious to parents that children of five or eight or even eleven require this involvement. They tend to believe that school-age children depend upon peers for reciprocity, that whether they like it or not, peers will supply the mirror and the lamp.

Yet research shows that children do not automatically depend upon peers to tell them what's good and what's bad, what's important and what's not. The dependence on peers for this so-called "value orientation" occurs primarily among youths whose parents are uninvolved, inattentive and unsympathetic toward their children.

Even the attitudes and practices that children pick up concerning use of alcohol and other drugs come *first* from parents and then from peers. According to research conducted in the eighties, if children have poor relations with parents, feel low self-esteem, little sense of social responsibility and a lack of commitment to religious or social values, they will try to fill the vacuum with acceptance by friends.

Children look first to parents to be the mirror and the lamp—to mirror their concerns and shed light on what they should do. Only when that parental mirror and lamp are not available will they seek that guidance from children their own age. Peers generally want to be imitated or mirrored, often to shore up their own uncertain self-esteem.

Peers are not equipped to provide the lamp that brightens the way for the next step in development. A peer involved in the drug culture wants to be imitated, but has no concern for the consequences of this imitation.

It may seem like a paradox, but if a parent wants a child to become independent, the parent needs to remain highly involved with the child. It is the high levels of parent and child involvement, rather than permissiveness or overprotectiveness, that develop social skills and ultimately help a child to function successfully and independently. Involvement leads to independence. Indifference or permissiveness impairs independence.

Though it takes much more effort for a parent to set limits and be consistent, especially when a child is resistant and angry, in the long run these limits will be internalized and the child will function independently. All parents want their children to love them, but children don't always like the limits that must be set. Parents have to withstand this temporary disaffection.

Let's say a parent comes home from work and regularly tells the child: "Go up and do your homework." The child is in his room for two hours each night supposedly doing homework. Yet before the semester ends the parent is called in by the teacher who claims the child is doing very poorly in school. The parent has to intervene, take the boy out of his room, ask to see his homework, help him if necessary. Whether the child admits it or not, he will probably be gratified by the attention.

However, the parent shouldn't do the homework for the child. Somewhere between the casual instruction to "Go up and do your homework," and the actual doing of that homework for the child is the vast middle ground of concerned supervision, the type of guidance that makes room for interest and encouragement. You might say, "Yes, I had a little trouble with math, too." (That's the mirroring part. The child is not alone with his or her discomfort. You have felt the same way.)

"But later on I was glad I had stuck with it." (The lamp part—even though you're having trouble now, it's worthwhile to continue your efforts. The lighting of the way might continue, whereby you show the child that the subject that seems so remote and unrelated to his or her life, actually is connected to it.) "Sometimes science seems to have nothing to do with our everyday life, yet the pencil we write with is filled with molecules. We only stay in our seats rather than flying off into space because of gravity. And we have all these scientists like Louis Pasteur and Jonas Salk to thank for helping us stay healthy enough to sit and complain about homework."

Think of yourself engaged in an arduous task—say, the preparation of your income tax forms. Sometimes a word of support, humor or encouragement is what we need to persevere and finish the task. Your children need at least that much from you.

A therapist in Beverly Hills who treats children of movie stars is often hired to help these kids with their homework. The fact is, their own parents haven't found time. The therapist's help is not as valued by the children as the help they might have gotten from their own mother or father. It's important to use therapists and special experts when necessary, but they are not meant to substitute for daily parental interaction. Buying your way out of involvement with your own children is not the answer. Carve out the time now to be with your child. Your involvement during the years from five to twelve will have benefits during adolescence and beyond.

If you're concerned that you aren't smart enough, or educated enough, to be helpful to your children, you're wrong. It's not the specific knowledge that you share that spurs them on. It's the feeling you convey that what they do is important to you. When she was a teenager, Joanne's mother had to leave high school after one year to support her family. Yet she always took a lively interest in what Joanne was learning. Sometimes it was the sharing of a school experience. Sometimes it was the wish that she could have finished high school and gone to college. And sometimes it was the way in which the things she learned in grammar school continued to help her throughout life—things like basic rules of English usage—she always seemed to know them better than most television commentators, like when to use "I" and when to use "me." It wasn't what her mother said that made Joanne want to excel in school and become a writer. It was her encouragement and concern that counted.

making parenting a priority

Parents may be happy to learn that they continue to be needed throughout childhood and into adolescence. On the other hand, such news may create anxiety for overburdened parents. Parents today actually have less time for their children. Compared to 1960, adults in households with children have ten to twelve fewer hours available each week to spend with their children. Stanford University economists Victor Fuchs and Diane Reklis, who evaluated the status of children in this country between 1960 and 1990, found the lack of time for children to be only one of many signs of trouble and decline. They found that economic necessity, including diminished opportunities for young husbands and the prevalence of divorce, has forced a majority of young mothers to work outside the home.* Fifty-two percent of mothers of babies less than one year old work, according to the Bureau of Labor Statistics. Among parents with school-age children (five through twelve), the figure is 72 percent. That means nearly three out of four mothers of school-age children are working outside the home.

Whether mothers are married, unmarried or divorced, they are usually the ones responsible for arranging child care, making sure children get to after-school activities, helping them with

*Victor Fuchs and Diane Reklis, "America's Children: Economic Perspectives and Policy Options," *Science*, Volume 255, January 3, 1992, pp. 41-43.

their homework. Gradually, many fathers are taking on a greater share of these responsibilities. They are experiencing that sense of being overburdened that mothers have felt for years.

These parenting pressures plus the economic pressures of maintaining jobs or advancing in their careers can create tremendous stress. It's difficult to make parenting a priority, since the rewards of parenting come long after the time and energy have been invested. While the effort is being made, parents get few incentives.

In tribal communities, mothers had communal support for mothering. John Bowlby, who has made a lifelong study of parent-child attachment, notes that earlier communities encouraged mothers to form bonds of attachment to their children. However, in our postindustrial world, mothers and fathers often feel isolated in what they see as a formidable challenge—the challenge of being a good parent in these very hard times.

We have the modern advantages of books and videos and experts on TV talk shows, but given our crowded, stressful lives, we are very likely to repeat old patterns. We are very likely to rear children as we have been reared—whether or not we regard that pattern as desirable, or appropriate for today's world.

We need to consider our own past and decide whether it should be emulated. If we don't take active steps toward change, those old patterns will be repeated. This is why teen pregnancy, substance abuse and child abuse tend to show up in one generation after another. It's also why characteristic patterns of parents—such as inducing guilt, being overprotective, demeaning or domineering—are also repeated. If we want to make some changes, we have to recognize that learning new ways of dealing with children will require patience, time and self-acceptance.

Working mothers do not have to fear doing irreparable harm to their children. Kids are resilient. But special accommodations will have to be made to make parenting a priority. If a person has to go to the office on Saturday when he promised to be with one of his children, couldn't the child be taken along? If an emergency meeting comes up, couldn't another evening that might have been a night for bowling or movies (or yes, some much needed rest) become a family night?

Once in a while a difficult choice has to be made between spending time with children and meeting other career and social obligations. A few years ago, Joanne was offered, on short notice, an opportunity to appear on an early morning TV show to publicize one of her books. But the invitation came a day before her son was to be inducted into the Freshman Honor Society. She had promised to be there at the special breakfast for the occasion, when her son accepted this honor. The author chose to be there for her son, perhaps not a wise career choice, but she received more satisfaction from that grateful audience of one, than she would have from the audience of millions on TV. Working parents can't attend all their children's functions, but realizing that their involvement is vital to their children may help them to find periods of time when they can give them their undivided attention.

It's difficult to enhance children's self-esteem if our own feelings of self-worth are low. We may have to build a support network of family, friends and professionals to help with the tasks of parenting, and to enhance our own self-esteem before we are capable of bolstering the self-esteem of our children. Fortunately, such support is available. Parent support groups, special groups for families dealing with problems of alcohol and substance abuse, mental health agencies, church- or synagogue-related services—these resources proliferate daily. Some of the national self-help and family support networks are listed in the appendices at the end of this book.

Though we tend to repeat the patterns of the previous generation—especially as they relate to love, discipline and sexuality—we are capable of learning. We are capable of fulfilling the special needs of children of this generation.

Let's look in more detail at those special needs and how we can fulfill them.

School-age Children and the Question, ''Who Am I?''

Between the ages of five and twelve, children don't seem to change much physically, not until they go through puberty. Puberty may occur before age twelve, but the majority of school-age children between five and twelve simply get taller and proportionately heavier. Their outward appearance does not alter radically. The external changes of the school-age years are gradual. But very important internal changes are taking place having to do with how a child sees the world and how a child feels about his or her self.

Children of seven and eight, for example, are just beginning to learn to multiply and divide. They are just beginning to understand that things aren't always what they appear to be. A half cup (four ounces) of juice that fills a tall thin glass isn't a whole cup (eight ounces). A whole cup of juice (eight ounces) that only fills half of a large glass isn't a half cup (four ounces). This mental ability to understand that a quantity can remain the same though the containers may differ is called conservation.

In their social interactions, children are just beginning to distinguish illusion from reality. They are just beginning to learn when someone is lying and when he or she is telling the truth. As these social and cognitive abilities mature, the child's world becomes a bit less egocentric. A four-year-old sees the world as revolving around herself. But as children move into kindergarten, first and second grade, they begin to see themselves in relation to other children. Children begin to form opinions about themselves. During the years between age five and age twelve, children decide

  if they are smart or stupid
  if they are popular or unpopular
  if they are athletic or clumsy
  if they are bullies or victims, leaders or followers
  if they are pretty or ugly or just okay
  if it's good to be who they are
  if they can say "no" when they want to
  if they will be influenced by some peers to smoke, drink, or
    take drugs
  if they will follow suggestions of ads to drink or smoke

You are still their most important teacher. As children move into the wider world of school and after-school activities, they have many other "models" of behavior, many other teachers. Your children will be learning from schoolteachers, from children they meet, from adults they see on television and in movies. But the messages you provide, by what you do and what you say, by your love and your example, are still the most important lessons.

the most effective mode of parenting

The mode of parenting that seems most likely to produce children with high self-esteem is an authoritative, rather than an authoritarian, style. The crucial difference in these two styles is open communication. The authoritarian parent simply lays down the law. The authoritative parent is willing to listen and be responsive to the child's point of view. The permissive parent doesn't communicate but simply lets the child do as he or she pleases.

The parent must be a mirror and a lamp. The parent must be a sounding board and a source of enlightenment and guidance. Harsh authoritarian parents, as well as laissez-faire permissive parents, fail to mirror children's concerns and fail to shed light for them. Both the parent who says, "Do as you please," and the parent who says, "Do only as *I* please," are failing to engage in the type of reciprocal interaction that will ultimately enable children to make good decisions on their own. What parents need to develop with their children is a system of co-regulation. The parent sets the rules and regulations but gradually gives the child opportunities to regulate his or her own actions. With this foundation laid in childhood, the child matures and eventually is able to regulate his or her own behavior according to values learned from parents.

love and limits— the roots of self-esteem

You have already begun to build your child's self-esteem by love. When your children were babies, you touched and comforted them, smiled at, gazed at, and talked to them. You cared for their physical needs—feeding them when they were hungry, changing them when they were wet or dirty. And you cared for their emotional needs—cuddling them when they cried, showing them lots of affection. You also put them to bed when they were tired, even if they whimpered about it.

When your children were toddlers, you continued to give them lots of love, but you also had to set limits. You started to make some simple rules. You had to say "no" if they were about to hurt themselves or break something.

When your children were four or five, you continued to give them your hugs and kisses, adding praise when they did something good or tried to do something good. You added guidance, teaching them some simple tasks and skills, answering their endless questions. You continued to set limits. Your limits or rules included a reason. You showed respect for their feelings and their intelligence. Perhaps you kneeled down to their level while you explained why they couldn't hit another child, or grab all the toys.

As your children mature from kindergarten through grade school, *you need to continue to show your love.* You need to spend time with them. School-age children might not want you to kiss them and hug them in public. That doesn't mean you can't kiss them and hug them at home. They need those hugs and kisses.

They might not want you to do everything for them now, or even with them. That doesn't mean you can't show them what to do and let them try it on their own. They need your encouragement.

School-age children have now made friends of their own. That doesn't mean they don't need you to check out those friends to make sure they're nice kids. Get to know your children's friends. Let your children know if you're concerned about their friends and why. Talk to them about selecting friends.

Your children might be busy during the week, as you probably are. That doesn't mean they wouldn't welcome a family outing, a basketball lesson, a chance to make popcorn or cookies with you, a time to talk to you. When you think about managing your time, be sure to manage these easy to overlook but vital moments.

You will gradually stimulate children's independence, not by doing for them what they can do for themselves, but by encouraging them to do these things on their own. And, when they succeed, congratulate them.

This process of encouraging self-reliance and gradually letting go is symbolized in our experience by the changes over time in the Halloween ritual. When children are very young, a parent naturally must accompany them on their trick or treat rounds. When they are a bit older, the parent is likely to walk behind, just to make sure they do not encounter any danger. But then the time comes when Mom or Dad gives the warning about what to eat and what not to eat, and carves out the boundaries of which houses to approach, but the children are on their own. In some communities it may never be safe to engage in independent trick or treating. But even in more dangerous neighborhoods, there are other opportunities to gradually grant independence.

The divorce situation complicates this gradual process of letting go. The custodial parent may wish to shield the child from differences and difficulties with the other parent, but unless these difficulties entail a real danger to the child, this attempt at shielding is not helpful. Your child might return from visiting Dad for the weekend and complain, "Dad doesn't let me do anything myself. I can't watch TV or play without his watching me." It's not helpful for you to say, "You just tell him he has to let you watch TV and play without his hovering." It's best for you to explain, "Dad does things differently, but he may have his reasons. When you're with Dad, you need to follow his instructions, and work out your differences directly with him."

There are many other special considerations that apply to children whose parents have divorced and to children who have lost a parent. We've devoted Chapter 8 to helping your children survive divorce or the death of a loved one. Once a parent has allowed for the special period that follows a divorce or the loss of a loved one, the comments that we make about parents and children apply to all children.

Limits or rules and the way you set them are more important than ever. It's hard to see and sometimes hard to notice, but your child is developing a different way of looking at the world. Children of this age are developing a sense of right and wrong. They are beginning to understand that intentions are important.

Did they break something in the house? Now it's not as easy to deal with as it was when they were four. Now you have to find out how it was broken. What were their intentions? Was it an accident? Or were they trying to do something wrong?

For example, Mom comes home and finds her perfume bottle broken. Was the child alone and trying to use some of the perfume that Mommy uses? Is there a rule about going in Mom's bedroom? Was the child with another child who was trying to take the perfume? This is a wonderful opportunity to let your child know about the limits in your house, about sharing and respecting other people's property, about stealing and telling the truth. You can set your limits with love.

Here's a sample dialogue to give you the idea.

PARENT: How did this happen?
CHILD: I just wanted to see how it squirted.
PARENT: Did your friend want to see?
CHILD: (Silence.)
PARENT: Was it your idea, or your friend's idea?
CHILD: (Silence.)
PARENT: I noticed your friend smelled a lot from perfume when I walked in. I noticed my pretty comb is missing. Do you think your friend might have wanted it?
CHILD: (Silence.)
PARENT: You're getting older, so you want to try things that I use. But you have to ask permission. Even if you hadn't broken the bottle, it wouldn't be right to take my things without asking.
CHILD: We each took a squirt, but then Dana wanted to take the bottle home and I said no and we kind of fought about it and, I'm really sorry. I know Daddy got that for you. It was so pretty.
PARENT: I believe you're sorry. Do you believe your friend is sorry?
CHILD: I didn't know she was taking your comb.
PARENT: I want you to have friends over. But I don't want you to be with people who steal.
CHILD: But Dana is popular. She's on our soccer team.
PARENT: You can play soccer with her. But you can't have her over.

CHILD: I'll give you money for new perfume.
PARENT: I'm glad you told the truth. I'm glad you didn't want to steal. You save your money. And I'll save mine. Then when Christmas comes, maybe we'll each have enough to give each other some perfume.

A similar opportunity presents itself if you find your child has been playing with matches. Say you find a hole in a tablecloth or a piece of furniture, a hole obviously made by a match. You need to find out how this came about, whether the lighting of matches occurred because your child wanted to show off, or because another child encouraged yours to do it. You may learn in your conversation that your child is afraid to say no to this older or more popular child, a person who, in your child's eyes, is more powerful. This may be the first time your child has experimented with something that could be dangerous. Certainly, lighting matches could cause damage and serious consequences.

Situations like these let you find out whether your child might be associating with children who can be harmful. Your handling of the problem can send a clear message: "I'm concerned about your safety. I can't let you break the rules of the house, rules that have a reason behind them. A person who wants you to break those rules, to do harmful things, is not welcome here. That person isn't being a good friend to you."

It's also important not to shift all the responsibility to the friend who was over when the incident occurred. Let your child know that he is responsible for his own actions. Perhaps he was unable to stop the other person from doing the wrong thing, but he doesn't have to participate. Even if your child doesn't admit to participating, it's a good idea to let him know how you feel. "You say that you didn't light any matches—only Fred did. But if you did light them—perhaps because it looked like fun to you—you are responsible. Fred can't take all the blame if you decide to get involved. Remember, you can decide what to do. You can make a choice."

Letting your children know that they have the power to choose is very important. You can let them know this by reminding them when they make a poor choice—or when they choose to let someone lead them to do the wrong thing. You can also let children know when they have made the right choice. Let's say your child reports that everyone in the school was teasing the new kid in second grade, but your child wouldn't do it. Let her know that you're glad she chose not to do something hurtful. Choosing not to join the bullies is difficult. You're glad she made that choice.

One punishment that is not effective is to turn your back on the child for the wrongdoing—put him or her in the doghouse of indifference. Ignoring children, rather than making clear how you feel about their actions, doesn't shed light for them. It puts them in the dark as to how to behave next time. They know they did something wrong, but they have only guilt to guide them, and feelings of shame. Instead, they need the light that you can provide. They need to find out what they did wrong, why it was wrong and what the consequences are, along with a hopeful indication that you expect them to make the right choice next time. Perhaps you never made a clear rule about lighting matches, taking money for treats when you're not home, trying on your clothes or using your things. Your child's mistake presents an opportunity to make these rules clear.

Limits are necessary. Loving limits will help build self-esteem. Rules set now will help your children later on to say "no"—to drugs and liquor and unwanted sex. They will teach your children to make those limits part of their own behavior—the way they might make your gestures or taste in food part of their behavior. Later, they'll be able to set limits for themselves, even when you're not around.

If you don't set limits now, your children will keep pushing to find out, "When have I gone too far?" If you fail to pay attention when they break rules now, they may break more important rules later. Many teenagers actually take drugs to get their parents' attention. Many teenagers actually have babies to find out: "Do they really care?" Start today to set loving limits.

Limits should be set with love. As children mature, they become capable of making more serious mistakes. The bigger the mistake, the angrier you may feel. In fact, you may feel justified in unleashing a significant dose of anger. If you come home and find something broken or burned or missing, you have a right to feel anger. You might feel like lashing out, hitting your child, giving the child an extremely harsh punishment. Since we tend to repeat what we experienced at the hands of our own parents, if we experienced harsh discipline, we become even more likely to mete out harsh discipline to our own children.

But stop and think. Your child's mistake is your chance to teach that child. If you are overly harsh, or use a beating as the punishment, you will injure your child's self-esteem. Psychological and physical abuse, comments and actions that victimize a child, lead to feelings of humiliation, resentment and rage. By beating a child, you will teach your child that hitting and aggression are the ways to deal with a problem. Later on, the child may show that same kind of aggression toward you, or toward siblings, classmates and teachers.

Children do what parents do—not what parents say. If you can't control your anger, if you use abusive words or physical punishment, your children will eventually do the same—even if you tell them hitting and swearing are wrong.

Give a punishment if it becomes necessary. But explain why you're giving it and let children know you are giving the punishment because they did the wrong thing—not because they are bad or evil. It's what the child did that's wrong, not who he or she is. Focus on the child's actions and let the child know you believe he or she will do the right thing next time.

For a five-year-old who has just grabbed a toy from another child or hit that child, a swift retaliation is necessary. If the action has happened before and there's been a warning, something pleasurable needs to be taken away on the spot. "Nancy, I've told you not to hit in order to get your way. Give the toy back, apologize and say good-bye. We're leaving the playground."

For an older child, removing a privilege is effective. But the rule needs to be clear before a punishment for breaking the rule can work. Say the rule in your house is "Homework must be completed before watching TV." Your ten-year-old son didn't do his homework but he's watching television. No television tomorrow. You find he's failed to do homework all week, he misses the Saturday hockey game and spends the day catching up on his neglected homework. But he doesn't need to hear about his infraction for the rest of the year.

When Lewis was a child, he failed to do his homework and he talked back to the teacher. The teacher had him stay after school for a week, missing basketball practice and writing on the blackboard each afternoon one hundred times: "Smart alecks never win. Recent sad examples, Hitler and Mussolini." Lewis became an investigative reporter finding corruption in places like the public school system. He laughs about the punishment now, but it was foolish and ineffective, because it shamed him without turning his attention to learning. Mussolini and Hitler were not accurate reflections of his wrongdoing. Stating that they were, one hundred times a day, provided no lamp to light the way to better behavior. The punishment engendered anger and resentment, a determination to get back at unjust authorities.

Your children are old enough now to understand what the rules are and why you have them. If your children are getting into trouble, try to find out why. Do your children have enough worthwhile things to do? Are they hanging around with friends who are troublemakers? Are they in need of more love and attention? They may need some new activities to hold their interest. This could be a chance for them to meet new friends and feel better about themselves.

recognizing your child's individuality

Your child is not a lump of clay that you can shape and mold any way you choose. Even at birth, your child already had genes that would determine hair color, color of eyes and skin, whether the child would be male or female, what type of body build he or she would have at maturity.

Children are also born with some traits that will influence whether they are shy or friendly, active or slow-moving, bossy or meek. Remember when your child was a baby? Maybe she cried a lot and you had trouble comforting her. Maybe she was easy to please and liked to be cuddled. These actions express a child's temperament.

From the earliest moments together, parents may feel a compatibility—or sometimes an incompatibility—with a given child's temperament. A child who resists cuddling may seem to be rejecting the parent. A parent with serious doubts about herself or her ability to mother, or his ability to father, may take this behavior very personally and develop an antipathy for the child. A fussy child may be particularly difficult for a short-tempered parent to handle.

In nursery school, other personality traits may have emerged—whether your child was sociable or shy, quick to try new tasks or slower and more methodical. Your child's good and bad experiences also had some effect on his or her behavior.

We can influence some of our children's behavior. We might help them to be more comfortable with other people as they get older—less shy or less aggressive. Yet many things that affect a child's behavior or personality are beyond our control. This child may be the first-born and get more attention from adults—and also take on more responsibility. The child may be the last-born and be treated as "the baby," spending more time with brothers and sisters and not pressured to take on responsibility right away. Your child may be a boy born after several girls, a girl born after several boys or an only child. These differences are bound to affect the child's attitudes. For example, firstborn children and only children generally are pushed to achieve and more likely to feel comfortable with adults. Later-born children receive less pressure from adults and tend to relate more to peers. The point is that each child, even within the same family, has different traits, a different family constellation to fit into and different needs. Each child needs individualized attention.

Recently, one of the authors was speaking to a parent who had two children, one a high achiever, the other just entering a drug rehabilitation program. The father said, "I can't understand it. I always treated those two boys exactly the same." Perhaps that was one of the problems. The younger boy didn't need to be treated exactly the same as his brother. He wasn't the same as his brother. He needed his parents to recognize him as an individual.

Try to be sensitive. Try to know and respect your child as a separate individual. Try not to be constantly comparing your child to another brother and sister or a neighbor child. Some conflict between brothers and sisters or "sibling rivalry" is normal. Try not to take sides in these battles unless a child needs your protection. Try not to pick a favorite. This will just add fuel to the conflict. But if there is an incompatibility of temperament, or too much similarity, there's nothing wrong with admitting this vulnerability. Let's say you and your daughter are both very short-tempered. After a few blowups, it might be helpful to call the similarity to her attention and thus defuse the confrontations. Acknowledging such a stumbling block can clear the air and pave the way to a better relationship.

recognizing your own personal history

Like your child, you have a certain kind of personality. You also have a *personal history with unique life experiences*. You may have had lots of love, or not enough. You may have had parents who were self-centered and spent little time with you. You may have made mistakes that you want to keep secret. You may have had parents who drank too much, or parents who were abusive. You may find yourself doing something your parents did that you didn't like when you were a child. You may find yourself repeating words or actions you hated.

One of the problems all parents face is how to avoid becoming prisoners of their past, how to avoid repeating the mistakes made by their parents. Sometimes it helps to admit that such a struggle is going on.

For example, your child gets angry and breaks a dish. You are about to hit the child. You stop yourself. "Honey, I get so mad when you break things, I feel like hitting you. My mom used to hit me when I did something like that. I'm trying not to hurt you. But it's hard. I'm going to count to ten when I feel that way. When you feel angry enough to break something, I want you to say, I won't do it. I won't do it. I don't have to break this dish. I want to break it, but I won't do it."

You admitted a secret. You told your child you were once beaten. You admitted that you're trying to be more loving. The child can help. Together you can speak the language of love. Together you can build self-esteem.

In the same situation of a child breaking a dish out of anger, you might admit this. "When I was growing up, I got very little attention. No one seemed to care if I broke a dish, failed to take out the dog, forgot to do my homework. Sometimes I'd purposely do something wrong just to see if they'd notice. But they didn't. I don't want to make that mistake. What you do matters to me very much. I'll try not to harp on little things, but I want you to learn to control your anger and frustration when you do a job and to tell me if something is bothering you. That makes a difference to me."

You don't have to tell children all your past mistakes. But you do have to try to help them find out what they need to know. Admitting a few of your earlier mistakes may provide the personal connection that brings the lesson home. Let's say when you were in fifth grade, you and a friend unlocked your parents' liquor cabinet and tried some beer or whiskey. Perhaps later, as a young adult, you went through a period of drinking too much. Now you've stopped drinking. You find your child and a friend have tried wine coolers. This might be the interchange:

PARENT: I saw bottles of wine coolers in the trash.

CHILD: (Silence.)

PARENT: We don't drink wine coolers. I guess you decided to try them.

CHILD: Tommy brought them from his house. They taste like pop. They don't even have that much wine in them.

PARENT: It doesn't take that much wine to make a nine-year-old drunk. It doesn't take that much wine or beer or liquor to make a nine-year-old start drinking and not be able to stop.

CHILD: Come on, we just tried it.

PARENT: I know. I remember when I was in fifth grade and my friend and I thought it would be cool to sneak some samples from my parents' liquor cabinet. I just tried one sip of whiskey and a little bit of beer. I remember it made me dizzy, probably the way you felt this afternoon. In those days we didn't realize how easily people could develop problems with alcohol. Now we know how dangerous it is for kids to drink, even wine coolers, especially when they're your age. I don't want you to learn the hard way. That's why I'm making it a rule in our house. No drinking—not wine coolers or lite beer or anything else that sounds harmless but has alcohol in it. I love you. You're my son. You're a good ——— (student, ballplayer, trumpet player). You could become very good. You can't be the best you can be if you drink."

You let your child know that you made the mistake of trying beer when you were his age, but you didn't recount every mistake you made along the way related to drinking or cigarettes. You made your point and reinforced it with love and concern. You gave him the added incentive that avoiding alcohol would help him accomplish things in life.

If, however, you or your spouse actually has a serious drinking problem, then it's imperative for you to let your child know that Mom or Dad is struggling with this problem, that alcoholism puts the whole family at risk for problems with alcohol. There are a number of excellent resources for alcoholics and children of alcoholics. (Some of them are listed at the end of Chapter 7.)

When it comes to alcoholism, you must let your child know your family is vulnerable to the disease. If your child had diabetes, you would tell that child and let him or her know about avoiding sugar or taking insulin. If you or your spouse or people in your family have faced alcoholism or other drug abuse, your child is at a greater risk.

If you or your spouse suffered from too little attention, or a cloying amount of constant direction and supervision, your child is at risk of suffering from the same parental mistakes. Your awareness, your attempts to avoid these past mistakes, may require you to let your child know what you're concerned about, why you don't want to repeat the dangerous patterns from the previous generation.

Your child needs your extra warning, your limits. If you give these limits in a loving way, your child is old enough to appreciate that, to understand what you've said. Together you are speaking the language of love. Together you are building self-esteem.

involving your child in healthy activities

You don't have to spend a lot of money to give your children confidence. You do have to make time for them and give them lots of encouragement. School-age children can learn to do many things. They can learn to swim. They can learn to play an instrument. They can learn team sports, like basketball and baseball. They can learn to act in a play. They can build simple things. They can prepare simple recipes. They can learn to perform gymnastics, to ice skate, to play tennis or other physical games that require coordination. They can go fishing with you. They can pick blueberries with you or plant a vegetable garden. They can do simple household chores. They can ride bikes and learn songs.

But . . . they need a teacher to help them learn these things. Sometimes you will be the teacher. You will throw the ball and show them how to hold the bat. You will get out the ingredients and show them how to separate the eggs. Sometimes you'll have to take them to a place where they can learn what they need to know—whether it's a library, a gym, a museum, a community center, a skating rink. Sometimes you'll have to take the time to go to their ball game or their recital or their play. Whether or not you are the teacher, your involvement enhances their learning and their self-esteem.

If you have more than one child, you might find it difficult to spend equal time with each of the siblings. A number of things can be done with all the children. But consider the possibility of clearing some separate time for the younger brother or sister, time just for him or her. For example, if your older one has a piano lesson or a Brownie meeting that takes her out of the house for an hour, this might be the perfect time to share an hour with the younger child—an hour at the library, or working on some craft project, or planting an avocado pit that will later blossom.

Sometimes a child's social problems are compounded by indifference at home. Don't let children sit in front of the TV because they're shy, or because they can't make the basketball team. Help them find something they can do and then help them learn to do it well. This is a time to teach your children how to acquire skills, skills that will help them the rest of their life. This is a time to show your children that hard work and practice will help them reach a goal. This is a time to boost your children's confidence with a helping hand or a word of encouragement. With a little help from you, they can feel capable.

why are activities so important now?

During this time your child is still young enough to try new things, to make mistakes without feeling overly embarrassed. Your child is now beginning to learn some answers to the question, "Who am I?" At this age, children don't know yet if they're athletic or creative, if they can write a story or pitch a ball or compose a song.

If they can develop some skills now, they will have higher self-esteem when they hit the rough waters of adolescence. If they can develop a sense of pride in what they do now, they'll be less vulnerable to dropping out later. If they can accept and like themselves now, they'll be less hungry for love and acceptance later, less likely to drink or do drugs, or have sex—just to be loved and accepted.

So leave the TV off for a while and spend time with your child. You have a lot of love to give. You have a lot you can teach your child. Most important, you can teach your children to feel good about themselves.

You can teach your children that effort will help them improve. You can teach your children there are things worth working for. You can teach your children they can achieve some of those things if they try. You still have what they need, because they need the special encouragement that only you can give.

encouragement versus pressure

We all want our children to achieve. We want them to get good grades, to make the team, to get into the band or the school play. But there's a difference between encouragement and pressure. You can encourage children to try out for the team. If they don't make the team, you can either encourage them to try again, after practicing harder, or to try another activity. But you mustn't make your children feel that your love for them depends on whether they make the team. You mustn't make your children feel that your love for them depends on whether they get all A's.

School-age children can experience stress, the way you sometimes feel stress in your life. They might develop a stomachache because of it. They're afraid of disappointing you, but they don't believe they can do the job well enough, so they really get sick—to avoid the game or the math test or the recital.

You can help your children manage the pressures of their everyday life by showing them how you manage stress. If you see they're worried sick about an exam the next day, you can suggest that you do a few minutes of jumping jacks together, plan something pleasant for after the exam or spend a few minutes talking about why they are so anxious. Maybe there's something you don't know.

When her daughter Lisa was in the third grade, Joanne heard her crying in her room. She was trying to write a short poem called a haiku. In fact, she admitted she had fifteen haiku to write all in one night. "Fifteen," her mother asked, "in one night?" "Well," Lisa admitted through her tears, "I was supposed to do one each day." It seems Lisa's teacher had made a contract with her several weeks before. This represented her entire unit. She had procrastinated and left the entire job to the last night. Once the truth was out, Lisa was able to function. Her fifteen haiku were just mediocre, but she learned two ways to reduce stress: (1) tell the truth; (2) plan ahead. The teacher had also made a mistake in this case—expecting that a written contract made weeks before would be enough to ensure that third-grade children would complete the assignment. Joanne could have blamed the problem on the teacher. But are the people who give us work always sensitive to our needs? Telling Lisa that the fault was all the teacher's wouldn't have helped her handle the stress. And Joanne had to resist another temptation— doing Lisa's work for her. No parent likes to see his or her children unhappy. But the temporary sharing or mirroring of your child's unhappiness needs to be followed by lighting the way to actions the child must take. Lisa had to do the work herself as best she could.

Your children are always noticing how you deal with stress. The point is not to hide the tensions of the real world, but to show they can be coped with. It doesn't hurt, if you've had a particularly tense day, to share the experience. "Today, I thought I was going to explode. The boss piled on fifteen assignments that had to be done immediately. It was one of those times I just felt like shouting at him or quitting. Well, first I decided to count to ten. Then I made a date with my friend to go swimming tonight. Swimming really helps me get out some of those tensions. When I'm more relaxed, I can look at all the stuff I have to do and figure out how to handle it. Do you ever feel overwhelmed by your schoolwork, Nancy?"

What decades of self-help groups have taught is the value of hearing that someone else has the same problem you do. Your kids are not immune to the value of this type of sharing. Knowing that Mom or Dad felt anxious and figured out a way to survive the anxiety—a healthy way to survive it—will help your child now and in the years to come. Just as seeing you go right to the liquor cabinet or pop tranquilizers when you're stressed will plant the idea that escape through drugs is the way to manage stress.

enough responsibility, but not too much

Children from five to twelve years can now take on responsibility. They can be given a job or chore and be expected to do it. Maybe it's their job to take out the garbage, put away the groceries, make the salad. Most parents are working outside the home. They need help from their children. But at eight, nine and ten, they are still children. They may not be able to be the babysitter for a younger brother or sister, especially if they are in charge for hours. They may not be able to make the entire dinner.

Give your children a chance to try a new responsibility. Make sure they can handle it before it becomes part of their regular chores. Let them know when they're doing a good job. Give them a chance to tell you if they have more than they can handle.

For example, say your eight-year-old son gets home an hour before you do. Why not suggest, "Tim, it would be great if you could have the table set and the garbage out before I get home. Just seeing those two things done would make me feel that I can deal with cooking dinner. It would be a real help." If Tim doesn't do it, don't forget that you asked. "Tim, remember I asked about the garbage and setting the table? Did you just forget, or is there some reason that you can't do it?" You might find the dishes are too hard to reach. Or Tim is afraid to go out in the alley where the garbage cans are.

Or you might find he'd rather watch TV than take time to do these chores. If it's the latter, let him know that you're counting on him. "I was disappointed when I saw that I had to do everything. I need your help. Can I count on you next time?" And if Tim comes through next time: "Hi, Tim. I was so glad when I saw you had done those few chores. Just seeing that table set—with the hand-picked dandelions in the middle, too—made me feel I had a great helper on my side."

help your child
make healthy choices

Nurturing self-esteem means gradually teaching your child to make healthy choices. A person with high self-esteem feels he or she has a right to choose, the sense to make a good choice, the strength to choose what's best, whether or not others are making the same choice. School-age children will be confronted with a wide array of choices including:

> choices of friends
> choices of television programs
> choices of after-school activities
> choices of positive or pro-social activities, like Brownies, Cub Scouts, helping in a school clothing drive or church bake sale
> choices of antisocial activities, like lighting matches, petty theft, trying a cigarette, breaking a window

Your child is still young enough to be influenced by your values, your opinions.

fears

Between the ages of eight and ten, children's fears change. They used to be afraid of monsters and other imaginary characters. Now they are more likely to be afraid that someone might hurt them or kill them.

Eight-year-olds are beginning to understand cause and effect. They know what circumstances can cause physical injury. They see many examples on television and in movies. They're now more likely to fear getting hurt on the football field or killed in a plane crash than getting kidnapped by the bogeyman.

As children move into a wider world of friends and activities, they also develop fears of the embarrassing social situation—being rejected, being sent to the principal's office, not being picked for a team or a group.

Children's notions concerning death also change as they mature emotionally and intellectually. To five-year-olds, death is a monster. But to nine-year-olds, death is real. It can come from a bodily injury, an illness, an accident. By this time they may have lost a pet or a family member. By ten years of age children begin to understand that all living things die.

At the same time that children's fears take on a more immediate and realistic form, children become more secretive about their fears. They get the idea that they're supposed to be more grown-up now—not to cry as easily, not to admit being frightened. You may have to be particularly sensitive to the way your maturing children are acting. You may have to provide "askable" moments—moments when you are available to them for asking questions. You may have to look for opportunities to bring your children's fears into the open.

Events on the news provide openings to talk about fears of accidents, whether it be news of a plane crash or a sports injury. Some fears can be allayed by talking. Some fears need to be addressed. If your child is extremely frightened of physical injury during sports, maybe the danger could be reduced. Maybe more skill through practice would give him more confidence. Or maybe changing from football to basketball would be wise.

Some fears just need to be talked about. Some require you to take action. A child may feel better simply by letting you know she was embarrassed when the teacher criticized her in class.

If the child's fear is that she has no friends and, in fact, she doesn't, maybe she needs help. The help begins with talking things over. Rejection is a part of being in the outside world. But you can help inoculate your children against the pain of rejection by your own warm support and communication. You might provide further assistance by getting her involved in a nonjudgmental type of social group or class where she's likely to learn some social skills.

If your child is having serious difficulties getting along with friends because of aggressive behavior or extreme shyness, try to get your child some counseling.

When there is a death in the family, that death needs to be

recognized and mourned. The child needs to grieve, even while you reassure the child that life and the world will go on, though someone dear has died.

Children need to be encouraged to talk about their feelings for the person—or the pet—who has died. It helps if they are allowed to participate in the rituals, such as a funeral or religious service, a wake or a period of mourning.

If youngsters who lose a mother or father do not get a chance to express feelings and mourn when the death occurs, that parent can become a ghost who haunts the mind and makes growing up a scary and dangerous process.

Divorce and death are part of many people's childhood experiences. For that reason, we've devoted a special chapter on the handling of divorce and death, and ways to distinguish normal reactions to loss from serious depression (see Chapter 8).

new models including peers

When your child was first born, Mother was his or her primary model of behavior. Gradually, your child's world has expanded—to include Mother and Father, sisters and brothers, grandparents, teachers, other children. Most of these models have been healthy and loving people.

Now that your child is older, he or she will meet and observe still more models—some good, some bad. You can't control everything he or she sees and does, but in the early school years you can still monitor most activities. As your child matures, staying in touch with his or her outside activities becomes more difficult but also more important.

Children now exist in two worlds—the world of family and the world of peers. Your child needs friends and needs to learn how to share activities. By encouraging your child to engage in productive activities, such as sports, music, theater, art classes, cooking classes, you give him or her an opportunity to make good friends. By the time your child is ten or eleven, friendship will involve sharing thoughts and feelings.

Children can be influenced by friends to do good or bad things. They can be encouraged by friends to share and help others, to do so-called "pro-social" things. But by the time your child is ten or eleven, he or she may also be more susceptible to bad influences. A child might be persuaded by peers to engage in antisocial acts—shoplifting, vandalism, experimenting with alcohol or drugs.

It's important that you remain aware of which children your child is spending time with. If you don't approve of something your child's friend does or says, let your child know. If you find a friend up to something dangerous, like vandalism or theft, let your child know that friend is unacceptable. Guide your child away from that so-called "friend."

Try to teach your children how to choose friends. Let them know what you think makes a good friend. Help them develop the confidence to say "no" to a friend who doesn't make them feel good, a friend who doesn't do good things. Encourage them to express feelings about anything that has happened, any time they felt they were forced to do something that didn't feel right.

For example, here's the kind of disturbing event that could easily happen to a seven- or eight-year-old, one that provides an attentive parent with a unique opportunity.

CHILD: Yesterday we saw a dead bird.
PARENT: That's so sad. Sometimes birds fall out of their nest. Sometimes they're killed by cats.
CHILD: Bob pulled its wings off.
PARENT: That seems cruel.
CHILD: He said it was dead and it didn't matter.
PARENT: But you look sad about it. Did it matter to you?
CHILD: I wanted to bury it in a little box. But after he pulled its wings off, I was afraid to touch it. (Child cries.)
PARENT: (comforting child) That's such a cruel thing to do.

It sounds as if Bob wanted to scare you, to show you that he was tough enough to tear off the bird's wings. I don't like people who do things like that. I'm glad you told me about Bob. You don't have to play with Bob. I'm glad you told me about what happened. It's always better to tell when you see something bad. And even if Bob scared you and made you pull the bird's wing, too, it's better if you tell about it.

Next time, you say "No. I don't do that." And you leave the bully or the cruel person. You're strong and smart. You can decide to say no. You can decide to leave.

This is only a brief interchange, but in it the parent mirrors the child's upset, encourages the child to express feelings, encourages the child to choose friends rather than being manipulated by others. The parent provides the lamp, lighting the way for the child to make choices about what activities are acceptable and which ones are cruel or destructive and guides the child away from the destructive influence. This little lesson offered at seven or eight may prevent an episode of sexual abuse or delinquency later. These interactions are the stuff of which self-esteem is made.

SUMMARY

As a parent, you are a mirror for your child, reflecting what the child is feeling, and a lamp for your child, guiding the developing person from the moment of birth to new strengths, new skills and greater maturity. You continue to be a mirror and a lamp as your children enter school and continue through childhood. Your guidance is particularly important in the area of lighting the way to greater self-esteem.

children still need you to build their self-esteem

Self-esteem is feeling good about yourself. Self-esteem is believing you can do things. Self-esteem is believing you can make choices.

all parents can become builders of self-esteem

Parents build self-esteem in children by:

> spending time with their children
> talking with their children
> listening and watching and finding ways to offer support, information, and answers, even when children don't actually ask questions
> respecting their children's feelings
> and encouraging them to share those feelings
> setting clear rules,
> but not being overly harsh with words or punishments
> encouraging achievement,
> but not constantly pressuring their children
> sharing their beliefs and values

and sharing some of what they've learned from their own mistakes and victories

self-esteem can save their lives

Children who feel good about themselves, children who have high self-esteem, are less likely to:

1. drink alcohol
2. use drugs
3. start having sex too early
4. start having babies before marriage or before they are old enough to be responsible parents
5. engage in sex with many partners, sex simply to gain acceptance or unprotected intercourse

   Drugs and sex with many partners increase one's possible exposure to AIDS. Since children with high self-esteem are less likely to use drugs and engage in unsafe sex, they are therefore less likely to be exposed to AIDS and other sexually transmitted diseases.

People who experience high self-esteem as children are less likely to:

1. feel hopeless during adolescence
2. feel unloved as adults
3. attempt or actually commit suicide

self-esteem can make life more satisfying

Children who have high self-esteem are more likely to:

1. do well in school
2. enjoy activities
3. make friends
4. make healthy choices
5. feel they control their lives
6. feel good about their work
7. feel good about their relationships

Children who have high self-esteem will make mistakes, but they are more likely to learn from their mistakes. They are less likely to be hurt by or die from their mistakes.

children do what you do

Your actions are even more important than your words. Sometimes behavior is divided into words, called verbal communication, and actions, called nonverbal communication or body language. We've all encountered people who say, "That's just fine"—yet their body and face convey anger and dissatisfaction. Is there any question as to which you believed—their words or their body language? Chances are you believed what they did more than what they said. That's why the way you answer a child's question—the expression on your face, your gestures, the look in your eyes—is sometimes more important than what your answer is.

Telling an angry child who has just hit a playmate or sibling: "You've got to control yourself!" but showing the body language of rage is not teaching the child self-control. Demonstrating a sensitivity to the child's upset is more important than angrily lecturing on self-control. Putting your arm around a child when you answer a question and giving him or her your full attention may be more important than the answer you give.

The way you set limits—whether you do it with hate and uncontrollable anger in your face and body language or simply with concerned authority, whether you're fair and consistent or scary and unpredictable—these things are more important than what words you say, what punishment you choose. As you respond to peers your children choose, as you encourage them to assume responsibility and handle stress, you can continue the give and take, the special reciprocity that reflects their concerns, yet provides enlightenment to guide them. You can continue to be a mirror and a lamp.

3
CHILDHOOD—A
WINDOW OF OPPORTUNITY

When children reach the age of five or six, a window of opportunity opens for their parents, but, unfortunately, many parents don't even notice. They've paid strict attention during their children's vulnerable infancy period, during the terrible twos and the adorable threes and the adventurous fours.

Each stage has brought dramatic physical changes and obvious mental and motor advances—talking and walking, reciting colors and tying shoelaces. But the remarkably fast pace of physical growth during infancy and early childhood slows down about the age of six. In the first six months of life, your child's weight and height may have tripled. But each year after the age of five, instead of a 300 percent growth rate, height increases only 5 or 6 percent and weight only 10 percent.

the changing landscape
of a child's mind

It may seem that nothing much is going on. In fact, a revolution is taking place, but *the territory that's changing is the landscape of the mind*. Though the child's body barely seems to be altering, the child's mind is expanding into new territories and the child is acquiring a brand-new way of looking at the world.

Instead of relying on the most recent images to solve problems, as the four-year-old would, the seven-year-old has concepts and rules. For example, your child is wearing a new shirt. You jokingly say, "That shirt is so nice, I'd like to borrow it."

At four your child might have replied, "When my shirt grows up, you can wear it. At seven, your child understands the concept of growth and stability. The child knows that shirts can't grow but people can. The child no longer must rely on seeing a small and big shirt, or a small and big person to grasp the parent's joke. The seven-year-old can now maintain concepts in his "mind's eye."

The mental process called "cognition" undergoes a qualitative change in this new era of childhood, which enables children of six or seven to interpret sensory events—such as eating, drinking, watching television, seeing words on a page—in a new way. Not only will they have more words and numbers at their disposal, but they will be able to manipulate these symbols in the process of thinking, reasoning and solving problems.

For example, children of four might begin to see relationships between a group of different flowers, but they can deal only with classifying one feature at a time. They can put all the pink flowers together, or all the flowers with long stems, but by seven they can put all the long-stemmed pink flowers in a group. They are beginning to fully understand relationships—between the properties of flowers and between people.

At the age of three a child is unable to put herself in someone else's shoes. She is egocentric. She sees the world as revolving around herself. At the age of four or five, this egocentrism declines and by seven the child can actually put herself in another person's shoes, as shown in the example below.

the dawn of social awareness

If a child loses her temper and yells at or hits a playmate, she can understand how the other feels. This can be the beginning of learning to consciously control the impulse to hurt by words or actions. A younger child might obey the rule about no hitting for fear of not being allowed to play. The older child begins to have "empathy" for others. It is both the desire to please the parent and the desire to make playmates feel good that motivates a child to cooperate rather than bully others in a group. The new mental and social awareness of these years enable the child to have relationships—actual friendships with others.

a new perspective

The world looks different to the seven-year-old. Changes in perspective and reasoning open up areas of exploration. The world becomes a fascinating place, a place in which the child with his or her increasing skills can begin to feel important—not in the egocentric fashion of a toddler but in the more mature attitude of the older child who realizes: "I can do things in the world. I can make a difference."

Unlike the toddler or preschool child, the child of six or seven begins to have a bank of memories. The present images are joined by images from the past. Memory increases each year between five and ten years of age. A five-year-old can recall only four or five numbers. A ten-year-old can recall hundreds of numbers and manipulate them by adding, subtracting, multiplying and dividing.

encouraging new capacities

Parents' behavior can encourage these growing mental capacities. A child learns better when he or she is free from anxiety and has a motivation for learning. Screaming or scaring induces anxiety and prevents learning. As for, "Your older brother knew how to add and subtract at your age"—that doesn't help either. Invidious comparisons to siblings or neighborhood children induce feelings of inferiority, which slow down the learning process. Your praise and approval are significant motivation. Gifts and money rewards are not necessary to motivate learning.

Another strong incentive for learning is the opportunity to share experiences with parents or beloved adults. Tony's favorite uncle loved baseball and opera, which led Tony to quickly learn the Dodgers' batting averages and arias from *La Boheme* and *Tosca*. No money or grades were given. Learning was a way to be closer to a cherished person.

With the acquisition of memory and a sense of the past, children acquire the ability to use experience to modify their behavior. For example, in first grade Stan tried to make friends with a new boy in class. The child didn't respond. The teacher explained that the new student was shy and the others should give the person time and try again. In second grade, another new student came to class. Stan tried to make friends. His first effort was met by withdrawal. Stan remembered what had happened last year. He waited until the next week and invited the new student to go with him to a soccer game. The student accepted. The two became friends.

new vistas of learning

The window of opportunity that opens for school-age children involves an opportunity for scholarly learning and learning about social interaction. As her potential for social interaction expands, the child is increasingly concerned with the agreement of her concepts and those of other children and adults. For example, if you ask a four-year-old what's good, the child will use the last sensory motor experience: "An ice cream cone is good. A boat ride is good." But at seven or eight, whether or not he or she can put it into words, the child has a concept of good. Good is what makes the child feel happy *and* what people the child cares about approve of.

discovering the self

The child begins to have what we commonly call "self-awareness." The vast expansion in the child's cognitive abilities—including the ability to stand aside and take another's perspective—allows the child to label physical and emotional sensations he experiences. A four-year-old who feels fear, tension, or butterflies in the stomach can only cry. But a seven-year-old is able to reflect on what he feels and take appropriate action.

To a four-year-old, a parent might say, "Don't talk with strangers. Never go with a stranger." To a seven-year-old, you can reiterate those rules, but also add: "Listen to your feelings. If you feel bad feelings, tense, nervous, jumpy feelings, that's a danger sign. Don't go with or spend time with a person who makes you feel that way. Don't do anything that feels bad to you."

A parent should encourage the process by helping a child to

identify and express good and bad feelings. This skill can be vital to your child's mental health. It can help him or her avoid potentially harmful situations. And it can reduce stress and increase feelings of well-being. As the child matures, the ability to share and communicate good and bad feelings will increase that person's chances of having good human relationships. It's usually the bad feelings that are the most difficult—for the child and the parent. Denial of bad feelings can be a serious source of family and interpersonal problems.

When Heather was twelve, she was molested by a stranger. Her family was one in which negative things were never discussed. Her parents didn't argue or openly express anger. Her father was a teacher, her mother a comptroller. Neither commented when Heather seemed to be acting strangely. They simply stressed that she get her homework done. And she did. Heather graduated high school with all A's and a full scholarship to college. What was not recorded was Heather's inner turmoil.

A year after the abuse experience, a year in which Heather's upset had been ignored and therefore denied by her parents, Heather became sexually promiscuous. She came to believe that the sexual abuse she had suffered was her fault. So while she continued to be a perfect student, she secretly became sexually active with many different partners, often people who were uncaring and unsavory. In her senior year of high school, she became the girlfriend of a dropout who had become a drug dealer.

In her freshman year of college, which she was attending on a full scholarship, Heather became pregnant by the drug dealer. She dropped out of school and had her baby. But at that point she began to get help. Her past experience came out, the initial traumatic abuse and the subsequent situations in which she let herself be used. When her mother was asked if she ever had any inkling of what was going on during these years, her mother admitted that she had read something in Heather's diary when Heather was only twelve. She called the girl's accounts of her experiences "pure fantasy," "a slime pit." She denied that they had any validity—as she and her husband had always denied their own negative emotions, their own anger.

Most of the time, children's sad or angry feelings will concern less significant events, but your sensitivity to those feelings, your encouragement that the child express the feelings, will pave the way for the child's emotional development. You have the opportunity to lay down the foundation for their communication skills. And if they do have a traumatic experience, you have the opportunity to help them handle that experience now, before it can have lasting effects on their adolescence and beyond.

developing and honing decision-making skills

The window of opportunity opens wide at this period of life. The child makes quantum leaps in self-awareness and memory, and develops a new ability to generate ideas. A child can now look before he leaps. A child can think through a problem. He doesn't have to act it out. This is a time when children can actually imagine many solutions and develop skills for decision-making. Between the ages of five and twelve, children have fewer of the clear and present dangers that teenagers face. This is a wonderful time for parents to respond to their children with a new style of interaction. Instead of simply laying down the law or telling a child what to do, a parent can help children evaluate their thoughts.

For example, a seven-year-old comes home from school and reports, "Mindy says I should only play with her. If I try to be friends with Jenny and Paula, she won't be my friend anymore." A parent could say, "That's ridiculous. Mindy is being just plain stupid. You have to make other friends." But by doing this the parent stifles the child's problem-solving before it blossoms and discourages independence.

Instead the parent can take a moment to listen and encourage the child to make an appropriate decision.

PARENT: What do you think about Mindy?
CHILD: I'd like to play with other children.
PARENT: I think you can, especially if you try to include Mindy.
   OR
PARENT: What do you think about this?
CHILD: I'm afraid to lose Mindy. She's my only real friend.
PARENT: I wonder if Mindy's afraid to make friends and afraid to lose you, too.

At the time decision-making skills are just developing the parent still needs to help the process along. For example, parents can share a similar experience. "I had a friend like that. She was very possessive. I didn't want to lose her, either. I went along for a while, but then I noticed she was making other friends, so I decided to do the same." A parent needs to continue to guide the child, but in a way that encourages the child's participation. "You can have Mindy and another friend over. I'll be around. We'll show Mindy that it's possible to enjoy more than one person."

recognizing other advances in thinking

Though children will be getting mental stimulation from school, parents can help encourage a new type of thinking that children at six or seven are able to manage—inductive thinking. This is thinking that proceeds through trial and error, thinking that is creative.

Children now have a greater attention span that permits them to be reflective and imaginative, but they are not yet hampered by the fear of making a mistake that impedes the adolescent. Creative dramatics, art, music and activities involving math and science that encourage inductive reasoning are especially appropriate. As an added benefit, creativity will enhance the child's position in the peer group. (In the past this creative capacity has been especially helpful to girls, but the breakdown of stereotypes should lend advantages to both the creative boy and the creative girl.)

Another aspect of children's thinking is also advancing—their deductive capacities, which improve their ability to use rules to solve problems. Jean Piaget, who spent a good part of his life observing children to determine their mental development, found a significant change in the quality of children's thinking about age seven. They are able to coordinate operations, to think about two logical areas—time and space for example. They are able to understand that a quantity can stay the same even though its shape or container changes. They are able to have "mental representations" of a series of actions. For example, a four-year-old can walk to the store but a seven-year-old can "see" the route without actually following it and trace the route to the store on a piece of paper.

Seven-year-olds can reason about parts of a whole to classify objects. They are able to perceive subtle relationships between objects and gradations. A four-year-old might understand that darker means very dark. A seven-year-old understands darker means darker than another object. Piaget called this new group of cognitive abilities "concrete operations."

At about the age of twelve, people begin to be able to think about the future. They can imagine fanciful possibilities as well as scientific hypotheses. This type of thinking Piaget called formal operations. But even a twelve-year-old has difficulty making personal decisions based on possible consequences in the future. A parent can talk about future consequences with a young person of twelve, but it is still difficult for that person to modify his or her behavior because of what might happen in the future. At ages eleven and twelve, despite a growing sense of the past and the beginning of perceiving the future, children are more oriented to the present. But their perception of the present is infinitely more complex than during their preschool years.

development of a self-concept

As their mental abilities expand and their understanding about relations of objects and people deepens, children develop what is called a self-concept. This concept of the self will have a profound effect on the child's ability to make healthy decisions. In this area a parent plays an absolutely crucial role. For most children, the way in which they are treated by parents is the most significant factor in shaping their self-concept and determining whether they feel high or low self-esteem.

what parents can do to enhance children's self-esteem

Keeping in mind the importance of self-esteem, you probably are asking, "What can I do as a parent to give my child a good self-concept, to enhance my child's self-esteem?" Fortunately, researchers have identified parental characteristics that parents of children with high self-esteem seem to share. We're adding suggestions so you can realize some of these possibilities in your own family.

the importance of a parent's own self-esteem

Parents who have high self-esteem themselves are better able to encourage children's good feelings about themselves. What can a parent do if she or he suffers from low self-esteem? A parent can examine his or her own family background. Was the parent punished with undue harshness? Was there an episode of sexual abuse, an incident or an ongoing pattern of incest? Was there either frequent conflict or indifference exhibited by parents? An individual can get help in dealing with past experiences that may hinder parenting.

Parents can also look for ways to enrich their lives to increase personal feelings of self-worth—courses or additional training to give them new opportunities for a better job; creative opportunities with music, theater, crafts; volunteer work that allows them to feel important by helping another person to read or find shelter; spiritual support through responsible religious groups. Knowing that your psychological well-being is profoundly affecting your child may be the excuse you need to take better care of yourself.

family compatibility

Children with high self-esteem experience greater family compatibility and ease, and a clearer definition of each parent's area of authority and responsibility. This extends to any two people raising a child— husband and wife, parent and grandparent, single parent and ex-spouse, parent and live-in lover.

Conflicting messages from authority figures cause anxiety and confusion for children. Put yourself in the child's place.

Steve complains, "Mom says I should spend lots more time on homework. Dad says the important thing is to be good in sports. If I please Mom, I make Dad unhappy. And vice versa."

Diane says she is confused: "Grandma says drinking is the work of the devil. Mom always asks me to get her a beer when she comes home from work. If I don't give Mom her beer, she's mad. If I do, Grandma's mad at both of us."

Zach's parents are divorced. They don't see eye to eye about money: "Mom says I must save every penny. When I visit Dad on weekends, he gives me money and insists I spend it on having a good time."

The list of conflicting messages is endless. Since we can never be perfectly compatible with our mates or people with whom we live, it's impossible to avoid all conflict. What is possible is to recognize serious ongoing conflict and do something about it.

In the above examples, if Steve does two hours of homework per night, then he can spend three afternoons and one weekend day on basketball. Grandma should stop talking about drink and the devil, which frightens Diane. Mother should stop involving Diane in bringing her beer. If Mom has a serious drinking problem, Grandma and Diane can go to Al Anon or another community counseling service that helps the families of alcoholics.

The divorced Mom and Dad who disagree about the uses of money should talk privately about their differences. Can they agree on a compromise? For example, Zach gets an allowance. If he saves half of it, he can spend the other half on having a good time. Mom gets to say, "Dad and I see things differently here. I was always taught to save what I got for a rainy day. Dad was encouraged to spend freely. Here's our compromise: we have these differences, but we agree on one thing. We both love you."

the importance of parental encouragement and parental example

Parents who have high expectations for children, who provide sound models of such high expectations and give consistent encouragement and support, are more likely to have children with high self-esteem. This is a tricky proposition because a parent's expectations must be geared to a child's capabilities. A boy joining Little League who is an average athlete should not be expected to win every game. If he simply improves his skill during the season, that should be applauded.

A girl who is afraid of the water at the beginning of the summer and is able to float and tread water by the end of the summer has accomplished a great deal and should be celebrated. A brilliant competitive athlete may need a higher standard, or a goal related to teamwork so she broadens her abilities.

Sometimes a child's limited achievement potential can be a tremendous disappointment to a parent. A mildly retarded eleven-year-old boy struggled to achieve at the level of his average math classmates. His potential, no matter how hard he tried, was limited to simple calculations. Despite his mother's support in getting him to do his homework nightly, and sometimes tutoring him, his self-esteem suffered because her expectations that he achieve at an average math level were impossible for him to meet. The important thing is to have expectations suitable to your child's abilities. And as your child matures, he can participate in goal-setting. Sit down with your ten- or eleven-year-old. Ask what he or she is expecting to achieve in school or sports or outside activities. If you feel the expectations are unreasonably high or low, you can discuss this and suggest an adjustment.

Laura was a bright girl but a bit lazy. She set her goals low so she could just slip by. Her sister Amanda was a hard worker but an average achiever. She tended to set her goals high and then put herself under enormous stress, never feeling she had quite made the grade. The girls' parents had to get Laura to reach higher and work harder. They helped Amanda in two ways. They helped her find an activity where she could aim high. In other areas they helped her to pitch her goal to a medium level and experience the pleasure of having fully accomplished the goal without undue stress.

affection and acceptance
as nourishment for the self

The children of parents who are accepting of them and express that acceptance through close rapport and everyday gestures of affection and concern tend to have higher self-esteem.

Can anyone hear, "I love you," too often? Has anyone ever felt a parent was too caring? Most of us can easily think of those who chip away at self-confidence by indicating in word and gesture—"You can't do it." "You're not good enough." Individuals who have been victims of both physical and psychological battering say the psychological abuse is worse. Remarks that chip away at confidence are like a water-torture treatment. One is always waiting for the next drop to fall. On the other hand, nothing can feel as good to children as knowing their parents feel proud of them. Sometimes these feelings need to be expressed more openly, so that the child has the pleasure of hearing by words and feeling by a kiss or hug that he or she has succeeded in your eyes.

respect and reasonable rules

Parents of high self-esteem children are more likely to enforce established rules carefully and consistently. These parents are more likely to use rewards to affect their children's behavior, but when children break the rules, they are more likely to use a straightforward, appropriate punishment than harsh treatment or total withdrawal of love. In other words, they use what we have called loving limits, an authoritative rather than a dictatorial or authoritarian approach to rules and discipline.

standards and limits

Parents of high self-esteem children carefully define standards and limits. They emphasize the rights of their children and seek their children's ideas. They respect their opinions and as the children mature, they grant concessions. Remember the many mental abilities the child is acquiring now—the greater degree of social understanding. A parent encourages that progress with some give and take, unless danger might be involved. The child who plays with matches is never a child you would want as a playmate for your child, whether at your home or his. But if your child has a friend you have met, a friend who seems trustworthy, you can feel comfortable giving the two friends permission to do special things together, such as going to a ball game, having a sleepover. By the time your child is eleven or twelve, he or she will be making plans independently. By this time you may have developed enough trust not to check up on every moment of the child's day; but new friends and late night or overnight activities still require your scrutiny.

discussion versus force

Parents who enhance children's self-esteem stress discussion and reasoning rather than force.

Let's say a child of nine wants an allowance. He has a history of squandering any money he gets on candy. The authoritarian, dictatorial parent is going to give the child a flat "No," when he asks for an allowance. The parent might even throw in negative comments about how wasteful the child is, how when he was a boy he had to work for every penny, and now his son has anything he wants. If the child sneaks some change, or gets angry because he doesn't have an allowance and the other kids do, the parent might hit the child to make that no final. By so doing, the parent conveys anger, resentment and little if any confidence in the child's ability to make healthy choices. He has learned nothing about how to handle money judiciously. Father's policy of hitting or shaming the child teaches the child to feel angry and resentful, and at the same time inadequate.

But a parent who employs discussion and reasoning can use this opportunity to teach the child greater responsibility. The parent needs to explain why he's concerned about giving the child an allowance and see if the child is willing to promise to limit the amount of his allowance he will spend on candy. The parent can suggest other ways to use the allowance, such as saving part each week for a special item or event, using part of the allowance to build a collection (of stamps, books, model planes, baseball cards, etc.) that will bring hours of pleasure, instead of the quick fix of a candy bar that is eaten in a few minutes and gone. By talking it over, parent and child can arrive at an amount for the allowance and the portion of that allowed for candy that seems realistic. They should also agree to try this for a short time, say a few weeks or a month.

If the arrangement is working, the child can have a raise in allowance. If the child is spending all the money on candy, the allowance can be cut in half. At some point, this child is going to have to make choices about money. The only training he's going to get in this area, until he's an adult, is from his father and mother. If the child never has an experience of making these choices, he would be more likely to spend his money foolishly or to be unable ever to enjoy spending it.

protectiveness versus incentives for independence

Parents of children with moderate self-esteem are more likely than parents of children with low self-esteem to strike a balance between protectiveness and encouragement of autonomy. They are less likely to be anxious about a child sleeping over at a friend's, but more likely to think a child should be protected from jobs that might be too hard for him.

Children between the ages of five and twelve need to feel a sense of industry: I am what I can do. They must be encouraged to do some things on their own. Yet they clearly require an adult hand to guide them. Imagine three mothers bringing their six-year-olds for a swimming lesson. One mother is insistent her child jump in the pool, claiming he's done it before. The boy is frightened—he claims it's too deep, too cold. The mother turns to the other adults, insisting, "He can do it. I don't know what's wrong with him." When he refuses to jump in, she takes him and throws him in. He quickly paddles over to the shallow end and the mother turns to the others: "See, I told you he could do it." What she failed to see was the look of sheer terror on the boy's face as she threw him into the water—terror and betrayal.

A six-year-old girl is at the shallow end with her mother. She's riding on Mom's back, as one would expect a younger child to do. But her mom seems to be encouraging the babyish play. The child asks, "Can I try jumping in?" Her mom says, "No, you might hurt yourself," and continues to play with her.

The third mom is standing in the pool, her arms under her child, teaching her to float. She keeps her hands under the girl for a few moments, then slowly, hardly making an extra ripple, removes them. She whispers in the ear of her daughter, "You're floating—all by yourself." "I am?" the child asks in disbelief. "You can float!" says her mom, and the two smile proudly.

Balancing autonomy and protectiveness becomes more difficult as the challenges become greater, but the gradual removal of one's support plus the continued encouragement toward independence is the way to make parent and child feel a sense of pride.

a child's developing sense of morality

Parents have another opportunity during these middle childhood years of rich inner activity—they can affect the development of their child's conscience. People from many different schools of thought agree that moral development depends to some extent upon a person's cognitive maturity. Beginning at age five or six, children become capable of recognizing the difference between an intentional wrongdoing and an accidental wrongdoing. They become capable of making a choice guided by an understanding of what is right or wrong. There are many psychologists who believe there are two pathways for this moral growth to proceed—one is by identification with a moral parent, the other is by fearing loss of love or parental approval.

The child who identifies with a moral parent and is taught by the use of loving limits is more likely to internalize moral standards, rather than just acting out of fear. Children who act according to internalized moral standards rather than behaving merely because they fear detection and punishment report that their parents are less likely to use physical threats of force, deprivation or direct commands and are more likely to use love-related methods.

These children also had more opportunities than the group who acted out of fear of finding out what they did wrong when they were punished. "I have to insist that you stay in after school because you hit your sister." "You can't watch TV at the usual time, because you didn't do your homework." "You won't be able to go to the movies with us, because you haven't done the dishes, put away the tools you used, or taken the garbage out." These children learned that their actions, or failure to do what was expected, had consequences. Their choices—good and bad—made a difference.

These children were better able to evaluate and criticize their own behavior— "I know I shouldn't have lied about doing my homework." And their parents were more likely to be supportive of their admitting a wrongdoing, so the children knew they could regain their parent's approval by admitting they had done the wrong thing and showing they intended to do the right thing. "I'm sorry you lied about the homework yesterday, but I'm glad you told the truth today."

Parents need to make it clear that their disapproval of disappointment has to do with the wrongdoing—not with the child. This way parents give a message that lying is wrong, but the child is basically good and capable of making the right choice.

Parents who express disappointment and disapproval of the child—"Only a terrible person would lie about his homework"—make the child anxious, and conscience-ridden about being a bad person. This type of emotional blackmail impairs a child's autonomy, self-confidence and self-reliance. The parent who denigrates the child as a person may control and dominate the child more thoroughly, but that parent is also creating the type of inner rage and impaired self-esteem that make that child vulnerable to domination by peers, experimentation with drugs and behavior geared to gaining acceptance at any cost.

Guilt in the service of moral behavior is useful. Guilt that becomes generalized into an irrational sense of shame for normal thoughts and feelings can be very damaging.

Between five and twelve, the child's concept of guilt changes from a rigid inflexible notion of right and wrong learned from parents to a sense of equity that takes into account the specific situation in which the rules were broken. For example, a child's great grandmother is ill and in a nursing home. The child's parents decide not to tell the great grandmother of the death of a cousin who lived far away because they fear that the news will worry her and add stress to her condition. The rulebound seven-year-old may adhere to the belief that one should tell only the whole truth and that lying, under any circumstances, is wrong. A twelve-year-old might say that while withholding the truth is lying, there are times when protecting someone from the truth is more important than telling it. By the age of twelve, most children have developed the foundation for making choices and understanding whether or not another person's choice was fair or moral.

What an astounding transformation has occurred in the guise of these apparently tranquil middle years—an egocentric individual rooted in the present and unable to comprehend the feelings or motives of others has become a person who can think about the past and glimpse the future, a thoughtful individual who can experience the feelings of others through empathy and use those empathic feelings to guide behavior, a person with a conscience who can understand why people do what they do and decide whether an action is right or wrong *before* it is executed. In short, with the help of loving parents, the child emerges from these middle years with the potential for making good choices.

SUMMARY

A window of opportunity opens for parents when their children reach the age of five or six. Subtle but dramatic mental advances provide an opportunity for the child of this age to think about the past, to understand relationships of objects and of people, to develop a concept of self that is positive or negative. Parents can influence their developing child—to feel positively about herself or himself, to make healthy decisions, to recognize the difference between right and wrong and overall to choose the right behavior. Parents can guide their children while gradually encouraging them to make independent choices.

Parents can encourage high self-esteem in a number of ways. First, they can deal with their own psychological well-being, engaging in activities that tend to heighten their own feelings of self-worth. They can get help for problems from the past that may impair their ability to be good parents. Second, Mother and Father can define for themselves, and thus for their children, areas of authority and responsibility. This is particularly difficult for divorced parents. Yet once one recognizes the destructive nature of conflicting messages, the capacity for compromise can be found.

Third, parents whose children have high self-esteem expect their children to achieve and do the right thing. Their expectations are tailored to the individual child; they are within the realistic range of what an individual child can achieve. Fourth, affection, expressions of concern and everyday communication engender high self-esteem. Establishing rules and enforcing them are a fifth characteristic of parents whose children had high self-esteem. Respect and a gradual widening of the child's responsibilities are a key factor in the way the parents of high self-esteem children enforce standards and limits. Finally, the use of discussion and reasoning, rather than force, and a balance between protectiveness and encouraging independence characterize parents whose children have high self-esteem.

Parents can guide their children to a sense of morality by their own example and by disapproving of wrongdoing, rather than disapproving of the child. Excessive guilt and shame aren't helpful. Empowerment conveyed by a parent's belief that, despite mistakes, the child is capable of making the right choice does encourage moral choices.

4
HELPING YOUR CHILD RELATE TO THE WORLD OUTSIDE THE FAMILY

Every parent experiences a slight pang when his or her child goes off to school for the first time. Though the child may have gone to day care or nursery school, the child's departure for that first day of real school is a turning point. It means the child will be exposed to a new world, the world of friends and teachers. The child will have to meet new standards and new challenges.

Confronting and eventually mastering these challenges will further strengthen a child's self-esteem. There will be some anxiety along the way as the child learns to deal with peers. Parents can help by understanding the pressures a child confronts and providing support and encouragement as the child moves into this wider world.

developmental tasks of the school-age child

Children going off to school will have homework and after-school activities, but they also have a number of so-called developmental tasks. These are broad challenges that will influence their later development, making them feel a sense of mastery and industry, or a sense of inferiority and inadequacy. These are the major developmental tasks of the middle years, from five to twelve:

1. Development of intellectual skills and the motivation to master intellectual and academic material.

2. Learning to interact with peers.
3. Development of occupational work habits.
4. Crystallization of sex-role identification—strong feelings that "I am a boy," "I am a girl."
5. Increased autonomy and independence.
6. Development of moral standards.
7. Learning to deal with anxiety and conflict.

The way children learn to handle these tasks will affect the way they deal with adolescence and adulthood. There are three arenas in which these challenges are played out: at home, in school and in the peer group.

School entrance helps to reduce dependent ties to home. The parent waving to the child on that first day with a tear in her eye understands this immediately. At school there will be new adults the child must obey and whose acceptance he courts—sometimes to the point of "falling in love" with a teacher. Ideally, school and individual teachers will contribute to the child's mastery of intellectual skills, the ability to persevere in problem solving and establish long-range goals.

continuing to be an advocate for your child

But, even after your child is attending school all day, it's up to you to be an advocate for your child, to monitor the school situation and make sure the child is shouldering his responsibility and the teacher is creating an atmosphere for a good learning experience. In a majority of cases, teachers are doing the job, some with more dedication and talent than others. Occasionally, a teacher's insensitivity or lack of understanding creates a hostile environment for a child. The teacher may be making the types of mistakes we've described that parents can make— humiliating a child who misbehaves, setting expectations too high or too low.

A parent needs to check out the situation if a child doesn't want to go to school or seems to be suffering from unusual stress or if the child's enthusiasm seems to wane.

When Rachel was ten, she seemed to be losing interest in

school. Although she had always been enthusiastic about school, she now seemed apathetic and even negative. Her mother went to school and discovered a strange combination of circumstances. First, the teacher was very hard of hearing and did not wear a hearing aid. Second, Rachel's vision had changed and, unbeknownst to her parents, she now needed glasses. Rachel hadn't mentioned anything because she thought she wouldn't look pretty in glasses. Her seat at the back of the class prevented her from seeing the teacher, and prevented the teacher from hearing her.

Finally, she and another girl were the only ones in the class working at a level one grade above the others. They were essentially left to teach each other and were understandably getting bored with this method. The picture became clear at the parent/teacher meeting and action was taken. Rachel got glasses, and at her parents' demands, the principal found a way to enrich her curriculum with periods in an accelerated class. The following year the teacher was transferred. He had not yet gotten a hearing aid, nor had he learned to hear students asking for more stimulation.

School is an experience that involves teachers, textbooks, peers and parents, but the parents are the only ones who can monitor these other elements and make sure they offer an environment in which the child can thrive.

Six-year-old James started first grade at a private school. Because the schools located near their home had large classes and were not outstanding academically, James's parents decided he would have more attention and a better learning experience in the smaller classes of the private school. Unfortunately, the school was located some distance from their home in a white community that harbored anti-black bias. James's mother warned James that some people might not treat him fairly. His father explained to him that a black person in this country has to face discrimination. But James was still confused and disheartened when the teacher treated the gentle boy as if he were a threat to the class. "She makes me feel like I've got bugs or something," James complained. When the class bully took James's lunch and hit him over the head, the teacher didn't notice. When James hit back, she punished James. A number of these episodes convinced James's mother that the teacher and the students were bigoted and were discriminating against James. James's parents went to his classroom and confronted the teacher about her biased treatment of James and complained to the principal about the school's failure to meet its responsibility to provide a fair learning environment in which all students could develop their competence and self-esteem. Since the principal refused to acknowledge the racism within the school, James's parents transferred James to another private but integrated school where he thrived.

Private schools aren't a guarantee of excellence and sensitivity. It's up to parents to monitor the school and intervene if it becomes necessary. Some parents may see fit to change the child's classroom. Others may insist that the school acknowledge and act to change its institutionalized racist behavior by appealing higher to the board of directors or through legal means. If you don't advocate for your child when a teacher or school is at fault, who will?

peers

School brings children into regular contact with age-mates or their "peer group." It is the peer group that offers a child the opportunity to learn how to interact with children of the same age, how to deal with dominance and hostility, how to relate to a leader and how to lead others. By talking to peers, a child learns to share problems, conflicts and feelings, which can provide reassurance. Peers help the child develop a concept of herself or himself. The way children are accepted or rejected by peers gives them what may be a more realistic picture of their strengths and liabilities.

Peer standards are bound to differ somewhat from those of parents. At home, the child must be *love-worthy*—good, adherent to the rules of the family, affectionate. At school, the child must be *respect-worthy*—displaying physical competence and outgoing tendencies. The penalties inflicted by the peer group can be ridicule, humiliation and rejection.

Traditionally, the children of immigrant groups were more likely to depend on peers to show them what was "American." This continues to be true for more recent waves of immigrants, but it also is true for people moving from one part of the country to another and for cultures undergoing rapid change. As Margaret Mead once said, "We are all immigrants in time." In periods of cultural change, children may put a greater emphasis on peer values and peer acceptance.

Integration into the peer group offers many satisfactions: companionship, the chance to play favored roles, the opportunity to participate in play activity such as games and group gatherings. Though a child may be rejected by a peer group, the child cannot totally retreat from the peer group since he or she must remain in school. Finding out that your child has been rejected by his or her peers is painful and frustrating for parents. Author Ray Bradbury once wrote a story in which a parent is willing to sell his soul to the devil if he can just take the place of his child on the treacherous battlefield of the playground.

healthy ways to
gain peer acceptance

A child may try to imitate the actions, remarks and gestures of the most active members in the group, but what if he still can't gain acceptance?

At eleven, Mark was short for his age. His academic skills had put him in contact with an older group led by an enormous boy who was two years older and almost a foot taller than Mark. He was regularly menaced by the big bully. His parents suggested judo lessons. Mark became skilled enough to appear in judo exhibitions and one day, when the oversized boy shoved Mark, Mark flipped the bully over his hip, pinned him and released him only when he begged for mercy. He gained the peer group's acceptance and a sense of personal confidence that lasted way beyond that difficult year.

When Nina transferred to a new school, she found the other fourth-graders rejected her. Her parents knew Nina liked stories and make-believe; she always wanted to dress up and pretend she was one of the characters in these stories. Her parents enrolled Nina in a nearby theater class and Nina was soon appearing in plays. Her peers came and gradually she was accepted and even celebrated by the group.

Children who tend to be very controlling or who make trouble or break rules to draw attention to themselves often need creative outlets for their needs and energies. A third-grade boy of this type was regarded as a bully until his father took him in hand and told him he could be a great leader someday. The man showed him that good leaders don't browbeat people into doing things their way. They accept and applaud contributions from the group. The father used examples from areas the boy liked, such as sports, to bring home the message and then gave the boy an opportunity to join a new baseball team that was forming. As soon as he saw the boy making efforts to work with the other kids, the father applauded him.

After being picked up by the day camp bus, eight-year-old Mary had a habit of taking off most of the clothes she was wearing and throwing them out the window of the bus. Her mother didn't know how to stop this. She admitted to Mary's counselor that the girl always seemed to do things to gain attention. The counselor decided she'd find a way for Mary to get some positive attention. She assigned her to be the playwright for the group's next drama session. Mary made up a story and with the counselor's help the group acted the story out. The counselor praised Mary and reported Mary's achievement to her mother. Mary never did her bus stripping again and was an enthusiastic camper for the rest of the summer.

A first-grader was extremely shy, to the point where he rarely spoke to classmates or teachers. His father encouraged him to play soccer with the other boys, but he retreated further. Then the father thought of tennis. Not being a contact sport, tennis seemed to hold more hope for his son. Sure enough, the boy grew to love the sport and eventually was chosen for the junior varsity team.

Yet another shy child showed some interest in music. She played the piano, but that too was a solitary activity, so when she was in fourth grade, her mother introduced her to the flute. This being an instrument for orchestra, the girl gradually became involved in the school orchestra and found herself with many friends.

Loneliness may be the price of not following peers who are up to no good. At nine, Don was in a class where the "popular" kids regularly went on shoplifting sprees. Don didn't want to participate. But he didn't want to tell on his peers. His mother tried to find out what was wrong, why Don didn't seem to have any friends. Don wouldn't tell. So she just tried to marshal Don's assistance. She urged Don to help her when she volunteered to serve food at the neighborhood shelter. Toward the end of the year, Don finally admitted what was wrong. A parent can't always make things instantly better, but caring and involvement can sustain a child through a difficult period with peers.

changing peer group standards

The peer group undergoes changes as its members mature. In the early years of school, the peer group is an informal gathering of children. The group has few formal rules and there is rapid turnover in membership. Expediency plays a significant role, so that children simply living close to one another may determine who's in the group. Later, when children are ten to fourteen years old, the peer group tends to be more highly structured—there may be a name for the group, special membership requirements like taking an oath or formal rituals such as regular meetings. This kind of group may range from the Boy Scouts or Girl Scouts to the social club with jackets or T-shirts.

The makeup of the group also changes in terms of boys and girls. Seven- to eight-year-olds associate with same-sex peers. By nine to eleven boys may feel anxious about associating with girls, yet boy groups and girl groups may interact tentatively. In some communities, boys and girls of ten and eleven are already beginning to go on dates.

Our culture is one that tends to rush children through childhood. The media, with its sexual messages, and parents, with their belief that everything social and academic is best done at younger and younger ages, exert pressure on kids to be grown up earlier. As Dr. David Elkind of Tufts University has pointed out, these pressures tend to hurry children, foreshortening their childhood and cheating them out of time they need to gradually accomplish the tasks of development appropriate to their age. You need to monitor these pressures and make sure things aren't moving too fast for your child. Establishing an informal alliance with neighborhood parents can help in this effort to keep the social pressures from accelerating too quickly.

The peer group becomes especially important during the period before and at the end of puberty when children are likely to feel a yearning to disassociate themselves from family and a need to be supported in their unsure fumbling for a sense of womanhood or manhood. Even at this time, girls tend to maintain close ties with parents, while boys are more likely to be involved with the group.

the growing importance of friends

Though a parent may feel some ambivalence about the child's movement into the peer group, a parent needs to recognize the importance of a group of age-mates. A child needs the experience of interacting with other children who share his level of cognitive development, his interests, needs, abilities and skills, as well as his problems and anxieties. A child needs to feel some sense of belonging to a peer group as the close family bonds of early childhood loosen and the testing of independence begins. A child needs friends.

If your child has no friends, this is a reason to be concerned. It may be an indication that your child needs counseling.

Though early friendships may be accidental and circumstantial—based on sharing the same activity or living on the same block—as the child matures, friendships are based on common interests, similar family backgrounds and general intelligence. By seventh grade friendships are likely to be stable and very important to your child.

Certain factors tend to foster peer group acceptance. Your child's individual traits and your family values may not always be in harmony with the demands of the peer group. Yet it's interesting to know which traits are attractive to other children. Generally, "popular" children are higher in social aggressiveness and outgoing characteristics. They display enthusiasm, active participation and leadership. They are cheerful, friendly, neat and pleasant-looking and are able to laugh. Some of these characteristics can be encouraged by gratifying and rewarding early interactions at home.

Teachers and counselors can affect the likelihood of a child's profiting from peer group experience. When Linda was ten, she attended a camp in which some of her peers excluded her because she was black. (She was the only nonwhite person at the camp.) The counselor wasn't in a position to make sure other blacks attended the camp, but she did rearrange the tent assignments so that the anti-black clique was dispersed and the camp experience turned out to be rewarding for all the campers. A skilled teacher or group leader can maximize acceptance and participation by all members of the group.

Another phenomenon that most of us have experienced is the change in standards of groups as one progresses from first through fifth grade. In one group followed throughout elementary school, first-grade girls believed it was important to "act like a lady" to avoid being quarrelsome or bossy. But fifth-grade girls stressed good sportsmanship and friendliness. First-grade boys admired daring; third-graders stressed fairness in play and fifth-grade boys liked other boys who were not bashful and were what they called *"real boys."* Confidence and a degree of competence in athletics carry weight with peers.

Generally, more intelligent and creative children find greater acceptance among peers. Boys more than girls stress size, strength and athletic ability. Children who are anxious, uncertain and withdrawn or rebellious and hostile are likely to have low status. Obesity is another negative factor for peer acceptance, which we discuss in more detail below.

building your child's confidence and social skills

Though parents can't guarantee peer acceptance for children, they can try to do things in the early years of middle childhood that will give their children the confidence and skills they need to function with friends. Exposure to creative activities, the chance to develop coordination and athletic skills and opportunities to interact with other children from a position of strength and confidence are ways in which parents can help improve children's chances for acceptance.

Parents can make sure children who need help for a particular problem, such as a speech impediment or learning disability, get therapy early enough. Failure feelings pave the way for depression and drug use in adolescence, whereas overcoming learning and social handicaps and experiencing mastery in childhood will reap benefits in peer acceptance and school performance later on. They can discuss problems of racial or ethnic tensions that their children are likely to encounter, while instilling pride and transmitting knowledge of their children's own special heritage.

The reasons a child is called names, ridiculed or rejected by peers vary widely, from superficial habits, such as the way a person walks or talks, to poor social skills, physical disabilities or malformations or social withdrawal due to anxiety or depression, but such experiences contribute to lowering self-esteem. Intervention that addresses the underlying cause of such rejection by peers may be necessary.

helping your child avoid weight problems

One liability that parents can help children deal with is overeating. Children are doing less and eating more. The result is more obesity. And obesity is a sure ticket to social ridicule and rejection. Studies show that one out of five children is obese and that obesity among children has increased 50 percent over the past two decades. Longer hours of television watching, with many more programs geared to children and teenagers, are aggravating this tendency. According to an A. C. Nielsen survey, children ages six to eleven years old watch about twenty-two hours of television a week.

Children of the nineties are snacking in front of the TV, are less active and generally less fit than children of previous generations. Currently, half of the girls between six years of age and seventeen can't do even one pull-up. According to the President's Council on Physical Fitness, significant numbers of young children are showing signs of later health problems connected with lack of exercise and improper diet. At least one risk factor for heart disease showed up in 40 percent of children ages five to eight years old. The American Academy of Pediatrics has called overweight children the single most important health issue for pediatricians.

What's a parent to do when a child begins putting on weight? First, keep in mind that *your* eating and exercise habits and the kinds of meals given your children will influence your child's eating and exercise habits. That influence persists into young adulthood.

In a University of Pittsburgh research project headed by

Leonard H. Epstein, three parent-child groups were followed for ten years. In each group an obese parent attended a treatment program with a child who was at least 20 percent overweight for his or her age and height. All the parent-child teams involved were given an exercise program and a low-fat diet. In the group where parents and children were given incentives for weight loss, the one in which parents were taught how to reinforce good eating and exercise habits with praise and special outings, the children became less overweight as adults than did those in the other groups. Epstein found that parents who were willing to serve as better role models during the program helped their children control their weight over the ten years.

Garnering advice from health professionals and nutritionists, here are some specific guidelines for parents on weight control for kids:

1. *Encourage natural exercise.* Children may balk about it, but they really can walk to many places instead of being driven there. Family walks, hikes and bike rides help set the pattern. Mothers who exercise, according to research findings, tend to have children who are fit. Setting the example and involving children is important. Team sports are important, but they may involve a lot of standing around and waiting, whereas daily walking or biking builds stamina and burns calories.

2. *Don't reward children with food.* It's easy to fall into the pattern. Sue does all her homework and you give her a cookie or an ice cream sundae. But using food as a reward or bribe is doubly destructive. It puts a high value on high calorie foods and it indicates that food is a measure of love and acceptance. Motivate children with praise or with your time and attention, or the chance to engage in positive activities with their peers.

3. *Combine mealtime with family time.* These days it's extremely difficult to have meals together as a family. The workday and the school day don't often coincide. But keep in mind that an ordinary meal eaten together is more important than a fancy meal eaten apart. Children also look forward to shared weekend meals. Make these appealing but healthy. Combining nurture and nutrition helps your child feel satisfied without indulging in fattening treats.

4. *Break the pattern of eating and watching television.* Limit your child's television viewing and don't allow children to combine eating and TV watching. Confining meals to areas of your home

where there is no television will make mealtime more sociable and less fattening.

5. *Encourage moderation rather than severely restricting calories and sweets.* Small portions of cookies or candies several times a week are more effective in the long run than totally forbidding children from any sweets. A small ice cream cone instead of a large ice cream sundae, one oatmeal cookie rather than a large piece of chocolate cake with icing can satisfy a sweet tooth. Smaller portions of foods that are low in fat content served on plates instead of family-style will work better than strict calorie counting. Stocking a variety of foods that includes fruits, vegetables and more grains and reducing sharply the amount of junk food in the house can help the entire family stay more fit.

Trends toward obesity and inactivity should signal parents to get more aggressive about health and fitness. A pattern of overeating and overweight can be dealt with early in the school years to avoid later rejection.

It's important that the child doesn't begin to think of herself or himself as overweight and unattractive. Actual and imagined rejection can cause an overweight child to start looking at the world as always reacting to their fatness. When thin girls and obese girls were shown a picture of a girl standing a short distance away from a cluster of other girls, the thin girls thought that the girl was walking toward the cluster. The obese girls said she had been excluded from the group. Obese children are, in fact, often excluded from the group. And the problem becomes more severe as the child goes through puberty and becomes even more concerned with her body image. The middle years offer a window of opportunity for parents to help children attain fitness and maintain normal weight.

helping your children avoid or move away from negative peer influence

Children generally want to be accepted by their peer group, which often prompts them to conform to the standards of the group. Some conformity to the peer group is normal and natural. But what happens when peer group influences and parent values come into conflict? Some children will be more susceptible to the peer group influence. Researchers find that these very susceptible children are more likely to come from homes that are not nurturing. They make the transition from home to school feeling insecure and in need of acceptance.

Those who choose negative peer influence over home values were also less likely to have formed a strong identification with same-sex parents during early childhood. If children don't find an appropriate parent or role model of the same sex to identify with when they are three, four and five years old, they will look for a substitute model to identify with later. They will be more likely to adopt the attitudes of the peer group leader, even if those attitudes conflict with what they've learned at home.

Children of divorce are not necessarily going to be at greater risk. Studies show that exposure to positive male role models is more important in a boy's adjustment than whether the father is actually present. In homes where teenagers were raising children without the benefit of a husband/father, the frequent visits of a grandfather had a strong positive effect on both the teenage mother and her male or female child.

A divorced mother may, however, need to make a greater effort to ensure that a male figure is available for her children. A divorced father with custody of his children has to make the same effort to have a female figure available as a role model.

Despite a parent's best efforts, it's possible for children, especially those of eleven or twelve, to gain the acceptance of a peer group that seems to have a very negative influence. If you suspect that a friend or peer group is dangerous—bent on getting into trouble, experimenting with alcohol or other drugs, encouraging your child to cut school and break family rules— you would do well to investigate. Have these friends over to the house. If your concern continues, discuss the situation with your child. Sometimes a child of eleven or twelve wants to be free of a powerful friend but doesn't know how to get out from under his or her influence. If alcohol or other drugs are involved, intervention is called for. This may mean speaking to the parents of the other child, requiring that your child attend a support group to help him or her avoid drugs and those involved in drugs, or even transferring your child to another school.

signs of maturity

As your child matures and gets closer to adolescence, you'll find that he or she is becoming somewhat more independent and more capable in school. Your child is having some meaningful peer interaction, making a few friends. Your child has a firm sense of being a boy or a girl and ideas about what those sex roles entail. Your child is developing a sense of right and wrong, making mistakes at times, but generally developing an internal detector or conscience to guide decision making. Your child is experiencing some anxiety and conflict as he or she faces demands of teachers and peers, but he or she is learning how to deal with that anxiety, how to resolve conflicts.

These advances are likely to occur by the time your child completes his or her twelfth year. These are signs that your child is mastering the tasks of this period and preparing for the challenges of adolescence. And even though you may feel sad to realize that your child is growing up and to some extent growing away, you can feel gratified that you have been a primary source of support, guidance and encouragement.

SUMMARY

Among the many developmental tasks of the middle years are the development of intellectual and academic skills and the motivation to master these skills. Parents can encourage that mastery. Learning to interact with peers is another major task of this stage of life. Though peer standards may differ somewhat from parental standards, positive interactions at home can help a child to be "love-worthy" and "respect-worthy." Parents can encourage social skill development by helping their child to participate in constructive activities outside of school—such as music, sports, creative art and drama projects.

Parents can help ease their child's entry into the world of peers. If a child is overweight, parents can guide the child into habits of exercise and healthy eating that can make the child physically fit and help him or her avoid excess weight—a condition that may invite rejection as well as health problems.

Identification with positive role models can help children avoid negative peer influence. At ages eleven or twelve, when drugs or drinking may become part of a negative peer group, a parent may need to intervene to prevent a child from becoming involved in seriously destructive behavior. With help from parents, and examples at home of managing stress, anxiety and conflict, most children can learn to deal with normal anxiety and conflict without resorting to drinking or drugs.

By the time children reach adolescence, most of them have made major advances—in terms of school accomplishment and making friends. They have a greater sense of independence and self-reliance. They are learning how to make healthy choices. And you have been instrumental in seeing that they are prepared for the challenges of adolescence.

5

TALKING TO YOUR CHILDREN ABOUT LOVE AND SEX

Too little, too late. This is our concern about many areas of parent-child communication. But nowhere is it a more apt and urgent consideration than with the area of sex.

have we overemphasized sex?

Many parents may feel that there's been too much emphasis on sex, that we have become a sex-obsessed society and they'd like to get away from that. They'd like to return to a time when other things mattered. They would like to reestablish the bonds between love and sex that seem to have disintegrated, especially in the last two decades.

Some blame Sigmund Freud for making sex so significant in his theories about human behavior, theories that influenced our thinking about human development. But each generation reacts to the mistakes of the previous one. Sigmund Freud reacted to repressive attitudes toward sex. In the lexicon of Freudian thought, life force or libido and sex are almost interchangeable. Infants have a generalized need for physical pleasure. About the age of five, according to Freud, children's generalized or polymorphous desire for touching and physical pleasure becomes more focused. Children realize they have genitals and also begin to desire the parent of the opposite sex. This desire, or Oedipal Complex, informs the five-year-old boy's behavior. The girl's version of the same desire is called the Electra Complex, but is given less importance. For Freud, revolutionary thinker that he was, still was influenced by a male-oriented culture.

Childhood, according to Freudian theory, is a period of "latency" when the Oedipal drive goes underground. It resurfaces in adolescence. Resolving this Oedipal Complex will eventually steer the individual to find an appropriate sexual partner.

However, contrary to Sigmund Freud's latency theory, the average grade-schooler is aware of and is probably curious about a variety of sexual topics. Children of this age are actually more interested in sex and people's attitudes about it than when they were younger. Remember that the preschooler is involved in the self and lacks the social understanding of the older child. The limited world of the preschooler and the young child's self-preoccupation are rapidly augmented in the school years by a variety of outside influences and sexual references. Television, music, magazines, movies, advertising, clothes, jewelry, cosmetics—all are laden with heavy sexual messages. The intensity of the pressure of these wider sexual influences was unheard of twenty-five or thirty years ago when most parents were growing up.

At the same time that children are more exposed to these sexual references, they are also conscious for the first time that certain types of questions make parents uncomfortable, so they may tend to refrain from asking them.

"Latency" may be a product of the child protecting the parents from discomfort. It is easy for parents who are uncomfortable discussing sexual matters to take the child's silence as a sign—to the relief of parents—that the child has nothing she really wants to ask. Parents who conclude this are, unfortunately for both parents and child, deluding themselves. Any child of seven to twelve years, unless he or she is totally sheltered from the adult world, is aware of rape, AIDS, child abuse, homosexuality, pornography, unwanted pregnancies, abortion and other bewildering aspects of sexuality constantly being headlined in the media, at school and among peers. Even when a child doesn't ask questions, parents need to keep talking.

If Freud and his followers placed too much emphasis on sexuality, at least they began the process of bringing this crucial area of human behavior out of the closet. If they interpreted everything as sexual, and too often used male standards of sexuality, their predecessors had made the mistake of denying everything that was sexual, especially when it came to children. As we approach the year 2000, perhaps we can also approach a more balanced view of sex and human development.

sex as a basic human need

Sex is inextricably tied up with love, the use or abuse of power and trust—which is the basis for intimacy. It is a basic human need, which tends to influence and be influenced by love, power and trust. Sex is like eating. We all have a need to eat, but from the earliest moments of our existence, the giving of nourishment becomes associated with love, later with attitudes about family, religion and ethnicity. The way food is given to us influences our feeling of whether we can have our needs fulfilled. It's a basic building block of trust.

Sex in the broader sense is similar. From the earliest moments of life, we have a need for human contact, for touching and comfort. These earliest physical contacts establish a basis for later attitudes. Though babies can't formulate these ideas, notions are formed about relationships even in these preverbal periods. To put them into words, the child as infant learns: "I can trust people around me to fill my physical needs"; or "When I have needs, they aren't satisfied right away. I am treated roughly, without affection. When I grow up, I can't trust people to fill my physical needs with respect."

Is there a connection between the touching of an infant and sex? Is that touching vital? Renee Spitz and others have proven that children in institutions who are not touched will die. Harry Harlow, who raised generations of monkeys using a terry-cloth-covered monkey shape and regular feedings, proved that monkeys who are given only nourishment but are deprived of touching will be stunted in their future development. They will not be able to go through normal animal stages of masturbating, mating and parenting. As a result of this lack of loving contact, their behavior becomes permanently distorted. Renee Spitz and Harry Harlow were among the many researchers who made it clear that the need for nurturing physical contact is basic. Failure to fulfill that need will result in distortion of human behavior, abnormal sexual development or death.

Before children reach the age of five, associations are formed that will influence their attitudes about the give and take of affection, the degree to which they can control what happens, whether they are touched enough and how they are touched. At about five, they are beginning to see the way that men and women interact. The advances they achieve in mental abilities and social awareness will help them formulate far-reaching attitudes about what it means to be male or female. These attitudes are profoundly influenced by parental warmth.

A look at the impact of early human affection on later relationships seems to support Harry Harlow's findings with monkeys and shows just how significant warm parenting can be. Dr. Carol Franz, a psychologist at Boston University, went back to a group of people who had been studied as children by a Harvard University team. These people were now forty-one. It turned out that the people who had experienced cuddling, hugging and holding by their mother and father as young children tended to have relatively happy marriages, to establish close friends and to enjoy their work. They also showed what Dr. Franz called psychological well-being, a sense of zest and satisfaction with themselves.

Parental warmth was more important for later relationships than such things as being from an affluent or poor family, or being from parents who were divorced or even alcoholic. According to this study, sustained parental warmth could even overcome stressful events in childhood. Coldness on the part of parents or rejection was even more damaging to a child's potential for happy adult relationships than lack of money, divorce or problems one parent may have had with alcohol.*

forging links between love and sex

Childhood is the time of forming a self-concept. This is the window of opportunity for parents to influence mental and social advances. This is also a time of unique opportunity for parents to influence children's attitudes about sex. It is a time when parents can forge links between love and sex, between

---

* Daniel Goleman, "Parents' Warmth Is Found to Be Key to Adult Happiness," *The New York Times,* April 18, 1991, p. B1; also reported in May 1991 in the *Journal of Personality and Social Psychology*.

self-esteem and the exercise of choice, including choices about sex. A child of seven who learns to value his or her personal choice is more likely to become a teenager who can say no to unwanted sexual advances.

the question of sex education

"Sex education" has become an area of controversy, with some parents feeling strongly that human sexuality is a subject that should be taught in school and others feeling just as strongly that this subject should be kept out of the schools. Given our understanding of sex as linked to other human activities, we can begin to realize that sex education is happening from the earliest moments of a child's life, and sex education continues, whether or not a child is exposed to a specific formal lesson on sex.

Your children are getting sex education—from TV and pop music, from billboards and bathroom walls, from playground jokes and adult talk shows. Sex permeates our culture. Children develop a patina of sexual savvy that simply masks the fact that they are ignorant. They may not be innocent of four-letter words or even gestures and words associated with sex, but they are ignorant of the connections between sex and love, sex and responsibility, sex and pregnancy, sex and disease. These are connections that you can establish.

According to Anna Freud, no child can help being occupied with sexual concerns in the years before puberty. This is even truer today. The best thing parents can do for their children is to make them feel safe about expressing their concerns and feelings and encourage them to continue asking questions about sex throughout their growing years.

If parents do not develop a comfortable environment that allows children to talk freely about sex and sexuality, their children are likely to learn about these vital life functions in undesirable ways—through sexploitation magazines and books, from equally uninformed boyfriends or girlfriends, by hanging out with older more experienced peers who don't have their interests at heart. Besides the obvious advantages of learning about sex from you the parents, wouldn't it be gratifying if your child could say later on: "Whenever I wanted to know anything, I went straight to my parents. My mother and father always honestly tried to make me understand whatever I was concerned and curious about. I can thank them for having positive feelings about sex and making good choices."

the limitations of
school-based sex education

Schools offer some sex education, but even with the best-qualified teachers and materials, schools are limited in what they can offer your children. They may have a mandate to explain the facts of reproduction—usually between grades five and seven—and later in high school some communities provide information about pregnancy and sexually transmitted diseases.

But schools cannot teach family values. Schools cannot teach religious or ethical beliefs. Schools cannot personalize the issues of sexual decision-making to tailor them to an individual child's needs or specific personal history. Schools have been accused of teaching only plumbing, of encouraging sexual activity by not preaching abstinence or premarital chastity. Yet schools have been straitjacketed by community demands that they not invade the territory of religious and moral values that belongs to the family. It is not surprising, then, that school sex education, if not supported by family communication, is ineffective.

School sex education, according to a survey of five studies conducted between 1980 and 1987, doesn't change teenage sexual behavior. What these studies show is that classroom education that is not supported by efforts undertaken by family and community has no impact on pregnancy rates, no measurable influence on use of birth control or teenagers' decisions about when to engage in their first sexual intercourse.

Other studies indicate that children want to have sex education from their families, but most parents won't talk about sex in detail, if they talk about it at all. As physician and sex educator Dr. Domeena Renshaw puts it, "No sex education *is* sex education. It says, 'We cannot talk about sex.' "

Though a 1987 study of Illinois teens revealed that teenagers still consider their parents their primary source of sex education, they claimed that parents did not provide enough information on the sexual urges and attractions a person can feel and many wouldn't discuss anything to do with birth control. Teens who received information were more likely to receive it from their female parent, and daughters received more information than sons.

why you should talk with your child about sex

You are offering messages about sex to your children, whether you discuss sex openly or not. The question is whether you are offering positive or negative messages. If you say nothing, the messages are negative; if you are reluctant to show affection, or if you have hostile attitudes about your own or the opposite gender, the messages are negative. Perhaps you don't want to discuss sex because you favor premarital abstinence. If that's so, consider that "informed abstinence" may be a more effective path than abstinence by ignorance.

Your communication now can pave the way for your children to become adults who choose when to begin sexual activity, adults who will be able to enjoy sex in a context of love, respect and understanding.

Children need correct information and they need to have information about sex tied in with love, family values, responsibility and the dangers of sexually transmitted diseases. Your role as a parent has always been vital, but with the outbreak of AIDS and the prevalence of other sexually transmitted diseases, sex education becomes an urgent mission. In a world where AIDS exists, sex education is a matter of life and death.

Sex education is also the only way to stop what appears to be escalating incidences of sexual abuse of children. In 1989 the National Center for Juvenile Justice was finding that the arrest rate for rape by thirteen- and fourteen-year-olds had doubled since 1976, and arrest rates for lesser categories of sexual assault were up by 80 percent. Those who perpetrate sexual violence typically are men who have been sexually abused as children. But now the turnaround time in this vicious cycle of the abused becoming the abusers seems to have shortened. Sex education can prevent your child from being victimized, and it can help victims to express feelings about past abuse, before those feelings fester and transform victims into abusers.

There is no question then that our children need accurate,

personalized, effective sex education; no question that parents are the best possible sources. That doesn't mean that talking about sex with your children will come naturally, or that you will automatically know what to say and when to say it. This chapter is offered to help you discuss sex with your children. What follows are suggestions based on what is age-appropriate. They are offered with the understanding that you know your child best. You know your family values best. And you will be adapting these suggestions to your children. You will be the final judge of how and when to discuss sex.

talking about sex with children ages five to seven

Remember that this period is a time when children are learning to have a sense of personhood, a sense of who they are and whether that identity is good or bad. A major part of a child's sense of personhood concerns gender. Gender identity is understanding that one is male or female and also having an attitude about what that means. It's comprehending what roles males and females have, such as mother or father, and whether a mother can be a policeman and a father can cook. Gender identity also attributes other qualities to male and female. Is it okay for a woman to assert herself and for a man to express sad or frightened feelings? Is it acceptable for a woman to make active choices about work, family, sexual behavior, or does she have to wait until a man makes the choice for her?

gender identity

A person's basic sense of whether he or she is male or female is actually established by the age of two. But at five or six, children's responsibilities around the house increase and continue to define what is appropriate for them to do. Do boys wash dishes, or only girls? Do girls mow the lawn, or only boys? Which jobs depend on being male and which ones are assigned to females? Children of this age also have those marvelous new mental abilities that sensitize them to people's attitudes about gender. Is it wrong for a boy to cry when he's hit by a baseball? Can a girl get mad when she strikes out? Is tenderness or achievement the province of only one gender?

Parents should be aware of gender stereotyping. Most people are brought up with certain notions of what boys and girls can and can't do. As Margaret Mead observed in her cross-cultural studies of male and female, every culture tends to assign certain roles for male and female. None of us can be totally free of stereotypes. Yet we need to recognize that boys and girls who will mature in a world of expanding possibilities for men and women must have occupational and social roles left open as they grow. And that means permitting boys and girls to experience and express the full range of emotions, to exercise all their mental capacities and physical skills.

If children are growing up in a single-parent home, they need to have opportunities to be with trusted members of both genders. They need to develop a healthy identification with their own sex and a sense of being accepted, appreciated and admired by the opposite sex.

sexual curiosity

Just as children are expanding their horizons to recognize that the world does not revolve around them, they are also recognizing that the world is not made up of all boys, or all girls. They will notice and be curious about differences in body parts and body functions.

Parents need to confer accurate names of sexual body parts and an attitude that these parts are good and under the control of each individual. Penis, testicles, scrotum, labia, vulva, vagina, breast, nipples— these words are difficult for many parents to utter. In most cases, our own parents used them infrequently, if at all. But proper names give a sense of dignity to the human body. If ever children need to communicate about changes in their body or any liberties taken by another person, they must have the vocabulary and feel comfortable using it. (If someone attempts to molest a child, it would be better if the child could report, "He tried to touch my penis," or "He put his hand near my vagina," instead of, "He put his hand near my poo-poo," or "She touched me down there.")

privacy and personal rights regarding sex

This is also a time when issues of nudity and modesty may come up. Children develop attitudes about modesty from their families. At about age six, they are likely to want to take baths alone with the door closed, to use the toilet and change clothes in private. These feelings should be respected by the family. Children of this age need to be taught that they control their own bodies and should never feel obligated or pressured into allowing another child or adult to touch their private parts.

facts of life geared to the age of your child

At five or six children are capable of understanding that a baby can begin to grow inside the mother from a seed or fertilized egg made up of a cell from the mother and a cell from the father. They are likely to think of all living things as having will and behavior of their own, so they may still believe that a baby begins and grows because it wants to, not because of a natural process instigated by others.

They can understand that a baby is born through a mother's vagina. They can observe and learn signs of affection and trust and show affection to parents and other family members. They can also learn that affection is given out of choice, not through coercion. A child doesn't have to show affection to a relative or family friend unless he or she feels good about it.

When children go to school they begin to pick up and experiment with sexual slang. "Fuck you" from a six-year-old needs a calm explanation of polite and impolite conversation. These words from a nine-year-old should engender a discussion of sex and the importance of respect when talking about sex.

At five, six and seven, children handle sexual information with an ease and matter-of-factness that will decrease as they get closer to puberty. This is a wonderful time to impart information and instill positive attitudes about sex.

Today they may ask:

Why is the sky blue?
Why do dogs bark?
Why does Dad have a penis?

If you answer today, if you seem to listen and care today, your children will come to you later with other questions.

Why can't I sleep with that cute guy?
Should boys try to sleep with girls right away?
Why do I feel depressed?
Will I ever have a girlfriend?
Is it true you can't get pregnant if you drink Coke before sex?

Encourage questioning. Pick up cues from your children's "body language." Help them to ask if they seem confused. Give a simple answer. Admit it if you don't know, but show that you will try to find out.

Here's a sample dialogue for the youngster.

CHILD: Where does milk come from?
PARENT: It comes from cows.
CHILD: Why?
PARENT: They have milk for their calves, but they have more than they need, so we can have some.
(Later.)
CHILD: Did you have milk for me?
PARENT: Yes.
(FATHER: No, Mommy had the milk.)
CHILD: Where?
PARENT: In my breasts.
(FATHER: In her breasts.)
CHILD: Did I drink it?
PARENT: Yes. Then when you were bigger, you had a bottle, and then a cup.
(Later.)
CHILD: We saw chickens hatch today. They came right out of the eggs, real funny-looking. Where did I come from?
PARENT: From Mommy and Daddy.
CHILD: How?
PARENT: You grew from a tiny fertilized egg in my body.
(FATHER: You grew from a tiny egg, fertilized by me, which changed and grew larger inside Mommy's body.)
CHILD: How did it get there?
PARENT: Women produce eggs—not exactly the kind with shells that chickens have—eggs from their ovaries that are small.

Men produce something called sperm in their bodies. A sperm is even smaller than an egg and it has a tail. That makes it swim. When a sperm swims inside a woman, it can meet an egg and fertilize it. Then a baby can start, very small at first. And it grows and grows inside a special place called the uterus that the mother has.

(Later.)

CHILD: How did it get there?

PARENT: What?

CHILD: That sperm.

PARENT: Dad put it there, because I wanted him to. We loved each other and wanted to have a baby.

CHILD: Oh.

(Later.)

CHILD: How did he?

PARENT: What?

CHILD: Put it there.

appropriate attitudes about sex

You may be wondering what your attitude should be about sex. Should you treat questions about sex just like other questions? Should you be lighthearted when you explain the facts of life? When Leah was five and heard her parents use the word *testicles*, she commented—"Sounds like popsicles." Mom and Dad couldn't help but burst out laughing. Then they worried, should they be laughing about such a serious matter. There are times when sex and especially people's attitudes about it will seem funny. There are times when sex seems holy, when one is struck by the wonder of the plan for male and female and the beautiful possibilities for love to be enhanced by sex.

Most people who study child development suggest that you treat questions about sex in a natural way, so that your children will not learn to be embarrassed about it. Your openness is more important than the words you use. Sex may be humorous, dangerous, sacred. It's natural to feel differently about it at different times and natural to convey these various feelings at different times. Don't be surprised if your children seem to lose interest in the subject, then come back later with more questions. Remember that your children want simple answers.

You are the teacher. And you know your children better than

anyone else. Tell them what you believe they are ready to know. Tell them what is accurate, not a fairy tale. Express something positive, loving and healthy, not something negative, full of terror or shame. Remember, your behavior is more important than your words. If you answer in a loving, caring way, that's the most important part.

CHILD: Well, how did the daddy put the baby there?

PARENT: The sperm comes from the father's testicles. The mom has ovaries where her eggs are stored. The sperm go from the testicles into the penis. The father sends them from his penis into the mother by putting his penis into her vagina. Mothers and fathers do this by getting very close. They do it when they love each other and want to have a baby.

CHILD: Can I see this?

PARENT: No, this is something private.

CHILD: Oh. . . . How does it get out?

PARENT: The baby?

CHILD: Yes.

PARENT: Well, first it has to grow inside for nine months. A woman has a special place where the child grows—her uterus. The child gets food through a cord called the umbilical cord. The uterus is like a balloon. It can get bigger as the child grows. That's why pregnant women (like your Aunt Janie, etc.) seem to have great big tummies that stick way out.

CHILD: Then does the balloon explode?

PARENT: No.

CHILD: How does the baby get out?

(If your child is shy, maybe he or she won't ask. Maybe you'll have to figure out that's what they want to know.)

PARENT: This is a wonderful thing, almost like a miracle. Women have muscles that help the baby move out through the vagina, which also stretches. That's the same opening the father's sperm went into. It gets big enough to let the baby's head out. Then the doctor helps. When you were all the way out, the doctor tied off the umbilical cord that helped you get food. You didn't need it. It formed your belly button. That's why everyone has a belly button. Now you would get food through your mouth. Now Mommy and Daddy would be taking care of you.

CHILD: Did it hurt when I came out?

PARENT: It hurt some. But when I saw you, I was so happy, I didn't mind at all. And Daddy was so happy, he cried for joy.

CHILD: Do I have a vagina?

PARENT: Yes.

OR

PARENT: No, you have a penis, because you're a boy.

CHILD: Will I get a baby?

PARENT: No, you won't have mature eggs until you are older.

OR

PARENT: You won't produce sperm until you are older.

PARENT: And you're human, so you will wait until you love someone and that person loves you and you marry and decide to have a baby. Humans can make choices.

CHILD: But I want a baby now.

PARENT: Humans can learn to wait. Now we've had enough questions. Later we'll talk again about babies.

sex as a natural process

Young children are not embarrassed about sex. At five through seven, sex, penises, vaginas—these are just discoveries they are making. This is the time to make them feel comfortable about the subject. Part of feeling comfortable is helping them to understand that sex and having babies are natural processes, part of a loving family life.

If you have a pregnant relative or friend, try to elicit her cooperation. Let your child know that that's what you've been talking about. If the pregnant friend is willing, let your child feel the baby kick, and give him or her a chance to ask more questions. Sex education is a way to build self-esteem. When you talk about sex with a child, you can help him or her feel good about being male or female, about being born into your family. You can connect sex with love. Only *you* can do that. That's why you are the best person to talk to your children about sex.

Sex education from age five to seven is a way to establish communication before the subject becomes complicated, before there is actual sexual activity. Talking about it now, when your child is just curious, can lay the groundwork for questions later, when your child becomes a teenager and is really considering a sexual relationship.

steps to overcome
embarrassment about discussing sex

Assuming that most parents growing up in our culture will feel some discomfort discussing sex with their children, here are five steps that may help allay your embarrassment.

1. Plan ahead as to what your answers will be about predictable questions concerning sex. Discuss these answers with friends, spouse, relatives.

2. Practice saying words like penis and vagina in these discussions with adults, or in the mirror.

3. There's nothing wrong with admitting your discomfort to your child. "When I was growing up, people didn't talk freely about sex and there were fewer movies and songs about sex, so I find it difficult to talk to you about it. But I know how important it is, so we're going to talk about sex anyway.

4. Remember that you don't have to do this alone. You can include your spouse or another trusted adult when you're discussing sex with your child, or you can have the other person supplement your talk.

5. You can talk to the child of the opposite sex; in fact, you can help your son understand girls' feelings or your daughter understand boys' feelings. Communication about sex starts at home. Your discussions with your children will enable them to feel greater comfort in making clear their feelings about sex to any future intimate partner.

what if you have negative
sex experiences in your past?

Sex may be an embarrassing subject for you because

- you were taught to be embarrassed about sex
- you were sexually abused by a stranger or by a member of the family
- you had sex with people who mistreated you or simply didn't care enough
- you had sex when you didn't care enough
- you had sex and it resulted in a child out of wedlock, a miscarriage or an abortion
- you never learned to enjoy sex yourself

If your personal history has left you feeling embarrassed and uneasy about sex, this would be a good time to deal with your concerns. It's hard to convey a healthy attitude about sex when you don't feel good about it yourself. Take advantage of the resources in your community for information and counseling related to past sexual abuse or current sexual problems.

Millions of people are uninformed about sex. Millions have been victims of sexual abuse. And almost everyone has made what they consider some sort of mistake regarding sexual behavior. Don't involve your child in your problem. But do take steps to solve your problem. You will be your child's sex educator from now on. Even though they may have some sex education in school, as part of their religious education or from your family doctor, you will be the person they see and talk to every day. A little training and counseling could help you and your child.

talking about sex with children ages eight to ten

These are the years to build a base of support and information. As your child gets older, he or she will rely more and more on friends—for better or for worse. Now is the time when you can still make your influence felt in positive ways.

One sex lecture delivered at age five or six is not enough. Communication about sex, while it is not likely to be a daily interchange, should be established as an ongoing process. As children's understanding of the world changes—and we've seen how radical these changes are in childhood—they need to have periodic updates on sex education.

Children of eight to ten want to know how things, including their bodies, work. They are still young enough to talk with you about sex without too much embarrassment, though it's not uncommon to encounter a group of kids this age whispering and giggling about sex and then abruptly stopping when an adult enters the room. Don't be put off by their secretiveness, or their claim that anything to do with sex is "yucky," or because they pretend to know everything already. They need more information now. By the age of nine or ten, some girls will be starting to menstruate. By eleven or twelve, some boys will be experiencing their first nocturnal emission, or wet dream.

Whether your children will mature early or late, they are bound to be curious. Now is the time to let them know you are ready to answer their questions. When they become teenagers, they will find it more difficult to discuss sex with you. Their need for privacy and secrecy will grow as they become older. They will be less able to express their feelings about sex, their anxieties and fears about their own sexuality and how they should behave. Now they are still open to your values and guidance.

making opportunities to talk about sex

At this age, your child may not come out and ask you how babies are made. But if you are listening, you can find an opening. For example:

The child gets mad and uses the four-letter word for intercourse.

PARENT: Please don't use that word.

CHILD: Everybody at school uses it. They use it in the movies.

PARENT: I don't like that word. It's a word for having intercourse that makes sex seem like a dirty thing. It's not.

CHILD: What about when someone doesn't want to, ya know . . . ?

PARENT: Sex should never be forced on a person. It's something two people should do only if they love each other, and only if they decide they both want to show their love that way. (Here's a chance to add your particular family values. "I believe it's something people should do only after they are married," or "I believe it's something people should do only after they are old enough to understand how to use birth control and how to protect themselves from diseases that can be carried through sex.")

CHILD: Jimmy says he had sex already.

PARENT: Well, I don't know Jimmy, but if he's your age, I don't believe that's true. Maybe he just doesn't know about sex, and he has no one to ask. It took me a long time to understand what went on and why people even wanted to have intercourse.

CHILD: It did?

PARENT: Yes. My parents never talked about it. I heard things at school. I read things in what we used to call "dirty books." But you don't have to find out that way. I can explain it to you.

CHILD: You don't have to. I think I know.

PARENT: Well, it can't hurt to talk about it again.

(At this point, you would do well to have a picture or illustration so that you can identify body parts and show your child exactly where things are located. With this diagram or drawing, you need to connect what they see on the outside to what's going on inside. For example: Here's a man's body. That's the penis. These are the testicles. Inside where you can't see, sperm are being produced and mixed with other fluid to make semen. When a man and woman have intercourse, the semen travels to the penis, comes out of his penis and goes into the woman's vagina. Semen is loaded with sperm—just a teaspoon, which is what usually comes out, has four hundred million sperm.

Don't forget to explain male and female to your child. For example:

PARENT: Here's a woman's body. The female's sex organs or genitals are very different. A female has an opening called a vagina. Above the vagina is a small opening where urine comes out. That's the urethra. And above that is something called a clitoris. It's a very sensitive part of the body, like a man's penis. Around the vagina are the labia, outer lips and inner lips. This whole area is called a woman's vulva. These words might sound strange and scientific, because people often use slang words for genitals. And in this family, we sometimes call a penis a ——— (peepee, etc.). But it's good to know the correct words.

humanize sex and
relate it to your values

Give your child a chance to ask questions, or just talk about this general subject. The child might want to know if you felt embarrassed about sex when you were younger, if your parents talked to you, if you worried about being pretty—or handsome, if you worried about girls or boys liking you. If your child just goes through this vocabulary of body parts with you, remember that you have more information that he or she needs. The discussion of what sexual intercourse is might come at another time, or immediately after the explanation of male and female organs.

Whenever you do discuss this, keep in mind what your ideals are about sex, how you would like your child to think about it, what connections you'd like your child to make. Even if you are currently a single parent or in some way ambivalent about sex yourself, consider what a healthy attitude would be for your child. At the same time, be sure you are not completely sidestepping the facts in favor of some rosy picture you wish to paint of people walking off into the sunset. Here's an example of how you might start.

PARENT: When people love each other, they want to show that love in many ways. One way is by having intercourse. But intercourse can produce babies and intercourse can be a way of transmitting disease. So people have to learn to wait to have intercourse until they are sure they are safe—protected from the risk of disease. They have to wait until they are sure that if their intercourse should cause a baby to start, they would be prepared to take care of that baby. That's why I believe _____
(Here's a chance for you to insert your values. People should wait for marriage. People should wait until they are older. People should know each other very well and be very careful about having intercourse.)

Your child may or may not ask questions readily, but you might notice that he or she appears to be puzzled and obviously wants to ask something. Encourage your child to come forward. Admit that you found sex a confusing subject when you were younger, that you didn't understand it all the first time you heard about it. Ask your child if he or she understands or has questions.

If the child is ten, he might be wondering specifically what's going to happen to him soon, when he starts changing into a man. Girls of ten know that in a year or two, or sooner, they'll begin menstruating. They wonder what that's like. They might need your help in actually asking these questions.

PARENT: You look a little confused. Ask me anything about this. If I don't know, we'll both find out.
CHILD: Do sperm just come out, ya know, all the time?
PARENT: Sperm don't come out when a man urinates. They come out when a man is sexually aroused, as happens during intercourse. At that time he ejaculates or expels semen. When boys are about twelve or thirteen they have their first ejaculation of semen at night. It's called a wet dream or nocturnal emission. A boy may be embarrassed if he doesn't know this is natural and normal. This is the very beginning of producing sperm.

relate sex to male and female

If you're a woman explaining these developments to your son, you might want to read about it and speak to someone who has insights into how these changes affect men. The same applies to a father explaining things to a daughter.

Meredith has a ten-year-old son. She has not discussed sex with him since he was five and asked lots of questions. When she saw the film *Parenthood,* she realized it might be time to have another talk, or have the boy talk with his father. In that film, a young man is confused, embarrassed and ashamed of the changes he's experiencing. He withdraws from the family, carries a paper bag around all the time and is totally miserable—until his mother finds out the mysterious paper bag contains an X-rated videotape and her son is in need of talking to a man about these changes—changes that he finds to his relief are normal. All along, he thought he was the only one who ever had a wet dream, the only boy who masturbated.

Meredith never realized boys could be so upset by puberty. She thought it was only girls who felt awkward and embarrassed. She brought her son a videotape of the *Parenthood* movie, watched it with her son and used that as a way to talk about the subject again. She learned that sex is a subject that needs to be broached at various times during childhood, and in ways that show sensitivity to children's changing thoughts and feelings. She also realized that her son knew very little about women and how their bodies changed at puberty.

When you are equipped with an understanding of both male and female attitudes and biology, you can encourage your child to find out about the opposite sex, whether you are the mother or the father. For example:

"You're probably wondering how things work with women, how their bodies change at puberty. They produce eggs, but that happens in a monthly cycle. Actually, the origins of those eggs are in a woman's body from the day she's born. But they don't mature until she reaches puberty and her monthly cycle of menstruation begins. That usually happens when the woman is about twelve. But there's no correct time. For some women this begins at ten; for others at fourteen.

"Ovaries release an egg each month. The egg goes into the Fallopian tubes. If a woman has intercourse when an egg is present, the sperm expelled from the man's penis swim up through the tunnel-shaped vagina toward the egg. One may fertilize the egg. The egg then gets planted in the uterus where it grows into an embryo, then a fetus. Finally it is ready and comes out as a baby through the vagina."

Your child may or may not ask questions along the way. But there are certain questions that you can assume are on their minds, whether or not they ask.

CHILD: What if there's no, ya know, sperm?
PARENT: The uterus gets ready each month to receive a fertilized egg. If there's no fertilized egg in the uterus, the lining of the uterus is discarded. That's what *menstruation* is. It's the body sloughing off this lining, which is mostly blood.
CHILD: Yuck.
PARENT: It might seem unpleasant and for some women it causes them a few days of cramps or discomfort. But it's also a wonderful system, because it means that when the time comes

that a woman wants to have a baby, the uterus will be ready. It's also a sign that a women is developing the biological capacity to become pregnant if she has intercourse.

CHILD: What happens to the stuff when a woman is pregnant?

PARENT: She doesn't menstruate. She doesn't have her monthly period. The lining of her uterus is being used to provide a place for the developing baby. A special layer of the uterus forms called the placenta. The fetus is attached to the placenta by its umbilical cord.

CHILD: And when she has the baby, what happens to that stuff?

PARENT: The placenta comes out during the birth process, and the umbilical cord, which has no feeling, is cut and the remaining little bit of the cord closest to the baby forms the belly button. A woman doesn't get her period again for about six weeks after she has the baby. Then things start going back to their usual monthly cycle.

CHILD: That's weird.

PARENT: It's also wonderful. Sex is very special. I know there are lots of jokes about sex and periods. I used to feel pretty embarrassed about that stuff myself. But then I grew up. I met your father. (I met your mother.) Now, for me, sex is something related to love and creation. That's why I want to be the one to discuss it with you, instead of having you learn about it from dirty jokes or magazines that make sex seem casual, unimportant, something that people do on the spur of the moment for their own quick satisfaction.

talking about sex with children ages eleven and older

The wide gap between male and female maturing makes it difficult to generalize about what is appropriate sex education for males and females at different ages. The fact that boys mature two years later on the average than girls may account for the tardiness of parental talks and sex education courses. If parents gear their timetable for sex education to this male schedule, children won't learn about the changes of puberty until they are twelve or thirteen. Information on menstruation and reproduction can come *after* girls have begun to menstruate.

Girls are usually one or two years ahead of boys in physical as well as social and emotional development. Girls are usually interested in boys before boys are interested in them. Boys may experience this difference as pressure from girls for friendships, or as higher expectations on the part of girls for a close or even romantic relationship. Girls may experience boys of this age as boring or self-centered. (Interestingly, this difference between a female's desire for commitment and a male's reluctance to commit continues to exist in many cases on into adulthood.) Parents can be helpful in assuring their children that this gap exists, but that it can be closed, and children should not develop a negative attitude toward the other gender because of it.

Children should be told about the wide variations in the timing of puberty. They will probably be concerned about their bodily changes a year or two before puberty actually begins. Discussions with children who are a year or two from beginning puberty need to be more thorough than they've been so far. Descriptions of female external and internal anatomy should include labia, clitoris and hymen, as well as vagina, uterus, Fallopian tubes, ovary and ovum. The menstrual cycle and hygiene during menstruation should be explained in detail. (In previous generations, hygiene may have been the only thing discussed about menstruation.) There is a difference between hygiene and making a girl feel as if menstruation is a dirty or shameful thing.

Girls may benefit from some explanation of the shift in the balance of hormones before the monthly menstruation begins, a shift that causes some women to feel moody, depressed or irritable. According to an American Medical Association report on adolescents, half of all American adolescents experience discomfort or pain during menstruation that often results in school absences.

A girl should be able to talk to her parents about menstruation and any problems she has with it. A girl will be better able to tolerate any discomfort if she has a sympathetic person to confide in. She can be encouraged to attend school despite difficulties she has when she menstruates. Girls need to be encouraged to understand that menstruation is not a reason to feel less capable of competing or achieving. There is plenty of proof for this—from female Olympic athletes to active women who are effective every day in whatever they do.

Boys need the same thorough explanation of their own anatomy —penis, scrotum, foreskin, testes, circumcision, semen, vas deferens, seminal vesicle, prostate gland— and of female anatomy. Girls need to understand male anatomy and pubertal changes, as well as learning about their own bodies and the changes that take place as they mature. Boys need to understand what nocturnal emission is and why their attitude about females is undergoing a change.

More important than your vocabulary list, is your ability to remember what it was like to go through puberty yourself. Remember what it was like to feel as if you went to sleep with a flat chest and woke up with the beginnings of breasts, or to experience a wet dream, or to find that you were sprouting pubic hair, or to have one's voice crack in the middle of a sentence.

It's no wonder that the early years of adolescence are likely to be the hardest for parents and children. If we look at the incredible changes that are occurring and the strange way they occur, we can begin to understand why.

everything's changing

Everybody changes from child to adult, but not in the same way or at the same time. Puberty begins when the body makes certain hormones. The hormones for puberty are special chemicals produced in a gland near the brain called the pituitary gland. These hormones send a message to the sex glands—the ovaries and testicles. The message is: it's time to make some changes.

Many changes are going on, almost at the same time. It's like a revolution. Adolescents grow taller, sometimes in a dramatic leap called the "growth spurt." (The average age for accelerated growth ranges from nine and a half to fourteen, though boys may not achieve adult height until their late teens.)

Increase in so-called gonadotropic hormones, such as testosterone and estrogen, results in the appearance of pigmented pubic hair, for boys one of the first signs of puberty. Boys get facial hair and their voices fluctuate from high to low in an unexpected and embarrassing way. This and the creation of an Adam's apple occur because vocal chords are enlarging. Boys also sprout underarm hair. Their skin gets oily and pimples may erupt. They experience new sensations and their first ejaculation. Even their faces change—the nose growing before the rest. If they are going to require glasses, that shift in eyesight may occur now. It will take at least two years for all the changes of puberty to occur.

Girls go through the changes of puberty about two years before boys do. They grow taller, their growth spurt begins between the ages of seven and a half and eleven and a half and peaks about age twelve. Since all this happens earlier in girls, they find themselves taller than the boys in their class. Their breasts begin to grow about one or two years before menstruation begins. Their hips broaden. Underarm hair and pubic hair sprout due to gonadotropic hormones such as testosterone and estrogen—some of the same hormones as with boys but in very different proportions.

Menstruation begins. This event, also known as menarche, usually occurs between age eleven and age fifteen, but some girls menstruate as early as age nine and others as late as age twenty, depending on an individual's physiological state and genetic factors. Pictures drawn by girls before and after the beginning of menstruation (menarche) show that girls see themselves differently after this event. Once they start menstruating, they stop seeing themselves as children and start seeing themselves as women.

am i normal? am i attractive?

With all of the changes going on inside their bodies and externally, they feel as if they are strangers in a strange land. One thing that most young adolescents lack is confidence. Perhaps because they are younger when puberty hits, girls are especially uneasy at this time. Their self-esteem may dip. They often face a change of schools just when their entire bodies have changed, so they may begin junior high school feeling terribly insecure.

They desperately want to know if they are normal, if they have the right-sized breasts, if they got their periods at the right time, if their skin will ever be free of pimples, if they will ever be the right weight. Some girls become obsessed with their weight and develop eating disorders such as anorexia, where they eat too little and become dangerously thin. Some overeat and become obese. Concern over appearance at this time may cause some girls to become depressed. These are conditions that require counseling.

This is the time when girls develop a notion of whether they are attractive or unattractive, a sense of their body image that is based on earlier feelings of high or low self-esteem. This body image—these feelings of being attractive or unattractive—is likely to stay with them well into adulthood.

you can offer reassurance and information

They may not seem to want it. They may not come and ask for it. But when puberty begins, your child may feel confused and insecure. You can try to find opportunities to share some of your feelings and experiences as a young adolescent. Try not to turn it into a lecture. "When we were kids, we never did anything wrong, etc."

Ask yourself, When did your body change? How did you feel? What ideas did you have that were mistaken? What did your parents tell you? At what age? How did you feel about what they said? What do you wish they had said or not said? What do you want to do differently with your child? What do you want to do the same?

Try to recall some of the funny or embarrassing moments from your young life. And while you're sharing those feelings, you can offer information and see if there are any questions.

For example, this is a conversation that Tracy had with her mother when they were putting away groceries:

DAUGHTER: Molly's getting a bikini. I look gross in them.
MOTHER: I noticed your friend Molly has really grown and developed.
DAUGHTER: Mom, you're so weird.
MOTHER: I remember when my friends started growing and getting breasts and having their periods. I was afraid my turn would never come.
DAUGHTER: You were?
MOTHER: Sure. I thought I'd always be short and flat-chested and never get the "visit" that friends complained about, that

made them seem like they all belonged to their own club, and I was on the outside.

DAUGHTER: So what happened?

MOTHER: I finally got it when I was almost thirteen. I started to feel uncomfortable during dinner. I went to the bathroom. My mother knocked to see if I was okay. I told her. And you know what she did? When I came back to the table, she told the whole family—my father and brothers, Uncle Al, and Uncle Billy, who was only eight then and didn't even know what it was. I was so embarrassed.

DAUGHTER: Did you get mad at her?

MOTHER: Yeah, I made her promise never to talk about it in front of anyone again. But I was kind of glad, too. I didn't tell her, but she made me feel like it wasn't a terrible thing. She made me feel like it was something to be proud of. I'd like you to feel good about the changes that are happening to you. Someday you'll be a fine woman.

DAUGHTER: I don't think so.

MOTHER: I know so. Lots of kids your age don't even know what's happening to them. Even people my age sometimes don't know. I had to read some books to remember it all. Let's talk about some of the changes.

In early adolescence, your child may resist any attempt to pass along information. There's a powerful need when the changes of puberty occur to start separating from parents, to break away from the child role, to declare unequivocally, I'm a person. Given this attitude, you may find, the minute you try to bring up anything to do with the physical changes of adolescence, your child finds something else to do.

MOTHER: I just want to be sure you understand some of the changes that you're experiencing now, or that you'll be experiencing soon.

DAUGHTER: I have to call Molly.

MOTHER: Sure, in a minute. I'm just going to mention five things.

DAUGHTER: Okay. Just five.

MOTHER: Breasts.

DAUGHTER: That's one.

MOTHER: I've got to say what happens. It starts with nipples getting darker and larger and there's just a little mound and you start thinking, this is all I'll ever have. Now some people don't get very big breasts and some get ones that are extremely big. At your age, everyone worries about the size and shape of their breasts. But beautiful people have all sizes and shapes. When people feel good about their bodies, they are attractive.

DAUGHTER: But how do you feel good about your body when it's gross.

MOTHER: You work with it, get exercise, eat things that are healthy and not too fattening. Your hips are going to get wider—mine got much wider, but some of my friends stayed narrower and I envied them. Still, I got used to my own shape. I used to struggle into jeans that weren't made for my figure. Then I realized, hey, this is my body and I'm going to wear what looks good on me.

DAUGHTER: Nothing looks good on me.

MOTHER: Give yourself a chance. You're going to be a beautiful woman.

discuss feelings
as well as physiology

If your child is going through puberty, he or she may be especially perplexed about physical changes and emotional swings connected to what comedians have called the age of raging hormones. These are the areas that parents are most likely to avoid discussing. Yet this is what young adolescents most need to understand, why they are experiencing these new feelings, and whether anyone else has ever felt this way. So if you can bring feelings as well as physiology into your explanation, you're much more likely to reach your child.

For example:

MOTHER: The part that's hard to understand, especially with women, is what's going on inside. You notice certain changes on the outside. The whole area of sexual parts between your legs is called your vulva.

DAUGHTER: Mom, you told me this when I was in first grade.

MOTHER: Did you have hair there before?

DAUGHTER: No.

MOTHER: Are you starting to get hair on your outer lips?

DAUGHTER: Lips, yuck, why do they call them lips?

MOTHER: They have to call them something. Sometimes they call them labia.

DAUGHTER: Oo, that's even worse.

MOTHER: There are the outer and inner . . .

DAUGHTER: Lips, okay.

MOTHER: And at the top there's the clitoris.

DAUGHTER: Another dumb word.

MOTHER: But it's an important part of your body. It's very small, about the size of a pea, but it's very sensitive to sexual feelings and touching. In that way, it's like a man's penis. This is a time when you might get the urge to explore your own body.

DAUGHTER: Mom.

MOTHER: Well, some girls rub these areas and experience sexual excitement that reaches a kind of peak and it's called an . . .

DAUGHTER: Mother!

MOTHER: Orgasm. Okay. Girls sometimes masturbate, and so do boys, even though the practice has been forbidden or considered taboo for a long time, even though it's normal. I also want you to know that the vagina has a ring of skin at the opening for extra protection and it's called a hymen. Almost everyone's hymen has a large enough opening to allow the flow of menstrual blood or the use of tampons without pain. Sometimes the hymen stretches to the sides from exercise or physical examination, or when a person first has intercourse. Sometimes a hymen is gone even though there has been no intercourse.

DAUGHTER: Did you have one?

MOTHER: Yes, so it hurt a little when I first had intercourse.

DAUGHTER: Oh . . . will it hurt when I get my period?

MOTHER: It might. Women are different. Some people get cramps during menstruation. They might feel very grouchy. Some don't feel much different physically or emotionally.

But one thing we've learned, women can keep on doing even strenuous things when they have their periods. Women have set world records in sports while they've had their periods. So even if you might feel a little uncomfortable during that time, you don't have to stop everything. And you shouldn't let anyone use that as an excuse for not having girls or women compete.

Take a moment to emphasize the connection between menstruation and the possibility of pregnancy. It's vital that your daughter—or your son—grasps this connection.

MOTHER: I do want you to be very clear about menstruation, because if you don't understand it, you don't understand how and when you might get pregnant. And that can certainly change your life.

DAUGHTER: You can get pregnant if you, ya know, have sex with a man.

MOTHER: Here's how and when that can happen. When the egg or ovum is ripe, the ovary releases it and it gets sucked in by the Fallopian tube, which looks kind of like a morning glory flower and functions like a vacuum. Now if a woman has intercourse during this time of ovulation, one of those millions of sperm that a man ejaculates during intercourse could join up with that egg and fertilize it. The fertilized egg would then go to the uterus or womb, which is low in the tummy and has a special lining with blood and food for the baby. The fertilized egg attaches itself and grows there. The woman is pregnant.

DAUGHTER: What happens if the egg isn't fertilized?

MOTHER: Don't forget an ovum is smaller than a pinhead. You couldn't recognize it as an egg. If it's not fertilized it just dissolves and the special lining prepared in the uterus leaves the body if there's no pregnancy. It comes out as menstrual fluid. That blood lining goes out through the vagina over about three to seven days. Some people get a heavy flow. Some get a lighter one. Some are very regular—every twenty-eight days. Some get it every twenty or every forty days. When girls first start menstruating, they might skip a period, but most women settle into a pattern as they get older.

DAUGHTER: Is it a curse? Ya know, how they say that?

MOTHER: I see it as more blessing than curse. Women can give birth. It's a wonderful, miraculous gift from God. It's also got some problems and responsibilities attached to it. It's a reminder that you are a woman. You have to take care of your body and be responsible for the choices you make. You have the chance to develop a human life within you. You can't use a gift like that any old time. You have to save it for the time when you can take care of a new life. And that time is much, much later. This is the time to take care of your own life.

let them know they can come to you

Your daughter may thank you and hug you. She may tell you you're weird or old-fashioned. She may say nothing. But you've given her something very important that she couldn't get out of a textbook. You've shared your love and encouraged her to feel good about being a woman. You've let her know she can come to you.

don't bypass boys

Surveys show that parents talk less to boys than to girls about sexuality and sexual responsibility. This is surprising and disturbing, especially at a time when boys can contract sexually transmitted diseases, including AIDS, just as easily as girls. It is also surprising, because boys and later men are often expected to know more about sex—a strange expectation in a culture that discourages boys from asking questions and doesn't seem to give boys the same benefits as girls when it comes to communication about sex.

Your son (or nephew or grandson) may not go through puberty before the age of twelve, but he will be aware of many girls in the class and some of the other boys undergoing this change. He will be curious and perhaps anxious about what is about to happen, if it hasn't started already. A mother can talk to a son about these changes, but she should also provide opportunities for the boy to talk with his father, an uncle, or older brother.

The best situation is to let the boy know that there are men and women he can turn to to discuss sex, as well as other concerns in his life. Sometimes a boy's curiosity about sex manifests itself by his getting hold of magazines, books or videos that feature female nudity. This may not look like a window of opportunity, but it is. Take advantage of it. For example:

FATHER: I noticed you had one of those magazines in your room.

SON: What magazines?

FATHER: It's okay. I don't blame you for wanting to look at beautiful women. I don't blame you for being curious about women's bodies.

SON: Dad, can we just skip it? I'll throw it out.

FATHER: You don't have to. I just want you to know there are other places to go to find out what you need to know.

SON: Like where?

FATHER: Like here.

SON: Things are a lot different now.

FATHER: Some things aren't. When I was your age I felt confused by sex and fascinated by it. It was my favorite subject, but I never asked questions, because I didn't want to act like I didn't know everything, which of course I didn't. My older brother told me stuff. I figured some things out. A lot of things I didn't learn until later. I'm still learning.

SON: You are?

FATHER: Sure. I understand what's happening to you much better than I understood what was happening to me. That's why I want to talk to you about—

SON: I've got basketball practice.

FATHER: I won't be that long. I just want to let you know that what's going on with you now, or what will start going on in the next year or two, is perfectly normal. There's nothing strange about you. That's what used to worry me a lot.

SON: Sometimes I worry it will never happen, that I'll never grow and get stuff the older guys have. Then sometimes I worry that it will happen and I won't know, ya know, how to act.

FATHER: I remember feeling that way. And then, I remember when I had my first wet dream. In the books they call it a nocturnal emission. It's the first time a boy ejaculates, the first time semen comes out of your penis. It might happen in your sleep and you might just wake up and find a wet spot. Or you might remember a dream about sex.

SON: What happens if you have one and you don't, ya know, do anything about it?

FATHER: You can have an erection without ejaculating. What happens is extra blood fills the spongy tissues in your penis. Your penis becomes firmer and larger and sticks out from your body. The erection usually disappears. The penis softens and returns to its usual size and position. The erection might be followed by ejaculation. Ejaculation happens when the muscles around the sex organs contract several times. Semen comes out in small spurts.

SON: What if you don't have enough semen?

FATHER: You shouldn't be deceived by the amount. There's usually about a teaspoon full, but that one teaspoon holds four hundred million sperm cells. It's just semen that comes out. Even though urine and sperm come from the same opening, they can't come out at the same time.

Usually a man has a special tingly feeling in his body. This feeling, which builds up and comes to a peak or a climax with ejaculation, is called an orgasm. A teenage guy doesn't have an orgasm and ejaculation with every erection. Whether you ejaculate or not, that erection will gradually go away.

Erections occur because of many thoughts, sights, even sometimes when there's nothing to do with sex. Almost all males have them off and on while they sleep. Sometimes they happen unexpectedly, like at school, or when you're just talking to a girl.

That first wet dream might be embarrassing, but it's a good sign, a sign you're growing up. After that, ejaculation might occur in different ways. It might happen from masturbating, which boys do. Most people feel it's not good to concentrate too much on masturbation. Some people feel it's wrong or a sin. I know it doesn't cause mental or physical harm. I know it's normal.

Later on, when you start going out with girls, ejaculation can occur when you're with a girl. You might be kissing or touching her. She might be touching you. It can happen even if she doesn't actually touch your penis, because it can be pretty exciting to kiss a girl.

I don't expect you to be having intercourse for a long time, but that's the other time when ejaculation occurs. By the way, penises come in different sizes and shapes. The penis grows larger during puberty, but whatever size it becomes, the size has nothing to do with virility—being a man in the sense of being capable of having sex—or fertility, being able to have children.

who should talk about sex with preadolescents?

This is an age when young people may relate better to the parent of their gender—sons to father, daughters to mothers. But the most important thing is that children going through puberty get the information they need.

If you're a single parent, you can talk to children of the opposite sex about sex. You can also supplement what you have to say by having someone of their gender talk to them—a minister or rabbi, a health teacher, a friend or relative who is sensitive and understanding.

you can listen

Once you have offered some of the basic facts of puberty and reproduction, learn to cultivate the art of listening. It's best not to assume you know what your children are going through, even though it may be similar to what you experienced. Instead, set up a situation that will allow you to elicit their feelings and allow you to listen. If your preteen daughter asks, "Why do people have sex?" instead of launching into another presentation of the reproductive facts, assume that something specific triggered her question. Say, "There are lots of different reasons—why do you think they do? "Asking several gentle questions allows your child to talk about things on her mind. A personalized, responsive approach rather than a hasty sermon can give her the kinds of facts she can relate to, the kind of information that could influence her behavior.

This is also a time to allow children to listen to adult conversations about sex if they happen to walk in on one that's going on, rather than to abruptly stop talking about sexual matters when the child enters the room.

a new style of parenting

The dramatic changes of puberty are accompanied by social and emotional changes in the young adolescent, changes that require an altered style of parenting. The preadolescent or young adolescent begins to test old rules of family life and this testing causes parents' anxiety levels to rise. The preteen may try cigarettes or wine or beer. He or she may experiment with drugs. We'll discuss this possibility in Chapter Six. The threat of experimentation in the adolescent years is bound to make parents apprehensive.

Parents may feel frightened for their children, or even guilty, as they rethink their own adolescence and ask themselves if they've been good enough parents so far.

Though it's normal for parents to feel stressed by their children's preadolescent behavior, it's up to parents to make a special effort to keep communication open. It's up to them to trust the child on the brink of puberty with more solid information and expressions of confidence, love and affection that will boost the child's self-esteem. Reassure your child that new curiosities and friendships are normal. The family will always be there. The child will be loved by the family, even as the child tries his or her wings.

At the same time, there's a need to reaffirm family values and basic family rules. So if the child has stayed out too late, or broken the rules, the limits need to be reiterated, the consequences of breaking the rules enforced. But along with the rules must come the message: "We love and believe in you even though we don't always agree with or approve of what you do. We are always ready to talk to you about anything that confuses or troubles you."

The truth is, there are times you may wish you didn't care as much as you do, times when you experience an anger akin to rage because you don't like what your child has done—no—you hate it. And at the very moment that anger bursts upon you, you know you can never stop loving your child. Most of the time, that thought will make you happy. During early adolescence, there are moments when it may feel like a mixed blessing.

SUMMARY

Children between the ages of five and twelve may not seem overtly preoccupied with sex, but they are forming important attitudes toward this basic need, attitudes that will be influenced by parents, as well as by peers, other adults and messages from the media. These attitudes about sex, built on the child's earliest experiences with affection and the fulfillment of needs, undergo significant development during the school years. Parents are uniquely suited to communicating appropriate information about sex, for they can place it in a context of love and family values.

Few parents feel completely comfortable talking about sex. They may lack education and practice discussing the topic, or they may have had a negative past sexual experience. But parents can become more comfortable communicating to their children, especially when they understand that appropriate sex education can protect their children from sexually transmitted diseases, including AIDS. Dealing with negative experiences from the past related to sex, through counseling, self-help groups or sharing with trusted friends, can help parents resolve personal problems, as well as helping them communicate vital information and a healthy attitude to their children.

Reassurance, love and support are just as important as scientific accuracy when talking about sex. As children approach adolescence, they may seem less willing to listen, more anxious to pull away from your influence. You may need to show more respect and support for the new people they are becoming, but they continue to need rules and guidance.

From ages five through twelve, children gain from seeing themselves as having control over their own bodies and over choices to give and receive affection. They need to be taught that they can say no to unwanted touching. As they approach adolescence, they need to grasp changes that will occur in their bodies, to understand what makes male and female capable of reproduction and what kind of feelings go along with puberty and the beginning of sexual maturity. As a parent, you can impart a hopeful, confident attitude about sex. You can make your child feel that he or she can always come to you to find out information or share personal concerns about sex. As children make the transition from childhood to adolescence, their demands for independence increase. It's up to parents to continue to be supportive and yet reassert family values and basic rules. It's a difficult balancing act but a vital one.

6

TEACHING YOUR CHILD
TO MAKE DECISIONS
ABOUT SEX

One of the most important things you can do when you talk to your children about sexuality is stress the significance of making responsible decisions. As you build your child's self-esteem, you are reinforcing her ability to make healthy choices. Nowhere is this more crucial than in the area of decisions regarding sex. This chapter will suggest ways for you to guide your children to healthy decisions regarding sex, throughout childhood and on into adolescence. It will also help you discuss AIDS at appropriate times and in appropriate ways.

importance of choice
and responsibility

Children of five, six and seven need to feel capable of respecting their own bodies and the bodies of others. Without feeling shame concerning their bodies, they need to grasp the basic notion of privacy and self-determination when it comes to touching and private parts. They need to be able to firmly refuse anyone who wishes to take physical advantage of them—whether it's a relative who wants to hug, kiss or stroke them in some way that feels uncomfortable, or a stranger who wants to woo them into a car.

Children of eight, nine and ten are curious about the details of puberty, what it feels like to be a teenager, for girls what it feels like to have breasts and menstruate, for boys what it feels like to have one's voice change, to become sexually aroused.

At eleven and twelve, when many girls are already menstruating and boys are about to begin the phases of puberty, young people want additional details—about love and sex, about intercourse and pregnancy, and about scary diseases, particularly AIDS.

Your talks with your child about human sexuality should always stress the importance of making decisions about sex. You should stress the right of your child to choose when and how and whether to be touched, to choose whether or not sexual activity is what he or she wants. You will be laying a foundation for later discussions about abstinence, birth control and sexually transmitted diseases. You may wish to wait until your child is into the teenage years to discuss in more detail which forms of contraception exist and which sexually transmitted diseases can affect people who are sexually active. (We've included some of these details in Appendix 1 for use when you choose to bring up these topics.)

stressing decision-making for children ages five to seven

When you explain basic differences between male and female to your child of five to seven years old, the child may want to know when he is going to have sperm and the body of a man, when she is going to have eggs and the body of a woman. You'll want to point out that even when they are old enough to produce either sperm or eggs, they will not be mature enough to have children. Even with the bodies of grown-ups, they need to wait until their thoughts and feelings catch up to their bodies. They will always need to use their thoughts and feelings to decide about when to be touched and when to have a baby.

Even at this early age, you can get across the idea that it's not good to have a baby when you're very young. A young child can understand that the baby might get sick when the young mommy wants to play and have fun, or when the young mommy needs to go to school. At that age you can say, "Having a baby takes thoughts and feelings—not just eggs and sperm. When it comes to having a baby, people need to wait and make a careful choice. When you get older, I hope you'll use your mind and your feelings, as well as your body. I hope you'll stop and think. I want you to have a happy family, with a mommy and a daddy who can take care of their children."

preventing sexual abuse

At this early age, you should definitely stress the idea that your child controls his or her own body.

You will want to specifically say that "Your body is yours. The only people who should touch your body are people you like, people who care for you. Some parts of your body are private, like your penis, or vagina, your rectum or what you call your behind. These are your private parts. You are the only person who may touch them, except at special times when Mommy or Daddy gives you a bath, or when the doctor examines you."

You need to instill in your child a sense of respect for the privacy of others and for other person's private parts. For example: "It's natural to be curious about other people's private parts, but their bodies belong to them. It's wrong to insist on seeing someone else's private parts. If a person wants to see your private parts, you say "no," you leave and tell me—even if that person who did the wrong thing is a person we know. If a person has touched your private parts already, it's important to tell me. Telling about things will make you feel better. Remember, swallowing a bad feeling is like trying to swallow a chicken bone. It always feels better to cough up that chicken bone. It will always feel better to tell about the bad feeling, to talk it over with someone who cares, like Mom or Dad or your teacher."

handling a disclosure
of sexual abuse

One of the greatest values of discussing sex at home, rather than relying totally on a teacher or minister or social worker to explain this for you, is that you can give your child permission to reveal anything of a sexual nature that might frighten him or her, or even something that has happened that he or she has been afraid to discuss. This means that you have to be not only talking to the child, but listening and watching the child's reactions. Let's say, at some point during a talk, your child is silent and turns away. You need to pick up on this clue and find out what's wrong.

(Child is silent and turns away.)

PARENT: What's wrong? You look upset.

CHILD: When I was playing at Sally's (Sean's), before she (he) moved away, I let her (him) touch my, ya know, penis (vulva).

PARENT: Did she (he) just touch it? Or did something else happen?

CHILD: No, she just touched it and said it was for, ya know, the f—— word you don't want me to say.

PARENT: Did you touch her (him) also?

CHILD: No, I . . . just, ya know, looked.

PARENT: Sure you looked. You were curious. But something told you this was wrong. You were right not to touch. And she (he) was wrong to touch you. Your body is your own and you don't let anyone touch. I know she (he) was curious. We each are curious to see the other person's parts. But they are private.

We don't let other people touch our private parts. We say no, and leave, or call home, or tell the mother or the babysitter. I'm glad you told me about Sally (Sean). You're a perfectly fine boy (girl). If anyone ever does anything or tries to do anything to you, always tell me. Don't keep it a secret and worry about it. I love you.

If your conversations with your child reveal a past episode of sexual abuse, be supportive of your child and take advantage of counseling services in your community. It's important that victims are not made to feel guilty or responsible for violations that occur. A child can overcome such an episode, if she or he has the chance to get out feelings about it and receive comfort and support.

When girls and boys go through puberty, the sexual desire of friends, or even someone in the family, may be inappropriately aroused. Divorce and remarriage may increase the chances for someone to take advantage of a half brother or half sister, a stepdaughter or stepson. Incest is a disturbingly common occurrence, a problem that requires immediate attention. Anyone who has been the victim of incest has suffered a severe trauma. The victim needs protection from any further abuse and an opportunity to overcome the feeling that she or he incited the event and deserved to be victimized. The responsibility for a child's victimization always rests with the adult.

emphasizing decision-making for ages eight to ten

From eight to ten, issues of choice can be even better understood, since children of this age have a clearer understanding of their own feelings and those of others. Children of this age can comprehend that actions and feelings aren't always in harmony. Unlike young children, who see the world as a product of their thoughts and feelings, children of eight, nine and ten are much less egocentric.

distinctions between love and sex

It is at this time that you can begin to distinguish between the feelings of love and the actions associated with making love. This is an appropriate time to talk to your child about love and sex. The example below suggests some points to be made.

"Intercourse can be an expression of the deepest feelings of love and commitment, a special way of saying 'I love you' reserved for husband and wife. But intercourse means different things to different people. Physically, it's the act of a man inserting his penis in a woman's vagina. This act is sometimes called making love. And sometimes that's what it is. But the urge for sex, the desire to have intercourse is, for some people, like a craving for a candy bar. After they have the candy, they want to try a different brand. For them sex isn't an expression of love, but a fleeting urge that needs to be satisfied. People have to be taught to feel and express love by seeing it and receiving it from their own parents. This makes them more likely to understand sex as something that can come after love, something very special that two people may choose to do. But some people don't learn how to love, don't understand that sex should be connected to love, because they have never been loved. Instead, they've been abused. People like that can get sex mixed up with showing power, controlling or bullying. They can make intercourse an expression of cruelty, such as the person who rapes a woman or molests a child."

Give children of this age examples of what you're saying. "Here are some other times when sex is not part of love, when sex is a bad choice:

> "When people don't want to have sexual relations, but they do anyway just to please someone else.
> "When people have sex without love because they think sex will make love happen.
> "When people pretend they feel love when they don't."

Your children need to understand that romantic or sexual feelings need not always lead to sexual activity. Let them know that falling in love means two people want to be together. They want to share their personal thoughts and feelings. They feel good about themselves when they're together.

Make clear that falling in love is just the beginning. Over time, two people may change the way they feel—they may fall out of love, or their first attraction, the first feeling of falling in love, may change to a deep love for and trust in each other.

Tell them that relationships involving deep love and trust can last; they are the kind where you plan things together, where you plan to have a family together. Most people think this is the best way to have sex, within marriage, within a relationship that will last.

Explain that sometimes people fall in love but they're not ready for sex or marriage. And they're certainly not ready for becoming parents. Let's say a person is thirteen or fourteen. The person is not ready for sex or marriage. But sex is not the only way to show feelings of love. Other things such as caring or talking are more important in a loving relationship. Two young people in love can show their love by being good listeners, doing special favors, giving something that is from the heart, like little gifts and showing thoughtfulness.

physical maturity and new responsibility

At ages eight to ten, you can let your children know that the special feelings of being older and having the body of a man or of a woman also bring with them some serious responsibilities. As you explain the details of menstruation and the changes that begin with nocturnal emission, let them know that this biological readiness will mean that they have new choices to make.

A woman can get pregnant and become a mother. A man can become a father and be responsible for a child. It's not too early for you to express your feelings about these choices, your belief that early sexual activity, for example at ages thirteen and fourteen and fifteen, means that young people will be risking pregnancy and other problems long before they can possibly deal with being parents.

Children of this age can understand that they will develop the bodies of grown-ups a long time before they can live a grown-up life. But they need concrete examples of what you're talking about. So, in addition to discussing appropriate aspects of love and sex including menstruation (see Chapter 5), explain when a pregnancy could occur.

"Now that you know how a woman can become pregnant, I also want you to understand when a woman can become pregnant. You [a woman] can become pregnant during the time your [her] ovaries release an egg, a time called ovulation. If you have intercourse during ovulation when an egg is present, one of the millions of sperm from the man's semen might fertilize that egg and that is the beginning of a pregnancy.

"I'm trying to help you understand what's ahead. I want you to think about the choices you're going to have to make before you actually have to make them. Most of all, I want you to know that you can come to me if you're having a hard time dealing with changes in your body or choices that worry you."

opening the door to health care professionals

For some girls between the ages of nine and twelve, talking to an objective, nonrelated person about their concerns, fears and sexual behaviors may be comfortable and reassuring. Introducing your daughter in her preteen years to your gynecologist may establish the beginning of a useful communication. You can bring your daughter with you to one of your regular visits and in her presence tell her and your doctor that the doctor has permission to talk confidentially without reporting to you. Many young women contract sexually transmitted diseases and have unwanted pregnancies because they don't have access to information and are afraid to reveal their concerns to parents. Helping your daughter establish a healthy relationship with an informed and considerate health care professional may reap great benefits in the future.

treating sexuality with respect

Children in our culture are exposed to language, jokes and images on film and TV that can denigrate sex. Conveying a sense of respect for sexuality is important. If you are religious, this may be done by conveying this feeling in a religious context. Whatever your orientation, expressing your respectful attitude about sex is in order.

"I know there are lots of jokes about sex and periods and pretty women. Some people make those jokes because they're embarrassed about sex. I used to feel embarrassed about it myself. But then I grew up. I met your mother [your father]. Now, for me, sex is something related to love and creation. That's why I don't like intercourse called by a crude name, or body parts described with dirty words. I want you to understand sex and consider it special."

emphasizing responsibility and sex for children ages eleven and twelve

Beginning at age eleven or twelve, when most girls are menstruating and boys are a year or two away from the beginning of puberty, instilling a sense of caution and responsibility regarding sex is even more important. This is important for boys, as well as girls. So fathers and mothers need to stress responsibility to sons as well as daughters. For example:

FATHER: I read a lot and see a lot on TV. I know some guys are having intercourse very early. They're also being pretty irresponsible about it. Don't forget those four hundred million sperm. They're produced in the testes and mixed with fluid from the seminal vesicle inside. All you need is one of the four hundred million to swim up and join with that egg, just one, and you've started a baby. As far as I'm concerned, a man is responsible for what he does. If he fathers a baby, he's responsible for it. And since you are too young to take on that kind of responsibility, it's important that you wait until you are much older to have intercourse.

Even when you're older, you have to protect yourself from any chance of causing an unwanted pregnancy or picking up a sexually transmitted disease by using a condom or a rubber. It covers your penis, keeps sperm from swimming up to meet an egg and form a baby. It keeps your penis from contact with fluids that might carry viruses, like AIDS or herpes or other sexually transmitted diseases. Magazines with nude women and X-rated movies only show bodies, but they leave important things out, things like pregnancy and STDs. Sex is a big responsibility. But you can always come to me if you have questions or concerns about sex.

discussions about other difficult subjects

It's hard to set age limits on the discussion of subjects involving sex. We've included in this chapter the kind of information we thought you'd be most likely to convey to your children through the ages of eleven and twelve. But we felt we'd be violating our own standards of giving enough information, if we left out a sample discussion on intercourse—not just the mechanics of it, but the feelings associated with it.

Parents of children on the brink of adolescence should be aware of changes in patterns of sexual activity. Teenagers are becoming sexually active at earlier ages, even as early as twelve, thirteen and fourteen. By sixteen, nearly half of the teenage boys and little over a third of the teenage girls become sexually active. By the time young people reach eighteen, at least 65 percent of the boys and 51 percent of the girls are sexually active. In some communities, the figures are much higher. In a study comparing a 1979 and a 1988 survey of sexual activity, researchers Freya Sonenstein, Joseph Pleck and Leighton Ku found that the percentage of seventeen-year-olds who say they have had sexual intercourse rose from 56 percent to 72 percent.* According to another more comprehensive report, from the American Medical Association entitled *America's Adolescents: How Healthy Are They?*† one out of every four sexually active high school students gets a sexually transmitted disease before graduating.

Even though children of eleven and twelve are very unlikely to be having intercourse, you may feel it's important to explain human sexual response in greater detail to them. Your child's questions, or other circumstances, such as an older brother or sister involved in a sexual relationship, divorced parents having sexual relationships with a lover living in the home or apartment—these situations may require a talk with your child about the feelings associated with sexual activity. Here is one presentation of the subject that may feel comfortable to you.

intercourse and human sexual response

"When people are attracted to each other, being close and touching makes them feel good in a special way. They become sexually excited. The woman's vagina gets moist. The man's penis becomes erect. They may kiss and pet, but they may want to be even closer.

"This is not a good time to make a choice, because it's hard to think clearly when you feel so excited. That's why, once you become sexually mature, you have to think about the possibility of intercourse and plan what you will do about it *before* you are alone in a situation where intercourse could occur.

"If the man and woman decide to have intercourse, here's what happens. They get very close and the man slides his penis into the woman's vagina. This feels good if both the man and

---

* Ellen Stark, "Teen Boys Get Condom Sense," *Psychology Today*, October 1989, pp. 62–63.

† Janet E. Ganz, Ph.D., Dale A. Blyth, Ph.D., Arthur Elster, M.D., and Lena Lundgren Gaveras, *America's Adolescents: How Healthy Are They?* American Medical Association (Chicago: American Medical Association, 1990) pp. 9–10.

woman have been kissing and touching until now, if both man and woman want to have intercourse.

"They move in ways that may cause the woman to have an orgasm and the man to have an orgasm and ejaculate. Because a woman's clitoris, the source of her greatest sexual excitement, is located above the vagina, she may or may not experience an orgasm during intercourse. Lack of foreplay or fondling before intercourse may prevent the act of intercourse from being sexually satisfying. Emotions and memories play an important role in sex and influence physical sensations. Anxiety or a frightening episode relating to sex from the past may prevent orgasm.

"Sexual satisfaction is much more likely to occur in relationships where both people feel loved and secure, where both the man and the woman can ask their partner to do what pleases them—and not to do what makes them feel uncomfortable. This is not likely to happen when both people are still feeling insecure about who they are and what they feel.

"Intercourse can last one or two minutes, or can last a long time. Usually the man ejaculates and his erection gradually goes away. People like to stay together and hug and feel close before and after intercourse. These feelings of closeness are what makes intercourse important. This is why intercourse belongs in a close trusting relationship.

"When young men and young women first go through adolescence, they are just learning about their own bodies. It's hard for them to be good sexual partners. So intercourse may be very unsatisfying or awkward. Neither the girl nor the boy is ready for a long-term caring relationship—either in terms of sex or in terms of the give and take involved in love.

"There are two other reasons not to have intercourse at an early age. First, intercourse can result in pregnancy. Second, when people have intercourse, they can also transmit diseases. For these reasons, I believe teenagers should . . . [This is where you need to state your convictions. You might believe teenagers should wait until after they are married before having intercourse. You might believe teenagers should wait until they are much older and have a relationship that could result in marriage. Yet we advise that you do not stop at stating your beliefs, that you go on to recognize the inescapable reality that large numbers of teenagers are sexually active.]

"Now I'd like to believe you will do exactly as I say, but I know that you are the sexual decision-maker. You will have to decide. Let's talk about what would happen if you decided to have intercourse.

"That decision leads to another one. Will you have so-called safe sex? Will you use a condom [or make sure your partner uses a condom]? If you decide not to use one [or not to insist that your partner use one], you are deciding to take two risks which I believe are matters of life and death. First, you are risking pregnancy—the responsibility for another life and a radical change in your own life. Second, you are exposing yourself to the chance of getting a sexually transmitted disease, such as chlamydia or even AIDS.

"Everything I've read on this and everything I've learned from my own life makes me realize that a pregnancy can really ruin a teenager's future—male or female. It could prevent you from getting a good education, which would help you get a job that was satisfying and paid well. It wouldn't be the best thing for your child, since you would be too young to give it everything the child needed.

"I'd like to see a child of yours have both parents around to help raise it. It's a lot easier that way. And don't forget, this is my grandchild we're talking about, so I want only the best for it."

Perhaps you won't cover all this territory in one conversation. With young adolescents, you're lucky to get stretches of time alone together that are not interrupted by phone calls from their friends or your child's own uneasiness with the subject. The important thing is to open the door on this hidden realm. Let your child know that there's a decision to be made and he or she is in control of the choices.

This alone may allow your child to express a variety of secret concerns. Adolescents may be afraid of strong sexual feelings, worried that it's not normal to experience an erection or lubrication in the middle of a history class just because a teacher made a certain remark, or wore an attractive outfit.

One of the hidden fears about sexual response that children and young adolescents may harbor is the fear of sexual feelings for a person of the same sex. Children may worry that a crush on the same-sex person, or masturbating—especially while thinking of a same-sex person—means that they are homosexual. It's not necessary to tell young children the details about the complexities of same-sex relationships, but seven- to eight-year-olds may be puzzled when they hear references to homosexuality or lesbianism. They do need guidance to avoid developing prejudices. As children approach puberty, they may have urgent questions about their own sexual identities.

homosexuality

It's important to let children and young adolescents who express concern about their sexual identities know that people can have crushes and sexual feelings for members of their own sex as well as for the opposite sex. This doesn't necessarily mean a person is homosexual.

Experts estimate that one third, or one out of three men in this country and about one out of eight women have had one homosexual experience. Many more report homosexual fantasies. Yet only one out of twelve men and one out of twenty women make the exclusive choice of same-sex partners. Among those who make this choice are many happy and successful people. Same-sex relationships may be equal to heterosexual relationships in their capacity for love and caring. But the stigma attached to homosexuality in our society and within many religions has created severe problems for homosexuals.

If your child is concerned about a feeling for someone of the same sex, or the fact that someone of the same sex expressed interest in or feelings for him or her, you can let him or her know that these things do not necessarily determine whether someone is "gay" or "straight."

Some people who later chose same-sex partners report that they experienced strong homosexual feelings even before puberty. So if your child has a passing interest, or if an older man or woman either forced or encouraged your child to engage in some sexual activity with him or her, this does not make your child a homosexual.

On the other hand, strong and ongoing homosexual feelings can't be ignored. If your child continues to be concerned about these feelings, give the child an opportunity to talk about it with a qualified counselor or therapist. Most counselors tell young people who know or believe they are homosexual not to be too anxious to make it widely known publicly. They advise that one's sexual preference is not the world's business, and that sexual preference may change. "Coming out"—or announcing to the outside world a homosexual preference—is a choice that should be carefully considered. Coming out is a choice made by an adult.

Most homosexuals are conflicted about telling their heterosexual parents. This will be complicated, and for the vast majority of families, a difficult fact to adjust to, since ours is a society that is particularly hostile to homosexuality. Yet the effects of denying one's identity, once that identity is discovered, can be more damaging than having to face the complications and psychological pain of telling parents.

Telling parents is often what young homosexuals dread most. Fear of parental rejection, of being the cause of grief to loved ones, may lead a homosexual adolescent to painful secrecy that can last a lifetime. Such children need all the support and understanding parents can give. Finding out that a child is homosexual may make a parent feel that he or she has failed somehow. A parent's own sense of sexual adequacy may be threatened by the knowledge of a child's homosexuality. This news may make some parents feel an overwhelming sense of loss and grief.

If, after the uncertain years of adolescence, your child becomes convinced that he is gay, or she is a lesbian, there are now national networks of support groups, as well as support groups for parents of gays and lesbians. Parents who need help in dealing with their own feelings or behavior may find it useful to get in touch with organizations like the National Federation of Parents and Friends of Lesbians and Gays. (Some of these are listed at the end of this chapter.) Other counseling services relating to homosexuality are available in many urban centers. People need to feel good about who they are if they are going to be good parents, just as children need to feel good about who they are if they are to become fulfilled adults.

when to discuss aids, other stds and contraception

Sexually transmitted diseases (STD's) are a particular danger to sexually active adolescents. Three out of four reported cases are of young people between the ages of fifteen and twenty-four. AIDS is now included along with syphilis, chlamydia, gonorrhea, human papillomavirus, and herpes as a disease to which a sexually active adolescent could be exposed. (We've included an explanation in Appendix 1 of these other STDs.)

We recommend that you do more than explain the physical changes of puberty, that you gradually communicate information about sexually transmitted diseases including AIDS. This is part of helping your children become decision-makers when it comes to sex. For their own good and the good of any future children, young adolescents need to start seeing themselves as people who are making thoughtful, informed choices about sexual activity, rather than people swept away by romantic feelings or a desperate yearning for acceptance.

why aids should be discussed during childhood

While you may want to leave the specific details of the various sexually transmitted diseases and methods of contraception to a later time when your child is possibly contemplating sexual activity, there is one sexually transmitted disease that needs to be explained and explained again throughout childhood and into adolescence. That disease is AIDS.

Your children inevitably will ask about AIDS. Even very young children hear about it—on TV and radio, in the conversations of the adults around them, from older kids at school. Increasingly, children actually know someone who has died of the disease. Many parents are uncertain about how to answer their questions in an age-appropriate way. In order to communicate about AIDS, you yourself need to understand it.

aids: the most serious std

AIDS stands for Acquired Immunodeficiency Syndrome. AIDS cripples the body's normal ability to fight invading germs and infections. AIDS refers to a whole set of infections and tumors that won't occur if the immune cells of the body are okay. The

AIDS virus, or HIV (human immunodeficiency virus) destroys these disease-fighting cells. A lot of other viruses and germs can then attack the body.

AIDS belongs to a family of viruses called "retroviruses," which copy their genetic code from RNA to DNA, the reverse of the usual pattern. Complications from mutations of the AIDS virus, and new forms of retroviruses bring portents that this fatal sexually transmitted disease will be around for the foreseeable future.

Traditional STD's can be treated if discovered. However AIDS does not yet have a vaccine to prevent it or a treatment that can cure it. Researchers are attempting to develop an AIDS vaccine. Despite promising indications from work done on a vaccine for monkeys, even the most optimistic experts do not foresee a cure for AIDS or a reliable human vaccine in the immediate future. Various drugs have been developed to alleviate suffering, combat secondary infections and prolong life. Yet the grim fact remains. Once HIV infection develops into the full-blown syndrome, AIDS is fatal.

what does hiv do?

What goes on inside the body is like the events on a battlefield. The body always has an "army" on reserve to fight off infection by germs. When a person has the HIV virus that person's immune system—the "army"—is gradually impaired. Eventually the body is unable to fight off other infections. The "army" has been destroyed by the HIV virus. A host of other infections attack bringing on full-blown AIDS.

In human blood, the "army" is made up of the white blood cells of different types. One type is lymphocytes. Lymphocytes can be B cells or T cells. Some of the T cells are helper cells. They send signals to the B cells to produce antibodies that fight organisms that cause disease.

T helper cells send signals to their brothers, T cytotoxic cells, which also fight off germs. Normally there are twice as many helper cells as suppressor cells. But people with AIDS have less helper cells than they should. (A person with AIDS has less than two hundred T4 helper cells per cubic millimeter of blood. The normal count for these cells is 1000.) Their defenses are down.

Their weapons are gone or greatly reduced. Their immune system can't fight disease.

AIDS is not transmitted in the way a cold or the flu might be. It is not spread in the air. You can't get AIDS from insects or birds or pets. You can't get it from touching objects someone with AIDS has touched—like plates, food, glasses, furniture.

AIDS is the result of a virus called HIV, which is transmitted through contact with contaminated blood or through the exchange of semen or secretions from the vagina or cervix during sexual intercourse, and by maternal-fetal transmission.

a closer look at
how aids is transmitted

The HIV virus cannot pass through undamaged skin. HIV can enter the body through the mucous membranes that line the vagina, rectum, urethra and possibly the mouth. It was initially thought that mucous membrane damage was required for the HIV to enter the body, but this is no longer believed to be necessary. Infection through contact of semen, blood, vaginal or cervical secretions with mucous membranes occurs during vaginal or anal intercourse and possibly during oral-genital sex.

Blood to blood transmission occurs by infected blood getting directly into the bloodstream. This can occur when unsterilized needles or other equipment are shared, as has happened with drug users, or when contaminated blood and blood products are accidentally given by transfusions to hemophiliacs or other blood recipients. Since March of 1985, the blood supply in the United States has been screened for contamination. But there is still the rare story of human error resulting in a patient receiving contaminated blood. Doctors, dentists and other health care workers need to take special precautions to avoid contaminated blood, and also to protect patients if they themselves are HIV positive. Tattoos and even ear piercing with unsterilized instruments are other possible sources of transmission.

how children get aids

Transmission from mother to child before or after birth so far accounts for about 1 percent of all the cases of AIDS. These have occurred in utero, during delivery and, in a few cases, by breast milk.

In 1990, children under thirteen accounted for between 1 and 2 percent of all AIDS cases. Of these, 77 percent were infected by mothers before or at birth; 19 percent through contaminated blood or blood products and only about 4 percent from breast milk. There was no case of a child contracting AIDS from another child.

Since 1989 the Center for Disease Control has projected that there would be about 1,500 to 2,000 infants infected with HIV each year. The spread of AIDS within the heterosexual community, means a larger number of children will be affected.

from hiv to aids

The HIV virus is the cause of AIDS, but people can carry the HIV virus and not come down with AIDS for many years. The time between HIV infection and suffering the serious illnesses called AIDS may be ten years. Even in the early stage, HIV cannot be detected for six weeks. It takes that long for antibodies that reveal the presence of HIV to be produced; in some rare cases these antibodies don't show up for as much as a year. Even after they have tested positive for HIV, most people don't show any symptoms for five years after the HIV enters their bloodstream. Some may have a brief spell of fever, fatigue, and swollen glands, but these symptoms disappear in a few weeks and most people who are HIV-positive feel fine.

In about five years after HIV infection, the person's immune defenses are reduced. Their T4 helper cell count, for example, has fallen to about half the normal level. At that time and for the next five years, treatment with anti-viral drugs such as AZT and DDI is usually recommended.

Finally, when the T4 helper cell count is down to 200, just one fifth of the normal level, the person's weakened immune system cannot fight off certain types of infections and diseases, such as a particular form of pneumonia and cancer. This late stage, which involves the onslaught of various diseases known as full-blown AIDS, can last two years. So far 200,000 people in America have developed AIDS and 125,000 of them have died. But an estimated one million living Americans carry HIV. Each year about 50,000 more people become infected with the HIV virus.*

Tests are available which determine whether or not a person has the HIV virus, but since symptoms may not show up for ten years, many people fail to get tested. Though some states used to require AIDS testing before marriage, this compulsory premarital screening has been abandoned. Mandatory testing for AIDS is under consideration for health professionals and others at high risk of contracting or disseminating the virus. Campaigns for AIDS testing are under way. Donated blood is screened for the virus. But testing remains a voluntary act, done only upon the individual's request.

how teenagers can contract aids

HIV is now showing up in the teenage population. Originally, it was only teenage drug users and those who had run away and worked as prostitutes who tested positive. Now, as unprotected sexual activity continues in the teen population, the numbers carrying the HIV virus are increasing. Sexual transmission—especially heterosexual—and drug use are the ways HIV is now getting into the teenage population. As of 1991, there were less than 1,000 teenagers reported as having full-blown AIDS, but this figure does not include teens who are HIV positive. It is suspected that thousands more teenagers are carrying the HIV virus. But teenagers are not routinely tested for AIDS. They are much less likely than adults to find out they are carrying the HIV virus.

One Miami teenager didn't know he was HIV positive until he donated blood for a school blood drive. His blood donation was screened and rejected. As Pedro Zamora now tells children in Miami schools, "A lot of us feel AIDS is never going to touch our lives. I felt that way too."† Pedro was thirteen when his mother died. He threw himself into schoolwork and athletics.

---

* Erik Eckholm, "Facts of Life," *The New York Times,* November 17, 1991, Section 4, p. 1.

† Eric Morgenthaler, "Pedro's Story: Teen Teaches Lessons for Life," *The Wall Street Journal,* September 4, 1991, p. 1.

And he became sexually active, getting involved with many partners. Pedro recalls only one discussion of AIDS—in seventh grade. A doctor came to visit the class, but he failed to mention sex practices, condoms or testing—in Pedro's case a deadly omission. This situation is changing as schools gradually incorporate AIDS education into the curriculum. The message hasn't reached everyone. Sexually active teenagers, who are healthy outside of being HIV positive, can be transmitting the virus unwittingly. Children need to know this before they are exposed. The only way to be sure your children know is by telling them yourself.

Because AIDS is connected with death, sex and drug use, parents worry about what to say and how to say it. We suggest that you make AIDS education a part of your approach to open communication with your children about sensitive subjects that they need to understand. They will be able to grasp different aspects of the problem at different times during childhood.

talking to children ages five to seven about aids

Most children of ages five to seven are full of questions. They are beginning to guess at the relations of objects and events to one another, but they can still mix up cause and effect, and they have difficulty with abstract concepts. Their thinking is still quite egocentric, which means answers to their questions need to relate to their personal world, a world in which people think and feel as they do. At this age, they may be fearful of this strange thing that kills people. They need you to allay their fears.

Sometimes their questions reveal their fear and confusion, such as the child who refuses to go near the drinking fountain, and then asks: "Doesn't that thing give you AIDS?" Or children may simply reveal their confusion by a puzzled expression, such as the child watching TV who sees the warning "AIDS Kills!" and simply looks upset.

Watch for opportunities to open up the subject. Let your child know that you find AIDS disturbing, too, and give the information in a simple, loving way.

PARENT: AIDS is one of the scary things I've heard about. It scares me because it makes people very sick, because people die of AIDS. But I'm not as afraid of AIDS since I learned about it. Do you know anything about AIDS? (Listen carefully to your child's answer.)

Perhaps your child will have some information. Perhaps the child will express fears or misconceptions. Be patient and reply in words the child can understand.

PARENT: I know AIDS is a bunch of sicknesses a person can get caused by a certain kind of a germ called a virus. The AIDS virus is called HIV. It's carried in the blood of infected people and in certain of their body fluids.

If you've explained sex to your children and feel they understand it, you can build on their knowledge, adding that the AIDS virus can be carried in the fluid that carries sperm, if the man has gotten the virus, or in the vagina of a woman. People can give it to each other when they have sex.

Try to determine what worries your child about AIDS, what he or she has heard about it. Children may be worried about catching it themselves. Reassure them.

PARENT: You can't get AIDS from touching someone with AIDS because the AIDS virus is not like the virus for colds or flu. It's not carried in the air. It's carried in the blood of the person who has the virus. You can't get AIDS from being in the same school as someone with AIDS. You can't get AIDS from bugs or flowers or pets. You can't get AIDS from plates or glasses or toilet seats. Now that I know these things, I'm not as frightened about AIDS. *When we have fears it helps to talk about them.*

If your child is particularly concerned about seeing children or babies with AIDS, explain how they got it.

PARENT: Let me tell you why some children have AIDS. Some children who have AIDS got it through blood transfusions. Some of the blood they got had that certain kind of germ in it called the AIDS virus or HIV. Now whenever children or grown-ups get a blood transfusion, the blood is tested so they won't get blood that has the AIDS virus.

Babies and very small children who have AIDS got it either from a blood transfusion or because their mothers had the AIDS virus in their blood and didn't know it. They passed it on to their babies. I never had the AIDS virus, so you couldn't get it that way. (If the child never had a blood transfusion, add the reassurance that they couldn't have gotten it that way either.) Now there are tests so that people know when they are carrying the AIDS virus and can avoid giving it to anyone else.

talking to children ages
eight to ten about aids

At ages eight through ten children develop a sense of right and wrong, a simple understanding of past and present, of the way matter can change from one form to another. At this age children can be told that the disease AIDS is "a whole bunch of infections and tumors that can occur if the cells that fight disease aren't working right."

They can comprehend that HIV—the AIDS virus—can lead to the AIDS disease. They can be told that people who share the same needle, such as heroin drug users, can get AIDS. And they can be told that the HIV virus is carried in body fluids that come out during sex, such as when a man ejaculates sperm.

School-age children should be told that transmission through blood is the only way one child can give it to another, and since they will not be handling the blood of a child with HIV, they have nothing to fear from a child at school with HIV. That person deserves their kindness and consideration.

You can also discuss with children of eight through ten why people are so afraid of AIDS, why fear and ignorance have caused people to panic and behave cruelly toward those with the disease.

talking to the preteen
and teenager about aids

Beginning at age eleven or twelve and on through adolescence, children are less likely to ask direct questions and more likely to need information to protect them from any risk of being exposed to the HIV virus. At this point parents may want to make books and pamphlets available to their children, as well as talk to them about AIDS. (Resources for such materials are included at the end of this chapter. Sample questions and answers about AIDS for young adolescents can be found at the back of this book in Appendix 2.)

Any explanation is more effective if a parent personalizes it and tailors it to the needs of the particular child. This is a good time to use examples of people they might know who are HIV positive or who have actually come down with AIDS. Magic Johnson is one such person who has forced young people to recognize the risk of AIDS.

"AIDS is a group of illnesses that happens after a certain kind of virus called HIV gets into the body. HIV can be transmitted through the blood of an infected person, such as when intravenous drug users share a contaminated needle, or during sexual intercourse through transmission by sperm or vaginal fluids.

"The letters A I D S stand for Acquired Immunodeficiency Syndrome. That's a fancy way of saying that the immune system—the army of cells that fight sicknesses caused by infections—is not working. The dangerous virus or HIV kills the cells that are needed to defend against all kinds of germs and bacteria and other viruses. When that happens, people get very sick. They have AIDS."

Preadolescent and adolescent people can understand that the choice to become sexually active can expose them to dangers of sexually transmitted diseases, including AIDS. Even though they may not welcome this information, they do actually want to have it and they prefer to get it from their parents. According to a survey reported in 1989 by Planned Parenthood and the Illinois-based Parents Too Soon, teenagers rely more on their parents than any other source for information on sex, but half say their parents don't provide enough information. Parents can help them by keeping doors of communication open, providing the kind of information on sex we've suggested and discussing AIDS as one of many sexually transmitted diseases.

You may wish to mention contraception when you talk about AIDS to children of eleven and twelve. Condom use is one of the ways that AIDS transmission can be prevented, a way that

they can protect themselves from AIDS and other sexually transmitted diseases. But let them know that condoms are not 100
percent effective. A failure rate of 15 percent discovered during
pregnancy testing indicates that the risk of HIV with condom
use can be the same. They also need to know that condoms are
made from different materials and only latex condoms used
with a spermicide are known to provide protection from transmission of the HIV virus. Also, young teenagers tend to be
unreliable in using contraception.

informed abstinence

At least in the early years of adolescence, informed abstinence—
abstaining as a choice made with full information about human
sexuality—is the safest route. Informed abstinence is a route
more likely to be chosen by a young person with high self-
esteem.

By helping develop children's self-esteem and build healthful
social skills through childhood, you are going far toward preventing AIDS, as well as unwanted pregnancy, alcoholism and
other drug use later in life. In the long run, low self-esteem is a
more significant threat to children and young adolescents than
AIDS.

Young adolescents need facts about AIDS, but these will be
meaningless if they do not receive support for flagging self-
esteem, and encouragement to make informed decisions about
sexual activity. Young adolescents need to know the way AIDS
can be transmitted through sharing of a contaminated needle,
but they also need a broader understanding of alcohol and other
drugs, what effects they have and why use of one can lead to use
of another.

The authors made an interesting discovery when they were
developing a series of books on AIDS for families. They realized
that explaining AIDS was going to require better parent-child
communication at many levels and on many subjects. Ironically,
it may be AIDS that finally prompts parents to talk to their
children more often, to give them information they've always
needed about sex and to let them know at each stage of development they are loved and valued human beings.

SUMMARY

As children mature, your communication with them about sex and related subjects needs to expand and include the concept of sexual decision making. Young children need to feel confident in asserting their rights to privacy and to refusing any unwanted advances. They need to feel comfortable talking to you about sexual curiosity and disclosing anything that may have occurred—from an episode of playing doctor to an episode of sexual abuse.

Children of eight, nine and ten can comprehend the difference between love and sex. They can grasp the notion that sexual activity brings with it responsibility, the possibility of pregnancy and the danger of exposure to sexually transmitted diseases. Children of eleven and twelve need a more detailed explanation of how one becomes pregnant. They may also want you to explain intercourse, including sexual response. Concerns about homosexuality may be fleeting worries without much foundation, or they may go to the heart of the child's identity.

Throughout all your discussions of human sexuality, keep in mind that a child needs to feel good about himself, confident about herself. The young person about to develop the body of an adult needs your support to make choices that will affect the rest of his or her life.

AIDS, a fatal sexually transmitted disease currently without an existing cure, requires special attention and special understanding. AIDS education needs to be part of a child's education about sex and choices concerning sex. Schools are now recognizing this fact, but parents are still the best teachers concerning this deadly disease. Though there are less than a thousand reported cases of AIDS in the teenage population, many more sexually active teenagers are HIV positive but do not know it. Teens are also at risk for AIDS if they become involved in intravenous drug use. Children who understand how AIDS is transmitted can be less fearful of those who have it, and at the same time, more aware of the precautions they have to take to avoid being exposed to it.

RESOURCES

Questions and Answers About AIDS for Young Adolescents, can be found at the back of the book in Appendix 2. Basic Information on Other Sexually Transmitted Diseases appears in Appendix 1 at the back of the book.

Public libraries, schools, state departments of public health and state departments of human resources, as well as many churches and synagogues now have books and pamphlets about human sexuality.

The American Medical Association publishes a number of booklets including a survey called *America's Adolescents: How Healthy Are They?* By Janet E. Ganz, Ph.D., Dale A. Blyth, Ph.D., Arthur Elster, M.D., and Lena Lundgren Gaveras. For information on these and other materials write: AMA, Publications Order Department, P.O. Box 109050, Chicago, IL 60610.

Planned Parenthood provides information on contraception and sexually transmitted diseases and on other subjects related to family planning: Planned Parenthood, 810 Seventh Avenue, New York, NY 10019, (212) 541-7800.

The National Federation of Parents and Friends of Lesbians and Gays is a support network: P.O. Box 24565, Los Angeles, CA 90024. (310) 472-8952.

There are a number of good sources for information on AIDS. The Center for Disease Control AIDS Hot Line is: (800) 342-AIDS; (800) 342-SIDA (Spanish).

National AIDS Information Clearinghouse is at P.O. Box 6003, Rockville, MD 20850. Or call: (800) 458-5231.

The Parents InTouch Project produces the *Families InTouch Series,* federally endorsed booklets for parents, children and teachers on sexuality, sexually transmitted diseases, AIDS, alcoholism and other drug abuse. Write Parents InTouch Project, 343 Dodge Avenue, Evanston, IL 60202. Or call (708) 864-5660.

7

FEELINGS, EMOTIONAL DISTURBANCES AND THE USE OF ALCOHOL AND OTHER DRUGS

Feelings and drug use are connected. Whether we take the professional perspective or the personal one, whether we look to case studies or to the people we know, we find that pent-up feelings—of boredom, worthlessness, sadness—often set the stage for alcohol use. So this chapter will deal first with feelings, ways that you can help your children express the whole range of emotions, including feelings of sadness, and ways that you can continue to help them express their feelings as they mature. Then we'll address the use of alcohol and other drugs by children and adolescents. We'll talk about how to help your children deal with pressures to drink and take drugs as they progress through school. We'll help you see how you and other members of the family function as role models. And we'll offer plenty of concrete information on the various drugs available and the signs of drug use.

expressing and coping with feelings

First and foremost, especially during the years five through twelve, your children need to learn to express feelings and to recognize that they are able to cope with anxiety and conflict without alcohol or other drugs.

Let's start with ages five and six. At this stage of their development, children need to learn how to identify what they are feeling and find acceptable ways to express those feelings. Here, to give you an idea of how to discuss feelings with a kindergartener or first-grader, is a page on feelings geared to five- and six-year-olds from the *Families In Touch Series* called *Getting to Know Me.**

> A person has feelings.
> Here are some feelings.
> I'm angry, because Mom made me stay in my room.
> I'm happy, because we're going to the zoo today.
> I'm sad, because my friend can't play with me.
> Here is a happy face. _____ .
> Here is a sad face. _____ .
> A person can learn to express feelings.
> Sometimes people express feelings by laughing or crying.
> Sometimes they do it by talking.
> Sometimes they do it by praying.
> Swallowing a bad feeling is like trying to swallow a chicken bone.
> It will always feel better to cough up that chicken bone.
> It will always feel better to tell about the bad feeling, to talk it over with someone who cares, like your mom or dad or teacher.

When you see your child trying to swallow feelings, let her know things will be better once the two of you talk it over. Reinforce this message by putting your arm around her, putting aside your other concerns and giving her a period of uninterrupted time. Perhaps the matter will turn out to be very small in your opinion—a misplaced toy, an unkind word—but this is your chance to show that your child's feelings matter to you.

You are telling your child: "It's okay to talk when you're hurting inside." Most important of all, this is an opportunity to have your child learn, firsthand, the benefits of talking things over. The child finds out that he or she does feel better after talking things over, and next time there's a problem, the child may not be so reluctant to share feelings.

* Joanne Koch, *Getting to Know Me, Families In Touch Series,* Book 2 (Evanston, Ill.: Parents In Touch Project, 1990), pp. 22, 23 and 31.

the connection between feelings and alcohol use

Trying to help children of eight, nine and ten talk about feelings will also help them talk to you about pressures to drink. Though the average age children report being pressured to drink is twelve, many children are offered alcohol or other drugs at even earlier ages.

By fifth grade, over one third of American students report being pressured to drink, according to a *Weekly Reader* survey. In some inner-city neighborhoods, reported University of Delaware sociologist James Iniciardi 1989, the first drink occurs about age seven and the first experience of becoming drunk by age eight. Yet another survey taken in shopping malls across the country of seven thousand people indicated that pressure to experiment with drugs had increased among the nine- to twelve-year-olds, with marijuana use doubling in the age group of nine-and ten-year-olds.

helping the older child continue to share feelings

As children get a little older, they may be less forthcoming about their feelings. This may be a time when a parent has to create opportunities for a child to share good and bad feelings, by spending relaxed time together—at a picnic, going fishing, playing ball, baking, working on a lawn project. The habit of sharing feelings within the family provides an emotional outlet that can prevent negative feelings and bad experiences from turning into more serious problems.

helping your child cope with sadness and disappointment

As your child is becoming more capable and socially aware, you can underscore the idea that some sad or painful feelings, some hardships, are a part of life. Financial difficulties, divorce, separation or illness may already have brought this lesson home.

But if your child's life has been relatively free of such hardships, you can at least give your child regular chores to do, and involve him or her in activities such as helping the homeless or bringing food to a shelter. Simply sharing with them some of your ups and downs, the everyday financial and emotional difficulties that most families confront, will reveal that people can learn to cope with anxiety and conflict without resorting to drugs.

Let them know that disappointments and frustrations can't always be avoided. Sometimes these temporary anxieties push us to solve problems or improve, as when we get a poor grade in school, strike out in a baseball game, and that pushes us to study harder or practice more. As a parent you can encourage your child to overcome these obstacles. When your child does bounce back and overcome a setback, congratulate the child. When your child is eight or nine continue to reinforce his or her efforts to tolerate frustration. This is a time to take note of people who overcome adversity without resorting to drugs or alcohol.

sharing experiences

By sharing his or her own past experiences, a parent can help a child understand the use and misuse of drugs and alcohol. For example, a parent might say: "A few months ago I had a problem at work. I was so aggravated, I came home and drank too much. I didn't solve the problem and wound up with a terrible headache. My problem got worse. A few days later, without the help of alcohol or drugs, I talked it over with my friend at work. We figured out how I could make my manager happy."

If a child is tense about a forthcoming exam, you might recall a time when you or a friend may have resorted to drinking or drugs to deal with school stress.

"When I was in college, a friend got so anxious about final exams, she took tranquilizers before she went into the test. She sat there for the whole hour, perfectly happy. She smiled when she handed in her exam paper. It didn't have one word on it. She had masked her anxiety for a few hours, but she hadn't solved her problem."

Remember to keep your examples concrete. Children of eight or nine think in terms of specific examples. Their ability to make abstractions and imagine the future develops later. The here and now makes the most sense to them. The closer you can bring this issue to their experience and the people they know, the better.

acknowledging pressures to try drugs

Once you've provided a few examples, you can let them know why you're concerned: "Sometimes people get used to escaping bad feelings by taking alcohol or drugs. It becomes a habit. And they seem to need more and more alcohol or drugs to make themselves feel better. I don't want you to be unhappy, but I do want you to learn ways to express bad or sad feelings. Together, we'll try to figure out a healthy way to deal with your problems."

Try to get the child into the conversation. "Have you ever felt so bad or embarrassed you just wanted to drown your troubles so you could escape that bad feeling?" Listen to the child's answer. "I guess that's the way celebrities like ——— once felt. [Use examples of young people your child would recognize, such as Drew Barrymore, Ally Sheedy, Darryl Strawberry, Melanie Griffith, Dwight Gooden, Kirstie Alley, Don Johnson.] They were drinking and taking drugs. But then they realized they couldn't solve their problems that way. They realized bad feelings wouldn't kill them, but alcohol and drugs could."

If you yourself had a period of using alcohol or drugs, you could speak from personal experience and explain that you had to learn this the hard way. "Before you were born, I wasted a lot of money on cigarettes, then I had to go to a special doctor to help me stop smoking. Cigarettes have nicotine. That's a drug I thought I needed. I found out it was terrible for my health, and could be harmful to my baby. So you helped me stop smoking. But I wish I had never started."

You can also ask your child questions and let the child be the teacher. One of the authors was amazed, recently, when she spoke with a group of ten-year-olds from a middle-class suburban neighborhood. They exhibited what seemed to be a precocious sophistication about drugs; they reported that some students got high in class, some came to class high, while others just drank and smoked pot on weekends.

Let your child know how you feel about the wave of early drinking and drug use. For example: "When I was your age, we didn't have people offering us drinks or drugs. It upsets me to think that you have to worry about this. I'd like to be an ostrich and just bury my head in the sand, so I wouldn't have to worry about this, but I'm your mom [your dad] and I can't ignore what's happening."

Later you might ask directly: "Has anyone approached you to smoke marijuana or have a drink? What did you say? I've heard of cases where rat poison or other substances are mixed in with marijuana. Because it's illegal, dealers have no way of knowing what's in these substances. A few years ago someone put poison in a certain aspirin substitute and several people died. At least we had a way to stop that and punish anyone who did that. But with illegal drugs, there are no controls, no one checking."

Acknowledge the pressures your child may be under in a sympathetic way. "You might feel very bad sometimes, or very curious about drugs. I hope you'll stop, if you're tempted, and remember what we've said. Remember there are always other ways to express bad feelings, and you can always share any feelings you have—good or bad—with me. Remember there are always other ways to feel good again."

Children in fourth or fifth grade can become very busy with homework and other activities. Many mothers and fathers of children this age are working full time, often outside the home. It's necessary to make a conscious effort to leave time during the week for relaxed interchanges with children. These talks shouldn't always harp on drugs and alcohol. If kids become accustomed to a give and take about what they're doing and feeling, the discussion of drugs and alcohol can simply become part of the many things talked about.

confronting emotional problems now to prevent drug use later

Once parents understand why children use drugs, they can develop their own strategies for preventing later drug use. If they can confront the causes of drug use early enough, they can help their children find other courses of action. In a California survey of over a thousand ninth- and eleventh-graders,* kids offered five reasons for using drugs:

1. to get away from problems
2. to experiment
3. because friends are using
4. to make themselves feel good
5. because they had nothing else to do

The survey is surprising because it shows peer pressure as only one reason, and not the most important reason, that kids say they use drugs. Kids, like adults, have an impulse to deny bad feelings and escape problems. As a parent, you need to help your children express feelings and confront problems. If your children's emotional problems seem overwhelming, or if they feel they have a problem and you can't help them deal with it, show them that they can get help, without resorting to drugs.

links between emotional problems and desperate measures, including drug use

You may assume that because your child is only nine or ten or eleven he or she won't be afflicted by serious emotional problems. You may have a tendency to chalk up persistent moodiness to the fact that he or she is approaching puberty. But as we note in our chapter on divorce, death and depression, depression can affect children, and is one condition that may lead a child to alcohol and other drug abuse. Either by itself or in combination with alcohol and other drugs, depression can lead to other self-destructive behavior, including attempts at suicide. A depressed child needs help. Ongoing feelings of hopelessness are not normal for children.

* Ken Barun and Philip Bashe, *How to Keep the Children You Love Off Drugs* (New York: *Atlantic Monthly Press,* 1988), p. 47.

Here are two actual examples of children whose families didn't recognize their children's depression until it was almost too late.

At twelve, George was attending advanced seventh-grade classes at a high school for gifted children. He was an excellent student and a courteous and charming boy until he was promoted to a new school. He found the teachers "weren't as nice" as at the old school.

Over the summer, his twenty-year-old brother, the brother's wife and their one-year-old baby had moved into his parents' home. George was very quiet in class, working very slowly and occasionally crying in school. But George was always very diligent. His teachers had not reported any problem. A few months after he started the new school, George's grades began to drop, particularly in science and social studies, subjects that required a greater degree of concentration and memorization.

George made no friends at the new school. He was frequently irritated and angry with his former playmates. Everything seemed "stupid" and he complained often of fatigue. At least once a day, after school, he even took a nap. His mother often found him crying out of frustration with his homework. On one such evening, his mother yelled at him for being so slow at completing his work. Since George had always been an excellent student, she had assumed he was just being difficult. She called George "lazy." Later that evening, his sister found him with his face submerged in the kitchen sink, attempting to drown himself. George said he wanted to die because he thought he was so hopelessly "stupid and troublesome." This desperate act finally made George's parents realized he needed help. He began seeing a therapist and he is coping much better. His parents learned to make a concerted effort to talk with George and listen to his concerns.

It's easier to overlook the feelings of grade school children. When infants or toddlers cry, we wonder if something is wrong, but when children in grade school or junior high complain, or seem "moody," we may be inclined to dismiss those feelings.

Anyone can have a bad day, but children who are consistently sad, those who show no interest in friends or schoolwork, need special attention. Regular opportunities in the course of family life to express feelings may alert parents to problems before they become serious. In some situations, a combination of circumstances may cause a child to plunge into a depression. At that point, even with the best intentions and efforts to cheer up the child, a child and the child's family may need outside help from a therapist.

Jamillah is an eleven-year-old sixth-grader. She was a good student and a pleasant girl until three months ago when several events occurred at just about the same time. She had the onset of her period and the loss of the one person to whom she could tell all her problems—her grandmother. Jamillah and her parents then moved to Chicago from a smaller city in the South. She didn't talk about her loss, or about the complicated feelings that went with getting her first period, the feelings of being no longer a child, yet not really a woman.

In Chicago Jamillah felt sad and friendless. She complained that the kids at school pressured her to smoke and drink. But her parents knew Jamillah was a good girl. They felt she just needed time to get used to the new surroundings. Jamillah's grades went down and she had frequent arguments with her mother.

Her mother thought that she was experiencing "hormonal changes" and tried to bolster Jamillah's self-esteem by sending her to a girls' club. Yet her mother criticized Jamillah for not completing her schoolwork. Jamillah said she was trying her best. Her mother then enrolled her in drama, hoping to raise her daughter's rapidly declining self-esteem and to stimulate her interest in activities. Jamillah found the performance pressure intolerable and began to cut drama and subsequently other classes.

Jamillah complained about her "stupidity" and "ugliness." Her concentration was poor. She had trouble getting up in the morning and cried easily. She found it impossible to make friends at her new school, claiming the only thing they talked about was drugs, alcohol and sex.

One day, before dinner, she watched a TV show in which a girl overdosed in a suicide attempt. Right after the program, she went to the kitchen, took a large glass of water and a full bottle of her father's hypertension pills.

She wrote four notes, one to her mother, one to her father, one to her deceased grandmother, and another to a friend in her hometown. She then took a bath. Finally, feeling frightened about what she had done, she told her mother. Her mother was completely shocked at the suicide attempt. She was surprised to find her daughter was "that depressed." She took Jamillah to the hospital where she stayed briefly. Jamillah and her parents went into psychotherapy and they are now doing well.

the drug roller coaster

Depression is not always related to the use of alcohol or other drugs, but often it is. Alcohol and drug use, while initially producing a "high," have the roller coaster effect of producing a concomitant low, which exacerbates depression. Drug-abusing teens are ten times more likely to attempt suicide than nondrug users.

providing outside help
before the onset of drug use

If parents heed indicators of emotional problems now—such as changes in mood, behavior and thought patterns and psychosomatic illnesses—they may avert drug abuse. Children who develop ulcers, suffer from migraine headaches, experience weight changes, have trouble sleeping or complain of physical pains may require counseling, as well as medical treatment. Persistent symptoms such as these won't just disappear. If they are ignored, a child is likely to seek respite through drinking or escape through other drugs.

Though it's not unusual for a child to experience an occasional bout of "What should I do today?," when a child feels ongoing boredom, sadness, dejection, apathy, despair, or expresses suicidal ideas, that person requires professional attention.

Therapy is also indicated when a child is unable to concentrate, experiences memory lapses, engages in constant self-criticism, expresses extreme anxiety and guilt or seems to suffer from an ongoing sense of low self-esteem. The number of friends any child has may vary and not every child will enjoy extreme popularity. But if your child seems alienated from others, hyperactive or extremely rebellious, therapy could be the answer.

You are the only one who can get help for your children before they resort to mood-altering substances, before they try to find escape or comfort in a drink or a joint. Emotional problems combined with alcohol or other drugs can be deadly.

links between drug use and suicide

Substance abuse may become part of a self-destructive, depressive, vicious cycle, which could, if not counteracted, lead to suicide. Alcohol and other drug abuse are the most important links to youth suicide. Over the past thirty years youth suicide has become the second leading cause of death among young people ages fifteen to twenty-four. "America's Adolescents: How Healthy Are They?" was the title question of a 1990 survey published by the American Medical Association.* It revealed that suicide among ten- to fourteen-year-olds has tripled over the past twenty years. Traffic accidents, also connected to alcohol and drug abuse, are the leading cause of teenage fatalities.† The Stanford University National Bureau of Economic Research study on the status of children conducted by Victor Fuchs and Diane Reklis reported that 6 percent of all American teenagers have tried to commit suicide and 15 percent have been depressed enough to feel on the verge of attempting to end their own lives. About one teen in seven describes herself (or himself) as having "come close to trying."

Among teenagers who commit suicide, there is a large percentage with a history of alcohol and drug abuse. Many of them began their drug experimentation as early as ages eleven or twelve. About half the young people who take their own lives have been drinking and doing drugs for many years. Their friends knew they were drinking and doing drugs; the parents usually say they were unaware of their children's alcohol and

* Ganz, Ph.D., Blyth, Ph.D., Elster, M.D., Gaveras, *America's Adolescents: How Healthy Are They?*, pp. 39–41.

†Victor Fuchs and Diane Reklis, "America's Children: Economic Perspectives and Policy Options, *Science*, Vol. 255, January 3, 1992, pp. 41–42.

drug problems. Those who have attempted suicide reported feeling hopeless, lacking friends and not being able to experience pleasure. Parents should not discount a child's aloneness and apathy, believing it's normal for preadolescents to withdraw. Children of eleven or twelve may indeed show more interest in peers than parents, but they should reveal enthusiasm for life, for friends and activities.

In addition to outside help through therapy, insecure or alienated children can benefit from strong family support and an opportunity to discover a sense of meaning in the world. Their involvement in religious or altruistic activities may help them to feel they are needed; their lives can make a difference.

Denial is often the way out for parents who notice that their child has emotional difficulties. Parents can feel besieged by the responsibilities of their children and their jobs. But it's vital that parents keep their eyes open and get help for a child who is emotionally troubled *before* that child also becomes chemically dependent.

explaining to young people why drugs don't help you cure problems

When your children are eleven and twelve, you may want to bring up this subject of depression and suicide, even if they haven't exhibited symptoms of emotional problems.

You can use the example of the roller coaster to make clear that drugs offer only temporary relief, not a solution, that they produce a profound low that follows that so-called high, and it is that low that is connected with depression and suicide.

Here is one way to help guide your children away from chemicals, suggested by the *Families In Touch Series: Older but Not Old Enough*, a book for children ages eleven to fifteen.*

"It's been found that about half the young people who take their own lives have been drinking and doing other drugs. Their friends knew they were drinking alcohol and doing other drugs.

* Joanne Koch, *Older but Not Old Enough*, *Families In Touch Series*, Book 6 (Evanston, Ill.: Parents InTouch Project, 1990), p. 49.

But the Moms and Dads of these people usually say they were unaware of their kids' alcohol and other drug problems.

"Perhaps you know someone who is caught up in a vicious circle of trying to feel better by drinking or doing other drugs, then feeling worse, more depressed than ever.

"Depression is a sickness that needs to be treated, whether it's caused by chemicals you take or possibly by some chemical changes going on in your body.

"If you have a friend who feels very depressed, or if you ever find yourself feeling very depressed, give yourself a break and talk to someone right away. You can always talk to me, but if for some reason you feel you can't, you can speak to a friend, someone on a hot line, a doctor, minister, rabbi or teacher. There are many people who care about you.

"If you ever have a friend who talks about taking his or her life, or seems severely depressed, tell someone you trust, someone who could help that person. Every human life is valuable."

where do children learn to use substances?

Children learn the habit of chemical dependency from adults, usually their own parents. They learn from what adults express verbally and what they do. Children observe parents carefully, just as parents take in everything children do and say. Remember, however, that in the early school years, children are more literal in their thinking. They hear a parent say, "I need a drink." They see the person take a drink and then notice what seems to be pleasure and relief. Seeing this enacted hundreds of times in the home makes a child think that drinking is a means of dealing with stress, perhaps the only means.

It's up to the parent to help the child understand that there are many ways to manage stress. It's up to the parent to show the child that sometimes physical activity or exercise, a change of pace such as listening to music, or painting, or seeing a funny movie, gives the needed relief from stress. It's up to the parent to be very clear when he or she is taking medicine or pills for a specific physical problem—not for quick relief of a mood problem. It's up to the parent to explain the difference between I *want* to have a drink and I *need* to have a drink.

If you can share some of your stressful feelings and make it clear to your child that you are finding ways other than drinking to cope with them, you will be providing a very helpful model. Children need to understand that negative feelings such as fear, worry and embarrassment are experienced by all people, but these emotions need not be drowned in alcohol—or escaped by some other kind of quick fix.

Feelings can be tolerated and shared. Tension can be alleviated by deep breathing, exercise and healthy diversions. Even if a person has to feel sad or angry or tense for a time, these feelings can be endured until the problem is solved. A person doesn't have to get rid of bad feelings immediately.

Parents should show children that alcohol and other drugs are not necessary, even if the parent takes a drink occasionally. If you show your child many ways of coping, then you can say on those occasions when you have a drink: "Sometimes I choose to have a drink, because it gives me a feeling of being relaxed for just a little while. But it really puts off the problem I have. It's not an answer. Most of the time I do other things about problems—talk them over, step back and have some fun and then return to the problem, go swimming or work out for a while."

There is no question that what you do and say will directly affect your child. The Pacific Institute for Research and Education found that children were more prone to drug abuse if their parents smoked cigarettes, were alcoholics, took other illicit drugs, used substances to manage stress or imparted an ambivalent or even a positive attitude toward drugs. Given a population in which 20.5 million adults of thirty-five or older have had some illicit drug experience, and 6.6 million continue to use illicit drugs, we have a large number of children at risk.

being an effective role model

The most effective role model is a parent who doesn't use drugs but is aware of the pressures in our society to use them. The least effective role model uses drugs and doesn't admit it. You may not be consciously aware of how many drugs most of us take in the ordinary course of events. When a parent takes an aspirin, he or she has to explain, "This is for a headache, not to change my mood." A parent has to explain that vitamins are for health reasons and such prescription medicines as antibiotics are to fight an infection.

Cigarette smoking and drinking should also be considered "drug use." Cigarettes are the first dependency-inducing substance used by kids. Children of smokers are at high risk of becoming smokers. They are also jeopardized by the effects of passive smoke. The American Cancer Society (ACS) reports that in households where both parents are smoking children from infancy through one year of age run twice the risk of bronchitis and pneumonia as in smokeless households. (The ACS offers information on a number of programs to help people quit smoking and stay off cigarettes.)

If you are a smoker, you may find that your children are starting to prevail upon you to stop smoking. In school, they're learning about the health problems connected with cigarettes, and they're worried about you.

One father finally stopped smoking after twenty-five years of cigarettes. By that time one of his daughters had picked up the habit. But as soon as he stopped and showed that it could be done, his daughter enrolled in a stop-smoking program. Parents should never underestimate the power of their example to influence their children.

Alcoholism may have a biochemical component that could, in some cases, be transmitted from one generation to the next. We do know that the example set by a parent who drinks does have a tremendous impact on the children. The National Council on Alcoholism states that the best predictor of adolescent drinking habits is parent's attitude and behavior with regard to alcohol use. Children of alcoholics are four times more likely to develop alcoholism than children of nonalcoholics. Currently there are 6.6 million children of alcoholics who are at risk of the disease—whether through inherited vulnerability or the learned influence of their parents.

If you are a parent with a drinking problem, at least acknowledge the problem to your children. Numerous agencies have sprung up to help parents cope with their alcohol problem and to help children of alcoholics avoid becoming alcoholics themselves. Some of these resources are listed at the end of this chapter.

The majority of Americans aren't alcoholics. However, they

do take a drink now and then. If you take an occasional drink, be aware that your child is noticing this and make sure you talk about what you're doing and why, in terms that the child can understand. For example, here's a dialogue that would help a child of eight or nine gain a realistic view of alcohol.

CHILD: Why do you drink, Mom?

MOTHER: Well, I like the taste of a glass of wine. It seems to make a good meal taste even better. And wine has a certain effect which is pleasant, makes me feel a little more light-headed, a little more relaxed. Yet many people can't take just one glass of wine or one glass of beer. Do you know any people like that?

CHILD: I'm not sure.

MOTHER: When we get together on Thanksgiving, did you ever notice how much Uncle Richard drinks. First he seems silly. Then he seems kind of mean. He's had lots of problems with his drinking. And the family worries about it. As an adult, I found I could take just a little bit of wine or beer. I decided I could do that once in a while.

CHILD: Why can't I have wine?

MOTHER: First of all, you're not an adult and so it's against the law for you to drink. When you get to be older, twenty-one years old like Cousin Anne, you will have to make a choice. You may choose not to drink anything, and honestly that's the safest choice. I hope you will never drink too much. Remember that time you ate all your Halloween candy in one night?

CHILD: I threw up.

MOTHER: Your body is smart. It lets you know. Don't overdo it. With alcohol, your body also lets you know. But some people get so attached to alcohol, they can't stop, even when they know alcohol is making them sick. Even though we sometimes see a movie or TV program where drinking seems to be fun or something to laugh at, it's not fun. It makes people throw up and have headaches.

CHILD: Then drinking isn't fun?

MOTHER: Not unless people can stop when they've had only a little, not if they get drunk or what we call intoxicated. And worst of all, people who drink and try to drive often hurt themselves and others. We have a friend whose daughter was jogging one day. A drunk driver drove up on the jogging path and hit her. She is paralyzed. She can't use her arms or legs. Drinking is a dangerous thing. For lots of people, it's a terrible problem.

Avoid complimenting people because they can "hold their liquor." Avoid inviting heavy drinkers to the house. Even if you deliver a "lecture" on drinking, when your children see people drinking and seeming to enjoy it, they will get a message that drinking is fun.

Do talk about drinking. The National Council on Alcoholism states that kids from nondrinking homes where drinking is never discussed are as susceptible to drinking as children from drinking homes.

update your understanding of alcohol and other drug use

As children get closer to the age when they will likely be offered alcohol or other drugs, you as a parent may need to update your knowledge concerning drugs and drug usage. Things have changed on the drug scene. And while you and your contemporaries may be drinking less, quitting smoking and recognizing that other drugs make no sense, your children's generation is trying everything earlier, including new drugs.

when do children start experimenting with drugs?

Your children will confront alcohol. They will have to make a choice. The average age of first use of alcohol is twelve years. First experimentation with other drugs begins on the average at thirteen years. But as you can see from the chart below, over one third of the nation's children feel pressured to drink at age ten.

PRESSURE TO DRINK*
Fifth grade (10 years) .... 39% report pressure to drink
Sixth grade (11 years) 46%

Seventh grade (12 years) 61%
Eighth grade (13 years) 68%
Ninth–twelfth grades (14–18 years) 75%

USE OF ALCOHOL AND OTHER DRUGS*
First use of alcohol...........................average age 12 years
First use of other drugs.....................average age 13 years

National Survey on Drugs and Drinking, Middleton, Connecticut, (Field, 1987)

More than half of America's young people have tried illicit drugs (57 percent) by their senior year in high school, according to the National Institute on Drug Abuse. More than one third (36 percent) have tried drugs other than marijuana by that time, according to the National Council on Alcoholism. One in six high school seniors has tried cocaine or crack. One third of high school seniors claim most or all of their friends get drunk at least once a week. Though girls may use more stimulants and tranquilizers than boys, they match boys' levels of use with alcohol, marijuana and cocaine. For some young people competing in athletics, steroids seem to offer a fast way to enlarge muscles and boost performance levels. Six and a half percent of high school males and 2.5 percent of high school females use or have used anabolic-androgenic steroids. The harmful effects of steroids are just beginning to come to light.

Though statistics may vary from one locale to another, the pattern of progression from cigarettes to alcohol and marijuana, to heroin or tranquilizers, then to LSD or PCP and on to cocaine seems to mark some children's movement from ninth through twelfth grades.

Now is the time to prepare your children for the difficult choices ahead. As you continue to help them feel self-worth and emotional well-being, instill in your children the advantages of healthy activities and the dangers of drug and alcohol use.

self-education

Before you can educate your kids, you must educate yourself. Remember that less than ten years ago, perhaps when your child was born, it was thought that marijuana had few if any harmful effects and cocaine was regarded as a nonaddictive substance.

"Crack" was virtually unknown. "ICE" or methampheta-mine—now regarded as one of the substances posing a serious threat to teenagers—was unheard of. Be sure that the information you secure is recent and reliable. To help in this process, we've supplied a list in Appendix 3 of frequently abused substances and their effects. More detailed information on a wide variety of substances is readily available. Resources for information and for finding treatment are listed at the end of this chapter.

how addiction occurs

The effects of drugs vary. But the addiction process applies to all of these substances—alcohol, cigarettes, marijuana, cocaine. Dr. Alvera Stern, a national authority on prevention of substance abuse, explains the process this way. The brain produces natural opiate-like chemicals called endorphins. Drugs, such as alcohol, serve as "look-alikes." They look like the natural endorphins. They fool the brain into believing they are the real thing. This process of fooling the brain causes the body to produce less endorphins, less of the natural opiate-like chemicals. The result is the body becomes more dependent upon the look-alikes, more needy of these substances. A vicious cycle is set in motion that results in a craving for the look-alike. This is addiction.

a united front

It's not unusual for parents to have differing views on alcohol and drugs, and differing personal habits. But this is one area that calls for a united front. Discuss the problem with your spouse. Even if you are separated or divorced, try to determine a uniform approach and a NO DRUGS ALLOWED stance—no tobacco, alcohol or marijuana. Many parents have found that forming parent groups and involving the community in prevention programs helps them strengthen their stand on drugs.

Since alcohol and cigarettes are legal for adults, many adults take a more lenient approach to these substances. But they are gateway drugs. Twelve- to seventeen-year-olds who are cigarette smokers are nine times as likely to ingest depressants and stimulants, ten times as likely to smoke marijuana, fourteen times as likely to use cocaine, heroin and hallucinogens. Half of all heavy drinkers also smoke marijuana regularly; 26 percent of marijuana smokers also used cocaine, hallucinogens or opiates as opposed to only 1 percent of nondrug users. And 93 percent of cocaine users first smoked marijuana. Multiple-drug use is the rule, not the exception. Combinations tend to enhance the effects of one drug with another; for example, alcohol heightens the mellowing out effect of marijuana.

You may argue that one joint won't turn a kid into an addict, but remember that the child who experiments with one drug and finds no ill effect may try others, in search of a satisfying "high." There is no way to detect who will progress into dependency. And any drug use puts children in a negative peer culture where they are more likely to experiment with drugs and other behavior that is illegal. Once in the drug culture, there is competition among peers to experiment with more dangerous drugs, as members of the group seek status. Any approval, such as, "It's okay to use alcohol or drugs at home," condones this behavior. Difficult as it may be to enforce, parents must assert that use of any substance is forbidden.

counteracting peer pressure to use drugs

"Fitting in with others"; "Because friends are using"; "I didn't want to be left out." These are reasons children of ten, eleven and twelve offer for using drugs.

If you are going to be successful in counteracting peer pressure, you have to acknowledge fully how important friends are to your children, how much they need to feel they belong to something. The drug "club" is the easiest one to join. Kids on drugs have a ready-made bond, not only in the obtaining and use of drugs, but in the talk about using. The negative identity offered by the club of drug users is still an identity. "Bad boy" or "bad girl" is still a sense of distinction.

You can counteract the appeal of the negative identity and the drug-using club by encouraging your child to engage in positive activities. The child who feels he's "no good at anything" is a ripe candidate for drug use.

Give your children alternatives to the drug "club" by promoting their skills and interests, so they can belong to the drama club, the ceramics club, the swim club, etc. Whether or not you are an athlete, you should appreciate the enormous benefit of physical exercise to your children, and try to promote it as a family activity. The brain, as we've noted, produces it's own mood-altering, opiate-like chemicals called endorphins. Physical exercise is one means of releasing endorphins that actually helps a person feel good.

The self-discipline gained by mastering a physical skill—whether it's baseball, tennis, swimming, basketball, gymnastics—offers gratification and opens the door to belonging. Physical exercise actually improves a child's posture, physique and complexion and builds a health consciousness. The child who cares about the condition of his or her body will be less likely to ingest dangerous substances. If the physical activity becomes a family activity, there's also the added reinforcement of sharing positive experiences.

You can also monitor and guide your child's friendships. Obviously, this becomes much more difficult when they are teenagers, but from ages five to twelve some vigilance and control are still possible. Paying attention to the friends your child spends time with can help you assess whether they are likely to experiment with drugs. Friends who are selfish and need to be the center of attention, friends who don't want to participate in activities or meet new people and visit new places, friends who are arrogant or seem indifferent to others are exhibiting signs of low self-esteem that are not likely to offer a healthy influence. It's worthwhile to try to meet the family of a friend your child plays with. Are the parents or a responsible adult at home when your child visits?

One third-grader befriended a new girl who invited her over. Michelle returned from Lila's house saying, "She's kind of strange." It turned out there was no one home at Lila's and Lila showed Michelle that she could light matches.

If there's a new friend and no parent at home, suggest they play at your house. If the friend has a propensity for dangerous activities, explain your concern to your child and insist that the visiting cease.

When children are eleven and twelve, it's more difficult to

monitor friendships, but if you determine that a particular child is destructive to yours, you can forbid that friendship. Make sure your conclusion is well founded, not based on dress, speech, race or other superficial factors. Explain your reason to your child. Explain that it's not a punishment, and you feel bad for the friend that he or she seems to be involved with alcohol, or drugs, or a group that's experimenting.

Show compassion for the friend, so the child doesn't feel obligated to stay with the friend out of loyalty. Never pretend that it's easy to make new friends, but let your child know that she will find someone who appreciates her and is not involved in drugs. If you are in a situation where you have to relocate, make sure you check out the opportunities for activities, the peer groups, along with the plumbing and mortgage payments.

helping your child refuse invitations to drink or use drugs

The actual offer of alcohol or other drugs is likely to come from friends or older siblings when no parent is around, and it's not easy for a child to refuse a friend or an older brother or sister. Children may feel they're insulting a friend if they say no.

You can help by acknowledging the pressures that exist. Perhaps you can relate your own experience with peer pressure—something a friend wanted you to do that you finally refused. Tell your child it was difficult to turn down your friend, but now you're glad you did. The friend is no longer a part of your life, but drugs could have been if you had started taking them.

Specific strategies for refusing have been developed by the "Just Say No" Clubs. When a friend makes an unusual offer, the first step for your child is to figure out if what the friend wants to do is okay. You can help your child identify situations that can easily lead to trouble: parties at a stranger's home, meetings at abandoned buildings, activities with an older group of kids. Suggest to your child that he ask his friend, "What will we do there?" "Are we allowed to be there?" Then suggest that your child ask himself: "Will my parents allow me to go there?" "What would they think?" "Will it make me feel good or bad inside?"

The second step is the answer. If your child figures out the offer is going to lead to trouble, he can say "no" in a friendly, quick way.

The third step allows your child to recover the initiative. It's a step that requires a child to have a certain amount of self-esteem. Step 3 is to turn the peer pressure around and suggest other things to do—baseball, swimming, a movie. Invite the friend to join. Then the friend is the one who has to say yes or no. With enough information and enough confidence, your child may be able to reverse the peer pressure: "Drugs can fry your brain. I can't believe you would do that." The child can allude to the dangerous side effects. But if your child feels uncomfortable assuming this role, he or she can just be firm about no, or give an excuse of having another activity, or change the subject, or give the so-called friend the cold shoulder and walk away.

At this age, kids don't want to be preachy or self-righteous. You might want to role play with them so they can say no with good humor and comfort. Pretend you are the friend.

PARENT: (pretending) We're all meeting at Mike's tonight.
CHILD: But he's in high school, isn't he?
PARENT: So what. He's cool. He's got great CD's.
CHILD: I promised Phil I'd bring some videos to his house.
PARENT: Videos. What's that. That's dumb. That's baby stuff. Mike's got a radical stereo, maybe a few six packs, maybe even some coke.
CHILD: Hey, I don't want my brain messed up or my heart suddenly stopping, like that basketball player, Len Bias. Besides, I promised Phil. He's my friend. See you around.

Your child is most likely to abuse alcohol. Chances are it's a substance with which you are familiar. That might make it more difficult for you to set down limits about it. Here's one way you might present the problem to your child. Let's say you're watching a TV program where a character has had too much to drink. The program portrays drunkenness as comical. Commercials for beer and wine coolers also use humor. This can be your opportunity to get your message across.

"Drinking sometimes seems funny. There are some people

who don't drink much but might overdo it once or twice. They might do silly things and seem to be having a great time. I've laughed at drunks in movies. But I've also seen some real-life drunks and it's not funny.

"I know that one out of every ten people has the disease of alcoholism. These people can't drink moderately even once in a while. They can't stop with one drink. I have a friend who lost everything because of alcohol. His wife divorced him. He lost his job. And he was such a bright guy.

"Even people who aren't alcoholics can do harmful things when they have too much to drink—things like get themselves and anyone in their car into accidents, shout and get into fights, hurt themselves and other people, even the people they love.

"Drinking kills. Accidents are the single most common cause of death for young people. This might be a good time to figure out what you're going to do if you're ever with someone who's had too much to drink or has taken drugs and wants to drive.

"Here's what lots of people your age are doing:

"They always make sure they have another way to get home from a party—an arrangement with parents, money for a cab.

"They never get into a car with a driver who is not sober.

"They try to convince anyone who's been drinking or taking drugs not to drive, saying, " 'You're my friend. I wouldn't want you hurt. And I wouldn't want you to have it on your conscience that you hurt someone else.' "

If you feel your child needs more reinforcement, you can discuss the problems of real people in the family or in the community, people they would know. Remember that this is not an age when children respond to abstract ideas. They need concrete examples, tangible proof from their own world that alcohol isn't everything the commercials promise.

the need for a healthy degree of suspicion

Despite your best efforts, your children may begin to experiment with substances. Be aware of any change in their behavior—such as markedly increased secretiveness, lack of interest in school or activities, more episodes of colds and flu, school absences and changes in grades. If you suspect drinking or drug use, check your children's belongings. If any evidence of drug use turns up, confront the child. If your children are using alcohol or other drugs, seek professional help. Most communities have programs in place to help young people who have become involved with drugs. Additional resources are listed at the end of this chapter.

red flags of alcohol and other drug abuse

Any of the things listed below may happen once, but when they happen regularly, that's a danger sign.

1. Extreme mood swings
2. Unreasonable anger
3. Lying and cover-ups, even for minor things
4. Change from old friends to new friends not known to parents or known to be involved with alcohol and other drugs
5. Extreme secretiveness and regularly avoiding contact with family
6. School problems such as drop in grades, absences, misbehavior
7. Change in activities and general boredom and lack of caring
8. Money—even large sums—appearing and disappearing without cause
9. Unusual "things" showing up, such as drug-related objects like pipes and roach clips, baggies in pockets, empty liquor bottles, lighters and matches
10. Physical changes like frequent illnesses, changes in eating habits, loss of weight, glassy-eyed look and mumbling

At eleven Amy entered a new junior high and quickly became friends with twelve-year-old Maureen, whose brother was into drugs. Amy's mother noticed changes in her daughter's behavior, her dress, her attitude. Amy's grades, which had always been good, plummeted. Amy's mother was convinced her child was experimenting with drugs. Amy had another group of friends from a camp she had attended the previous summer, friends who exerted a healthy influence. The mother arranged for Amy to return to the camp.

After camp, she had a talk with Amy and Amy admitted she was afraid of not following Maureen, even though she didn't want to get involved in drugs. Amy felt she couldn't go back to the same junior high and resist Maureen's influence. The mother and daughter arrived at a solution, which involved going to another school and making sure Amy had counseling during this transition. The solution took time. But gradually the old ties dissolved and new friendships were made. As an interesting footnote, when Amy finished college she wound up counseling teens who were into drugs.

Boredom is another reason children of ten, eleven and twelve offer when asked why they try drugs. Boredom is often tied to a lack of friends and no involvement in healthy activities. It's up to parents to show kids that there are other ways to relieve boredom. School children can be involved in several major activities a year. The range is enormous—from art, ice skating, karate, gymnastics, soccer, to guitar, gardening, Scouts and crafts like woodcarving and ceramics. Boredom may also be an indication that children have no responsibilities, such as cleaning their rooms, doing dishes, putting away groceries.

Sometimes parents pressure their children into competitive sports and skill contests. Some children enjoy such things as Little League or piano contests. For other children the pressure to win creates anxiety and serves to shake their self-esteem. Every child needs to be encouraged to practice and work toward a goal, but it's best if that goal is one they help to set. School-age children can be held accountable for homework, team practice, attending activities they've signed up for, household chores, doing dishes, cutting grass, picking up groceries. Work with them to help them grasp the meaning of becoming responsible and accountable.

make your family a haven

Don't underestimate the power of the family. It's natural to feel beleaguered in this age of early drug use. But remember that you can engender high self-esteem in your children by offering them love and setting clear limits. You can encourage them to express feelings and get help for them if they exhibit symptoms of emotional problems. You can increase their chances for finding acceptance through healthy activities. You can show them that everyday stress and even intense pressures need not force a person to use alcohol and other drugs.

Remind yourself of the way parents influence children to use drugs and avoid those patterns. High risk families—those where children are more likely to experiment with drugs—share certain traits. They do not express affection often. They ignore, neglect or abuse their children. They are either too lenient or too strict. They make too much money available to their children or they offer their children no experience with having an allowance or a small amount of money. They don't set clear limits or enforce those limits. These are families in which drug use is either not discouraged or not discussed, families in which parents and siblings are using tobacco, alcohol or other drugs or families in which the parent is dependent on the child, not just sharing feelings and giving the child a limited amount of responsibility, but burdening the child with adult responsibilities.

The family can be a haven from a stressful world, a place where a child can count on loving and being loved, a place where the limits are clear but the support is unlimited. But a family doesn't get this way automatically. Parents need to make a conscious effort to create such an environment. In a world laced with alcohol and drugs, a sanctuary is what children need.

SUMMARY

Expressing and coping with feelings are basic skills that children need for emotional well-being and to avoid drug use. Studies show that personal feelings of sadness, boredom and stress often cause children to try drugs. You can help children share feelings throughout childhood and into adolescence. Encouragement, making time for them, sharing your own feelings, especially those showing how you overcame stress or sadness without drugs, can help them express their own emotions. You can let them know that you're aware of the pressures to drink and use drugs. You can help them confront their emotional problems now to prevent later drug use. Let them know that drug use doesn't solve problems but rather puts them on an emotional roller coaster that can lead to depression, and even death.

As a parent, you can recognize the enormous influence you wield as a role model and modify your own habits regarding alcohol and other drugs. You can update your education about current alcohol use and use of other drugs. You can provide a united front within your own family of emotional support and support for children to refuse drugs. At the same time, you can recognize that experimentation may occur, and deal with it quickly and effectively if it does. Children need a haven from emotional stress and pressures to drink and escape through drug use. You can provide that haven.

RESOURCES

A detailed explanation of drugs and their effects appears at the back of this book in Appendix 3. The places listed on this page can supply a variety of other information on alcohol and other drugs.

National Parent's Resource Institute for Drug Education (PRIDE)
(404) 577-4500
50 Hurst Plaza
Suite 210
Atlanta, GA 30303

National Council on Alcoholism (NCA)
(800) 622-2255

National Clearinghouse for Alcohol and Drug Information
P.O. Box 2345
Rockville, MD 20852
(800) 729-6686

National Institute on Drug Abuse
Offers a variety of videotapes, films, pamphlets.
(301) 443-6245

Families In Touch Series consists of age-appropriate, federally endorsed books to help parents and children avoid alcoholism and abuse of other drugs.
Write:
Parents InTouch Project
343 Dodge Avenue
Evanston, IL 60202
(708) 864-5660

resources for adults and their families who use alcohol or other drugs

The American Cancer Society offers information on cigarettes and other drugs as well as information on programs to help smokers stop smoking.
(800) 227-2345

Alcoholics Anonymous, Alanon, Alateen, as well as Drugs Anonymous, Cocaine Anonymous, Families Anonymous, are all self-help agencies for abusers and their families. Local branches are listed in the white pages.

Alcoholics Anonymous
P.O. Box 459
Grand Central Station
New York, NY 10163
(212) 686-1100

Adult Children of Alcoholics
National Headquarters
(312) 929-4581

Al-Anon
Family Group Headquarters
P.O. Box 182
Madison Square Station
New York, NY 10159
(800) 245-4656

hot lines:

Drug Treatment Hot Line
National Institute on Drug
Abuse

(800) 662-HELP

Cocaine Hot Line
(800) COCAINE

In addition to these national agencies and hot lines, most states have resource centers for directing residents to prevention and treatment programs for alcohol and other drug problems.

8

HELPING YOUR CHILD SURVIVE CRISES—DIVORCE, DEATH OF A LOVED ONE OR DEPRESSION

Most children cope with the changes they undergo between ages five and twelve with at least moderate success. However, sometimes children must go through a crisis situation that really tests their coping skills, and those of their parents. This might be a period of separation, or the complex changes brought about by divorce. It might be the death of a parent, grandparent or other loved one. For some children, the transition from childhood to adolescence is particularly stressful. These children may experience feelings of depression and severe self-doubt as they go through puberty.

Parents need help in sorting out the "normal" reactions to loss and change from those reactions that deserve special attention. This chapter will help you speak to your children about divorce and death. It will help you deal with your children's grief over divorce or death by showing you what to expect and how to handle those normal grief reactions. And it will give you some guidelines for distinguishing between a predictable response that requires time and patience, and one that requires special attention through outside therapy.

separation and loss

Children experience loss in many ways. Loss is more commonplace for children than we realize. A long hospitalization, a move to a new city, a change of schools, separation due to military service, divorce of parents or the death of a loved one are some examples. Given the prevalence of divorce and death in the span of years between five and twelve, there is at least a 50 percent chance that your child will have a loss experience during his or her childhood.

the double burden for parents

Children's reactions to separation or loss are painful, distressing and sometimes even infuriating for parents. The problem is compounded because parents themselves are often suffering their own grief and pain when they are called upon to help their children. A mother going through a divorce, for example, is suffering a temporary depletion of her own self-esteem, a feeling of failure in a most important relationship, a significant reduction in income (typically at least a one third drop in income) and often the attendant need to get a job or find some additional caregiver to help maintain work and family.

The single-parent mother feels the need to support and understand her children. But she also feels guilt, anger and frustration when she sees their pain. Parents are conditioned biologically and socially to protect their children, yet experiencing the pain of loss and change is unavoidable when a child goes through a divorce or death.

Our advice is in no way designed to instill or increase guilt feelings. It is intended to help you help your children get through their grieving and prevent that grief from harming their future emotional development. Parents going through a divorce or the death of a loved one may need extra personal support in order to help themselves and their children. Research on divorce and death tells us that helping children express their feelings at the time of a parent's divorce or death may prevent a dangerous detour in the normal course of emotional development.

the importance of grieving

It is imperative that children successfully resolve feelings of grief. Experts agree that unresolved childhood grief can cause severe and long-lasting effects in adolescence and even into

adulthood. Adolescent and adult problems such as anxiety disorders, alcohol and drug abuse, depressions and even suicidal
behaviors have been linked to unresolved early losses.

divorce as a source of grief

Judith Wallerstein, social worker, author and director of a major
divorce counseling center, tracked a group of middle-class families from northern California over a period of fifteen years,
monitoring the effects of divorce on the children. She found that
the unresolved grief from a divorce affected children when they
became adolescents and adults. Fears of abandonment, self-
destructive behavior, abuse of alcohol and other drugs resulted
later in life from the festering of these unhealed wounds. In her
opinion, it was not the divorce itself, but the handling of the
divorce, the failure of parents to offer children the help and
understanding needed at this difficult time, that created the
problems. (Please see the Resources page at the end of the chapter for reference to the book *Second Chances* which includes these
and other findings.)

Divorcing parents may find divorce mediation a means of
helping them focus on the needs of their children. A divorce
mediator, working cooperatively with lawyers, helps the couple
work out custody arrangements and other aspects of the divorce, before these matters escalate into full-blown court battles. Court-mandated divorce classes are required in some
counties around the country as a way of trying to avert some of
the long-term effects of a conflicted, bitter divorce on children.

It is normal for a divorce to affect a child's behavior for a year
or two following the event. Whether or not children are affected
adversely over a long period of time seems to depend on the
way the parents handle the situation and both the mother's and
father's relationships with their children afterward.

To a child, divorce is the death of the family—the only family
the child has ever known. When a divorce takes place, one of the
parents will be leaving the home and remain away much of the
time. Many things will change—from material possessions to
the amount of attention the child receives from that absent parent. The child needs to mourn the death of that "familiar"—
accustomed, well-known, trusted—family before he or she can

understand that a changed but still loving family continues to exist.

Those who have studied children's reactions to a death in the family urge us not to underestimate a child's need to grieve. It is the suppression of that grief, the denial of grief by the surviving parent or the parent's anger at the child for difficult behavior following the loss that can complicate the process. Understanding, attention and support will allow the child to work through the loss and resume a normal life.

how to tell a child about death or divorce

If there is an impending loss, it is important to tell the child—not to keep it a secret. In the case of death, the adult to whom the child feels the closest should do the telling. In the case of divorce, both parents should tell the child together, so they can make clear that each loves the child and provide assurances of continued involvement. Those assurances will need to be carried out. If the parent who does not have custody remains involved in the day-to-day life of the child and works out a reasonably harmonious arrangement with the custodial parent, the negative effects of divorce are mitigated.

If a family member is dying, the child should be told by the parent but allowed to spend time with the loved one. Parents might be reluctant to take a child to a nursing home or hospital, but the chance to say good-bye to Grandma or Grandpa can make a tremendous difference to children in terms of their ability to cope with the loss. When survivors whisk the dead loved one away to a heavenly and unreal "nondeath," part of the child's mind remains in a kind of purgatory or limbo. Poet Sylvia Plath was ten when her father, Otto Plath, died after a long and difficult illness. Mrs. Plath thought she was protecting Sylvia when she contained her grief, excluded her daughter from the funeral and quickly moved from their seaside home to an inland dwelling. Later Sylvia wrote: "I was ten when they buried you. At twenty I tried to die/And get back, back, back to you."

If the death of a parent is sudden, a loving member of the family can tell the child, but as soon as possible the surviving parent should reunite with the child and repeat the news. The goal is twofold: the person closest to the child can offer the most comfort and can also limit the child's tendency to deny the news.

We know that the majority of children who lose a parent survive the experience. For some the loss taps a wellspring of creative energy. George Washington, Abraham Lincoln, Eleanor Roosevelt, Charles Darwin, Leo Tolstoy, Gustav Mahler, Babe Ruth and Arthur Ashe are among these successful survivors. However, the combination of a particularly vulnerable child, a surviving parent who can't openly grieve and the parent and child both denying the loss can be particularly destructive.

what children need to resolve grief

Psychoanalyst John Bowlby has written three volumes on human attachment, separation and loss. Bowlby has found that a child can resolve grief as successfully as an adult, given the following conditions:

1. The child had a reasonably secure relationship with the parent before the loss.
2. The child is given accurate and honest information about what happened and is able to ask questions and to have those questions answered honestly.
3. The child participated with the family at the funeral and at other rituals of grieving.
4. The child is comforted by the presence of a parent or another adult he trusts and on whom he can rely in a continuing relationship. (A list of Bowlby's books on this subject appears at the end of this chapter under Resources.)

overcoming your own resistance

You can help your child most by overcoming your own reluctance to talk about what has happened. It's okay to cry in front of your child and share your own pain. But after the initial shock, it's best to try to achieve some emotional distance if you are to help your child. It's better to find a friend whom you can use as a confidant, rather than putting your child in this role. If you are overwhelmed by your own feelings when you try to talk to your child, make sure you and your child have someone else to talk to—in the child's case, an adult friend, school counselor, or support group. For example, many schools now have groups for children whose parents have divorced.

reassuring your child

You may feel at a loss as to what to say to the bereaved child, or to the child who's just heard that a divorce is about to happen. The first assurance to give is that the child has not been abandoned. You are there now and will continue to be there. This can be done with words and even more powerfully with touch. An arm around the shoulder, a touch on the arm or knee, a gentle pat on the head—these gestures can be nonobtrusive and comforting.

Give assurances that you can reliably keep. If you're the parent leaving the house due to a divorce, don't say you'll visit every day unless you are sure you can do so. That would just compound the child's sense of loss.

making the loss real

You can help your child accept the reality of the information by emphasizing the child's own thoughts and feelings, reminding him or her of things the child has already noticed. Particularly during the years when children are developing their own social sensitivity, this approach helps them to trust their own thoughts, observations and feelings and builds their confidence in their own ability to figure things out.

For example, in the case of divorce, you might say: "I'm sure you've noticed that Mom and Dad have been awfully angry with each other lately—sometimes arguing, sometimes sad, sometimes trying to ignore each other. We can't be happy living together. We've decided to get a divorce." Or in the case of a dying grandparent: "Remember how pale and thin Grandma looked on our last visit? Well, she went into the hospital and the doctor says her sickness is really bad. He doesn't know exactly how much time she has, but she's going to die in a month or two."

Allow the child to ask questions. Answer any questions you're comfortable with honestly. Keep the focus on the child's concern. No matter what the child asks, there are disturbing basic questions underneath for which she is seeking reassurance: "Will you still love me the same as before?" "If your love for Daddy [or Mommy] can change, does that mean your love for me can change?" "If you can leave Daddy [Mommy], will you be leaving me?"

Let's say your child asks: "Are you in love with someone else?" You can say: "We are divorcing because Dad and I [Mom and I] have decided the two of us can't live together. Feelings about other people aren't what made the two of us decide to divorce. We were unhappy living together before I met ———. But our feelings about you haven't changed. We still love you the same, and we always will even though we won't be living together.

not the child's fault

A child needs to know that a divorce or death is not her fault, and that both parents will continue to love her.

Although it may be difficult to hear, allow the child to say he or she knew that things weren't going well. Let her complain about just how bad things have been. This encourages the child's confidence by showing she can understand what's happening. It also further proves that she is not the cause of the loss.

Offer concrete facts and times. "We've decided we'll be happier if we live in separate places. I'm moving out next week, but I'll be by at least twice a week to spend time with you." "Grandpa has a certain form of cancer that has to be treated in the hospital. They can make Grandpa comfortable there, but they can't cure him. He is going to die."

Be straightforward about the news, even if your own impulse is to cover it up, delay telling or keep the event secret. If the cause of death was suicide, this may be especially difficult, but it is preferable to lying. If the news reaches the child from a source other than you and he hasn't been told the truth, he will feel betrayed.

"I came home today. I didn't see Daddy. I heard the car running in the garage. When I went into the garage, it was full of exhaust smoke. Daddy was in the car. He looked like he was sleeping, but he wasn't. He was dead. I was shocked and I felt terrible. I felt maybe it was my fault, maybe there was something I could have done. But it's not my fault and it's certainly not your fault."

Younger children of five or six may still be thinking of the world in egocentric, magical terms. They believe all causes and effects are related to them, so they attribute the actions of their parents to something they have done—in the case of divorce, something they have done wrong. Even if they don't ask for the causes of the divorce, these children need to have it explicitly stated that the separation or divorce was not their fault. They must also be told that there was nothing they could have done to change the situation. Similarly, a death in the family requires a parent to make those same reassurances. There is nothing the child can do now, nothing the child could have done, to prevent the loved one from dying. And the death was not, in any way, their fault, even if they might have had a very angry thought or feeling about the person who is now dead.

At age seven or eight children become concrete thinkers. Part of the mental advances we've discussed earlier brings them to a new way of thinking about the world. Things are either black or white, good or bad. Subtleties and euphemisms are lost on them. Saying that "Uncle Al passed on to another world" or that "we lost Aunt Sarah" will confuse them. It helps to tie the event to the child's own perceptions and sensations. "I know you saw Grandma using an oxygen tank last time we visited. She was having trouble breathing." Or "I saw you cry when Dad and I argued last time. You were sad because you realized we weren't getting along. You were right."

The finality of divorce or death tends to be glossed over by some adults, but it is exactly that finality that must be grasped by the child. In the case of a death, let the child know that the dead person can't come back, but at the same time reassure your child by answering the unspoken questions: "Is this going to happen to me or to you?" Reassure him that death is a long way off for him and that you are healthy. If there is a divorce, don't let your child talk you into suggesting that Dad (or Mom) might come back again to live with you as your husband. Nurturing the fantasy of a family reunion only prolongs the child's denial that a change has occurred.

Between the ages of nine and twelve, children have developed more coping mechanisms to deal with death or divorce. They are more aware of their own feelings and they may be more open about admitting their sadness. Yet, they still may try to keep up a courageous front while hiding their suffering. If so, it's a parent's job to help the child express those buried feelings. Children of this age are less likely to blame themselves for divorce or death, but they still fear abandonment. In the case of divorce, they still feel angry at their parents' breakup. They may be torn between feelings of family loyalty and shame at their parents' behavior. For this age group, it is especially important that both parents maintain contact with their children and that the absent parent's contact be frequent and consistent to lend stability to the new arrangement.

As older children get closer to adolescence and dating, they may become especially resentful of the single parent's new relationships. A single parent shouldn't be surprised if a young adolescent acts morally indignant or withdraws sullenly when introduced to the divorced parent's date. The older child's conflicting feelings about the divorce are exacerbated if the divorced parent behaves like an adolescent about dating, flaunts his or her own sexuality, or comments on the sexual inadequacy of the former spouse. Another pitfall of single parenthood to avoid is making the older child an emotional surrogate for the absent mate or forcing the older child to serve as parent to younger sisters and brothers.

encourage the expression of feelings and questions

Encourage children to share feelings and ask questions. Encourage them to remember and to talk about the dead loved one. Help them by strengthening those positive memories. In the case of divorce, especially if one parent lives in another city or town, try to help your child keep positive thoughts of the divorced spouse alive. You yourself may not have positive feelings, but engendering hateful feelings toward the absent mother or father will not ease the child's sense of loss.

The combination of honest information and the support necessary to bear it enables children to respond realistically to a loss and—eventually—to accept it.

children's reactions to loss

Though children have different ways of responding to loss, there is a pattern to the process of grieving, various stages that need to be experienced. Specifically, there are four phases of grief: shock, numbing and denial; sadness, yearning and searching; disorganization, and apathy; and finally reorganization. These phases may skip around, overlap, return, but each phase has elements that occur in a predictable order. Trivial or devastating losses evoke the same reactions. It is the intensity and the length of the grief reaction that will differ. Profoundly disruptive events, such as a divorce or the death of a parent can require one or two years before the grief process concludes.

The problem with death or divorce is that it typically creates more than one loss. If a loved one dies—say a grandfather—the child's mother or father may also have to devote more time to the widowed grandmother and thus become less available to the child. If one of the parents dies, the surviving parent has a host of new responsibilities and emotional burdens. If a divorce occurs, Dad will be away much of the time and Mom may also have to be away more—perhaps working longer hours to manage the reduced family budget. When you understand these multiple losses and then see them through a child's eyes, you can begin to grasp the profound impact these events have.

phase one: shock, numbing and denial

Stacy has been an active and energetic five-year-old. She enjoys sharing games after nursery school with her Mom, who has been a full-time homemaker, and with her younger sister Rhonda. Recently and suddenly, Stacy's father moved out of the house and took a job in another city. Mom had to go out of state to deal with the impending divorce. The neighbor who is keeping Stacy during the day mentions her concern that Stacy seems sad and withdrawn. She spends most of her day sitting quietly with a sad expression and a faraway look in her eyes. It is difficult for sister Rhonda to engage Stacy in play, and when she does, Stacy appears to be just going through the motions, like a robot.

Such lifeless, automatic responses may alternate with underlying feelings of apprehension, and intermittent bursts of panic. Many children experiencing a loss, or—as in this case—a loss combined with the separation from a parent, will spend hours sitting and staring into space. This is a normal, natural protective response. When under stress the mind shuts down the emotions. Sometimes it also inhibits intellectual and even physical processes in order to protect us from becoming overloaded by the stress.

Strong reactions will follow, but usually sadness and anger are expressed only after a delay created by these built-in screening mechanisms. The initial numbing and disbelief renders the child's mind unable to grasp the reality and the pain. The psychological numbness makes the loss or separation bearable. This phase of numbness lasts between a few hours and a week. Then the numbness will alternate with feelings of intense distress or anger or both as the realization of the loss comes. The child may cry and sob, then be irritable, then long for the lost person.

When the lost person is a parent or a sibling, the child's sense of vulnerability is heightened. There is a combination of missing the lost person and a fear, "That could happen to me" or "Who will take care of me now?" In the case of divorce, if the father is moving out of the house, all the activities, qualities and roles of the father seem to be leaving also.

A younger child has no sense of the continuity of a family. Even the child of ten or eleven has only the vaguest sense of the future. What could it be like without Daddy (Mommy)? The child experiences what's called separation anxiety. She may refuse to go to school. She may refuse to do homework or participate in other usual activities. Feelings of anxiety and depression can also surface. "I'm not good enough to play in the recital this time." "Who wants to play basketball?" "I don't feel like eating."

A child can respond to death or divorce as an animal would respond to danger. Our bodies are programmed with what are known as fight or flight responses. Danger makes muscles tense. The heart races; bowels and bladder relax, breathing accelerates.

Loss triggers these responses. The thought of the lost or un-available loved one makes the child experience these intense physical reactions. The child may sigh when thinking or talking about the missing loved one. He or she may have difficulty sleeping. The combination of this insomnia and the stress creates fatigue and weakness.

HEIGHTENED VULNERABILITY

As a result of the physical stresses and changes in the bodies' usual rhythms, children going through a divorce or the death of a loved one are particularly prone to infections, allergic responses, skin rashes, respiratory ailments. The anxiety they are feeling may show itself in nail biting, hair pulling or picking at themselves. These symptoms may develop within the first few days of the separation, and after, as the loss sets in, or even later, as significant holidays or anniversaries remind the child of the death or divorce. Children who do not go through the grief process at the time of the loss are more likely to experience so-called "anniversary reactions" in adulthood—recurrent grief responses upon the anniversary of the person's death or departure.

FEARS

The child who has recently gone through a loss as a result of divorce or death may become afraid of the dark and continue being fearful for some time. He or she may have recurrent dreams symbolically related to the loss, or to a past experience with the lost one. A parent may hear a child crying, come into the room and find the child screaming with her eyes open, then find that the child is actually deep in sleep and unaware of events. These night terrors may be part of the fearfulness induced by the loss.

Many grieving children will want to cling to, or sleep with a parent. It's best to comfort children but encourage them to sleep in their own bed. Parent and child can help each other, but neither one should begin to think that the child is replacing the missing or lost mate.

Many children are afraid to express their resentment over the fact that a loved one has left them. It's easier for the child to idealize the dead or absent parent and resent the surviving one, the one who is on the scene and not threatening to leave.

As many as one third of grieving children become temporarily hyperactive or aggressive toward adults or peers, or destructive to property. With time and support, the anger can be expressed more appropriately.

In a television film called *Extreme Close-up,* a boy struggles to come to terms with his mother's death in a car crash. At first, he blames his father, his teacher, his counselor. Then, he realizes his mother's death was a suicide. At this point he becomes afraid that since he was "just like his mother" he will experience the same fate. With time and understanding, his anger subsides, and he comes around to accepting the loss.

DENYING THE LOSS

In the first phase of coping with loss, children may use the psychological defense of *denial.* Even though a parent tells the child that a loss or separation has to occur, the child refuses to believe it. Ellen, age eight, was told that the therapist she had been seeing every week for two years was relocating to another city. Ellen covered her ears, began shaking her head, closed her eyes and cried, "No, no, oh no!"

We all use denial, consciously or unconsciously, to prevent anxiety or at least reduce it when we feel threatened. It's as if Ellen were saying, "If I can't see it, or hear it, it isn't happening."

A grieving child may forget about the loss and expect the lost person's voice on the telephone. Weeks after a divorce, a child may run to answer the doorbell anticipating that Daddy has come home to dinner at the usual time. Some children refuse to believe the lost or missing person is gone and insist on trying to phone or visit the absent or departed parent.

If you are the surviving or separated parent, you may find these actions hard to take, but remember that these are actually healthy signs that show your child has had the ability to form a strong attachment and to love someone dearly.

The grieving child might even deprecate the lost or absent person, or even deny that person ever existed. Kevin, age twelve, reports his father left home two years ago. Later, when asked, "Where is your father now?" Kevin speaks sternly, though his eyes are filled with tears: "I have no father. I've never had a father." This kind of deprecation allows Kevin to deny the importance of his missing father—and to deny painful feelings of loss and abandonment.

Impending separations from beloved teachers or friends can bring on this same denial response. After several moves due to her parents' job relocations, Sarah is leaving yet another elementary school teacher. This teacher is one she has grown to like very much. The teacher is also sad to see her go and tells her, "Sarah, I can't tell you how sorry I am to lose such a good pupil." Sarah's face betrays no emotion as she says, "So what. You'll have new students and I'll have new teachers."

These types of denials give the child a brief respite from the feelings of grief triggered by separation or loss. Denial may persist for four to six months. If a child continues beyond that length of time to deny the loss or separation and to avoid the accompanying feelings, that's a sign that he or she is not resolving the first stage of grief. This should signal a parent that perhaps the child needs some additional help from a therapist or school counselor. Long-term denial can prevent the child from forming new relationships and getting on with life.

HEIGHTENED ACTIVITY

In this first phase of grief, children may also act out their anxiety by keeping very busy. Activities allow children to distract themselves from thinking about the loss and feeling the pain of it. The activity might become more and more frenzied or intense the more the child is reminded of the loss. Older children may use music, television, video games, the telephone, or even alcohol or other drugs to avoid thinking about the loss. Needless to say, adults may use similar routes of escape and denial.

HOW TO HELP A CHILD COPE WITH SHOCK, NUMBING AND DENIAL

You can help your child deal with this first phase of grief by taking five steps.

1. *Tell the child several times about the loss.*
    When first told of the loss, the child may react unemo-

tionally. She may need to be told again later for the news to register.

2. *When possible, tell the child before the impending loss occurs.*

If there is some forewarning, such as with a fatal illness, tell him beforehand. If one of the parents is going to be leaving the house prior to a divorce, give the child a chance to absorb this news. This will allow him to play and replay the experience of the loss and to practice his skills to cope with it. Given this preparation he may avoid a shock experience, or a lengthy episode of denial when the event occurs.

3. *Tell the child who will take care of her.*

The child must know not only who will take care of her, but also must be given some assurance that this person wants to, and knows how to take care of her. Some of the things you might do if the child were ill are appropriate now. Providing special foods, especially soft and warm foods like soup and hot chocolate; reassure the child and remind her of other times she was cared for. Offering warm and cuddly objects like stuffed animals, or tucking the child in lovingly with flannel blankets, can give the child a sense of security and protection. Reassuring sounds, such as those from a clock, a radio, the tape of a familiar song, may remind the child of more pleasant times and make her feel safe.

4. *Provide the child with a trusted, long-term caretaker.*

A bereaved child, or one who has recently experienced the breakup of his family, needs a sense of stability and continuity. For younger children, even normal separations from the remaining caretaking parent may become difficult. The child needs a long-term caretaker to comfort and sustain him.

If a child must go to day care, or a combination of school and day care, provide extra security measures. For example, Ralph is five. He's been in day care for two years. Ralph's parents are getting a divorce. His father has moved out of the house. His mother is his caretaker, but she must be away from Ralph a good part of the day. Now he goes to morning day care and afternoon kindergarten and an in-school program until Mom can pick him up. On a Monday, three days after his parents' separation, Ralph's mom put him in the car, preparing to take him to day care. But Ralph cried and kicked so violently, his mom was unable to drive him to the center. She has to find a way to get him to day care and school and get herself to work.

She can help Ralph in several ways. First, by getting him to focus on the day's routine, she can assure him that she will be there at the usual time to pick him up. She can focus on those activities that occur just before Mommy comes. She can give him an inexpensive watch so he can keep track of how long it is until Mom comes. But she has to be reliable. It's very important to Ralph that she consistently arrive at the time when he expects her. If possible, finding a reliable, consistent weekday baby sitter and reducing Ralph's transitions from mother, to daycare, to school, to afterschool could help restore his confidence and trust.

5. *Give the child some concrete symbol of your love to have when you are absent.*

With a younger child, it's a good idea to leave something of yourself with him, something he knows is important, that shows you are thinking of him throughout the day and that you will not forget him. This could be something like a good luck charm, something he might wear that he wouldn't have to worry about losing, like a chain with a cross or star.

When you say good-bye to a five- or six-year-old, reassure the child that you're not leaving because you're angry or unhappy with him. You just have to be at work. Remind him that you are thinking of him during the day, and that you will be back at the usual time.

Older children may not be as overt in expressing their needs. Especially at ages eleven or twelve, they may not want to admit that they need these kinds of reassurances. But your reliability and thoughtfulness, your willingness to provide symbols of your abiding love and continuous concern will be more welcome than the child may be able to admit.

phase two: sadness, yearning, searching

When we lose someone, a part of us wishes for and tries to find a different ending. A cycle of anxiety—searching and yearning, then sadness and despair—revolves around this core of hope.

This cycle is one every human being can understand, because it repeats itself when we move from one phase of life to another. Our best-loved childhood stories—"Snow White," "Lassie," *The Wizard of Oz*—have this loss and reunion theme—as do many of our grown-up fairy tales in movies and musicals. The happy ending is the wished-for ending that we know, as adults, is not realistic.

The difficulty in this stage of grief is the conflict between needing to give up the lost person and the wish to hold on. A child going through this stage of grief has the task of admitting to and suffering the feelings brought on by awareness of the loss, and gradually mastering those feelings.

A parent helps a child in this phase by letting the child experience the yearning and sadness, but then helping the child share those feelings with others who do not discount or minimize them. Only by this process can the child, little by little, let go of the hope that there can be the imagined reunion with the missing loved one, the happy ending.

This stage of grief is filled with conflicted feelings. The child wants to avoid any reminders of the past, then he wants to talk about the loss incessantly. The child insists on being alone with the feelings, then he wants to share the feelings. The child expresses an attitude that life is meaningless, then becomes busy with activities such as trying out for a play or sports team that bespeak some hope. The child is angry at the lost person for leaving, then feels guilt at being angry and even idealizes the one who died or left the home.

The intensity of these conflicts depends upon the hate-versus-love balance in the original relationship. Ambivalence about the parent creates a heightened conflict after he or she is gone.

It's painful to hear a child lauding the lost or missing parent, then spewing out hostility and resentment. It's hard on the child too. So hard that a child may try to rest and retire from the conflict by returning to an earlier stage in development, a time when the child felt competent and safe. This psychological mechanism is called *regression*.

Regression is common in children under stress. Brittany, a six-year-old, began whining like a preschooler. Nine-year-old Ben returned to bed-wetting. Twelve-year-old Kerry sought out the comfort of a lap. These regressions can be annoying and sometimes alarming to parents, yet they are normal and useful responses to the stress of loss. Children usually emerge from these regressions stronger and more confident to face the loss.

What if a parent is seriously distressed by regressed and babyish behavior? First, the parent should let the child know she understands and accepts the sad feelings that make the child want to be babied. Then she can say that it's okay to carry the old baby blanket, play with a baby toy—at home. It's okay to sit on Mom's lap and be rocked when the child really needs the special attention, but these are things that can't be done outside the house, or when Mom has to make dinner or is having company. If the parent feels she can't handle the regression, or the violent swings from love to hate that the child continues to express, the parent should seek professional supportive treatment or the bolstering of a support group.

More serious than the regressed child is the child who, after several months, has never acknowledged or admitted to the feelings of wanting to hold on to the loved one. When the conflict is so buried from awareness and expression, it can fester like a sore that readily breaks open with each new injury or threat of separation and loss.

At age seven, Shirley was told of the sudden and unexpected death of her young baby-sitter, Solvor. She and Solvor had had a warm and enjoyable relationship for one year. A week after Solvor's death, Shirley requested that she be allowed to keep two objects as mementos of Solvor—Solvor's nightgown and one of her glass animals.

Shirley's mother was concerned because Shirley wanted to sleep in Solvor's nightgown and in Solvor's bed. Despite her discomfort with the idea, Shirley's mother allowed this. After two nights, Shirley returned to her own bedclothes and her own bed. She was able to express her sadness at missing Solvor and accept the fact that Solvor was not coming back.

Why does a child continue to search for the lost or missing person when a parent has made it perfectly clear that the loved one is not returning? Why do some children conduct a physical search for the missing loved one—roaming around the room, going to places where the lost person used to be, repeatedly going over the memories and physical attributes of the missing person?

In fact, these searching behaviors, even the ones that may appear irrational or bizarre, are natural and possibly preprogrammed behavior. Once we have bonded to a person, our behavior is programmed to continue being close to that person. When something occurs to threaten that bond, we react forcefully to prevent that loss. When there is a separation, even a brief one, we act automatically to restore closeness to the person, only becoming angry about their having left us *after* they are successfully restored. When a child is lost in the grocery store, the mother searches frantically, finds the child, hugs and kisses her, *then* scolds her for getting lost.

This natural and automatic behavior occurs even when the loss is irretrievable. Grieving children experience this urge to recover their loved one, even though they may understand it is impossible. Over time, this behavior becomes less frequent, but the urge to recover the bond does not disappear. This attachment behavior remains ready to reactivate whenever certain memories or situations evoke the urge.

The searching behavior stops only after repeated unsuccessful efforts to regain the loss. Some of these efforts may involve bargaining with God, making bargains to "be good" or change some characteristic the lost person or higher power might desire. "I'll get all A's next semester if you bring Dad back." Children of five or six, who have not yet left the stage of magical thinking, are even more likely to believe that if they want something badly enough—such as the return of the dead parent or the remarriage of divorced parents—and if they are good enough, they will bring about the desired reunion.

It's natural to want to soothe a sad child, but promising a someday reunion only prolongs the pain. As long as the child believes he may retrieve the loss, his searching behavior will persist. So what is a parent to do?

HOW TO HELP A CHILD EXPERIENCING YEARNING AND SEARCHING

1. This period, with its swings between hope and despair, love and hate, going forward and going backward through regression, is very exhausting. Fatigue is common. Instituting earlier bedtimes and quiet times throughout the day is helpful. A par-

ent can help a child make the transition from activity to quiet times by soothing backrubs, warm baths, familiar stories, relaxing music. Rest helps a child replenish energy and shore up confidence.

2. Try to be patient. These behaviors are natural and a necessary part of learning to accept the loss. Impatience and criticism make it difficult for your child to go through the necessary sharing of feelings. Strengthen your own support network at this time, so you'll have an outlet for your feelings.

3. Support the child through these cycles of hope and disappointment. This is the "work" of grieving, the necessary process that leads to acceptance of the loss. If a child can't do this work, she may remain tied to the lost person, unable to proceed with her personal development, unable to form close relationships with others.

phase three: disorganization and apathy

The work of grieving is so hard, it depletes energy and leaves the bereaved person feeling no zest for life. The intense agony, anger, weeping, and searching subside. Though this new stage has its pain and difficulties, it is actually the beginning of recovery. At this time, the child is estimating the damages and preparing to rebuild. The child may feel overwhelmed.

Karen, age nine, had been difficult during the two months after her parents separated and divorced. She had been fretful, weepy, demanding extra attention, even breaking playthings and souvenirs. Now she has resumed her old routine. She's not so critical of her mother. She says she understands why her parents broke up and she claims she's glad that their bickering and yelling have stopped.

Mom was thinking, "Well, we're finally out of the woods." Then Karen's mom received a call from Karen's teacher reporting that Karen, usually a good student, was falling behind. She wasn't completing her assignments. She sat in class staring off into space. She didn't pay attention to instructions. The teacher requested a special conference to determine what was wrong and what to do.

Karen's problems are typical of this stage of grief. Concentration, attention and memory are often impaired by the grief process, making learning a problem. Teachers usually give grieving children some time to reorganize, but often they don't understand how much time this phase requires. Commands to study hard or do well are not likely to speed up Karen's acceptance of the divorce. Research suggests that even with good support at home, it takes most children more than a year to recover from a divorce or a death in the family. One half to two thirds of the children who suffer a loss still show signs of passivity and withdrawal into the second year after the loss.

There are four steps a parent can take during this period of disorganization:

1. Make a specific time and place to talk about the loss. Make sure there's time at home for the child to talk to the parent or another supportive person, such as an aunt or uncle, family friend.

2. Help the child remember what needs to be done. Verbally go over directions for chores or homework assignments and ask the child to repeat them. Make written lists for older children, use pictures for younger ones.

3. Reserve time for play or diversion. Even though the grieving child may fall behind in school, physical activity and time for fun are still necessary. The child may seem to have little enthusiasm for activities, but he still needs time with peers and without responsibility.

4. Provide encouragement. Help the child mentally prepare for important tasks by helping her to see herself achieving and triumphing.

THE DARKNESS BEFORE THE DAWN

Before a child turns the corner, he or she will go through a brief period of hitting bottom—ten days to three weeks of giving up. Hopelessness and despair are the most difficult aspect of grief for parents to observe in their own children. Witnessing a person realize that the worst has happened, watching the child feel helpless in the face of it, this is one of those times when a parent can legitimately feel, "It hurts me more than it hurts you." Normal tasks—waking up, going to sleep, eating, socializing— seem to be burdens. The child's speech and movements become slower. Lack of energy, exhaustion and pessimism prevail.

A child may even think of suicide to end the suffering, or to reunite with the lost person. Such thoughts are not uncommon. But if suicidal thoughts are severe, or if these thoughts and the symptoms of despair persist beyond a few weeks' time, professional help is indicated.

During this time of despair, a parent can be protective and supportive to help the child keep from feeling isolated and abandoned. A parent can validate the child's feelings, but a parent can't remove the pain; a parent can only help the child to endure it.

phase four: reorganization

There are no shortcuts when it comes to the grieving process. Parents may well be concerned that it's taking too long or is too intense, but eventually the child enters the last phase in the process—reorganization.

The child begins to feel: "I'm going to make it." The tears are less frequent and less profuse. The child's confidence is restored. He or she is more autonomous. The child makes new friends and is more attentive, more in control of himself or herself. Feelings of pain are replaced with feelings of caring and of poignancy. The child now seeks to find a meaning for the loss by gaining understanding of it. Art, music, books and religion are a source of insight. The child has returned to physical and psychological well-being, as if he or she has been on a long, difficult journey and has now returned home.

distinguishing between grief and pathological grief

Considering the length of the grief process and the extreme nature of a child's reaction to losing or separating from a loved one, how can a parent know when grief has gone too far? How can parents tell when mourning has turned into pathology?

The length of time a child continues to grieve and the ongoing intensity of the reactions indicate if there is a problem that needs professional help. Here are ten specific indicators of pathological grief.

1. increased feelings of low self-esteem and worthlessness
2. referring to the deceased in the present tense
3. suicide threats
4. withdrawal from people and refusal to interact
5. impulsiveness and self-destructive behavior
6. psychosomatic illness, especially symptoms of the deceased person's last illness
7. deep depression or anger that may include aggression and antisocial behavior
8. intense hyperactivity
9. unusual vulnerability to new separations
10. stoic refusal to show emotion

Pathological grief is caused by denial, distortion or a delay in the normal grief reactions. When the above symptoms show themselves in chronic proportions, when a parent is having difficulty controlling a child, additional help from a trained therapist is in order. It's a mistake to assume a child will outgrow this behavior.

Grief related to divorce or death usually can be worked through. The majority of children do endure a loss and return to a healthy developmental path.

distinguishing temporary sadness from depression

Elizabeth knew something was wrong with her ten-year-old daughter, but she couldn't say exactly what. "She's just not my Kimberley. There's something odd about her." One day Kim was cranky and irritated, the next mopey and quiet. Too often she would have temper outbursts and tears for no reason at all. Elizabeth talked to her mother, who reminded her that Kim might be changing as she was growing up. Maybe, Kim's grandmother wondered, these were the effects of puberty.

When Kim returned to school in September, her teacher insisted on a conference. The teacher was perplexed. Kim had been recommended as a model student. But the Kim this teacher observed, with her irritability, poor concentration, crying spells and her recent outburst that she'd be better off dead—this was not the Kim she had expected. This child needed help.

At the school's insistence, Elizabeth took Kim to her pediatrician, who referred her to a child psychiatrist. The diagnosis was depression. Kim's mother was incredulous. How could a child of ten suffer from depression?

Only since the early 1970s have doctors begun to recognize that children suffer from depression, as adults do. Before that it was believed that children were too immature to sustain deep-seated feelings of sadness and guilt, which were thought to be the hallmarks of adult depression.

Fortunately, young children don't often become severely depressed. Severe depression occurs in only 2 percent of children seven to twelve years old, but if one includes less serious periods of depression, the estimate goes up to 8 percent. And in adolescence the incidence significantly increases. Many of these adolescent depressions go undiagnosed and untreated. Remember that 15 percent of American teenagers, according to the Fuchs and Reklis 1991 Stanford Study, reported that they came close to trying suicide.

All these statistics tell us one thing. We must take depression in children seriously and deal with it when it occurs. Depressed children and adolescents are more likely to abuse drugs and alcohol. Depression can lead to suicidal thoughts and behavior. Even depressed seven-year-olds have suicidal thoughts. Their desire to die may be equal to that of a teenager. Specialists have suggested that children this age don't commit suicide because they just don't know how to accomplish it. These are chilling thoughts to a parent. But if a parent can help a depressed child early enough, it may be possible to help the child avoid more severe problems later.

how to know if your child is depressed

Communication is the best way to monitor your child's mental health. Communicate your own feelings to your child. This tells your child it's all right to have feelings, to identify them and to express feelings to others. This form of "permission" to share feelings is essential to children.

Listen to your children's feelings and encourage them to tell you exactly what they are feeling. As good communication continues, children become more comfortable expressing feelings, even when those feelings are painful. When children are trying to cope with the stresses and strains of adapting to shifts in family, peer, school and other relationships, talking can prevent them from becoming anxious and depressed.

All children have sad periods, especially when they are responding to a sad event. Normally, children bounce back from that unhappiness in a short period of time—hours or at most days. Unless there has been a death in the family or a divorce, sadness or irritability that persist two weeks or more is cause for concern.

If there is a mood change, look for these behavioral changes as well: boredom in school and generalized boredom; daydreaming in school and poor concentration; weight loss or gain; physical complaints such as headaches and stomachaches; physical agitation or excessive slowness in movements or speech; loss of interest in peers, hobbies or usual activities; school trouble such as poor grades, conduct problems, anxiety or refusal to go to school. Some of the behavior changes of depressed children are similar to those shown by depressed adults: difficulty going to sleep and staying asleep; pessimism, fear of death or preoccupation with death and dying; suicidal thoughts or behavior; fatigue and loss of energy; feelings of guilt or worthlessness.

Certain patterns of behavior can lead to depression if not confronted and treated. Any time a parent observes a child who has trouble making friends, a child who seems surly, is unable to apply himself to constructive work or behaves like a bully, the parent needs to realize that this child is developing a self-defeating mode of behavior that could, down the road, lead to depression.

Often what is depressing a child can be fixed—a teacher who is picking on him, a child who is bullying him, schoolwork that is beyond his capacity. But if the apparent problem is solved and the sadness persists, a parent should ask for a pediatrician's referral to a specialist.

A depressed child feels sadness that she cannot shake. The world looks different to her, hopeless. Too many parents try to explain the problem away or tell the child to snap out of it.

These types of responses can make the child feel more miserable. A depressed child's self-esteem is hurting. That child can say things like, "I can't do it. They won't like me. I can't try," and mean it.

In the normal course of events, when a child feels a bit down or lacking in confidence, support, sympathy and encouragement from parents will help the child feel better. One clue to depression is that this support from parents doesn't work.

gender differences in depression

Research on depression in children and teenagers is relatively new, but current findings show that after puberty girls are more prone to depression than boys, and they show symptoms different from boys. Dr. Peter Lewinsohn, a psychologist at the Oregon Research Institute in Portland, believes preoccupation with body image is the reason behind this.

"If adolescent girls felt as physically attractive and generally good about themselves as boys their age do, they would not experience so much depression," Lewinsohn told *New York Times* reporter Daniel Goleman.* Though girls and boys of seven and eight show no difference in rates of depression, by age fourteen the rate for depression in girls, according to Lewinsohn, is twice that of boys.

Girls' concern about appearance intensifies before puberty. By age ten, many girls become preoccupied with how they look. One need only go to a shopping mall to observe the preteen mania for fads in hairdos and clothes. For depressed girls, this concern becomes intensified and distorted. They feel ugly and unattractive. They may lose weight, and become obsessive about what they eat, or they may go on binges and then feel extreme remorse. A small number of these depressed, hypercritical girls may develop a pattern of pathological dieting and weight loss called anorexia nervosa or compulsive binging and self-induced vomiting called bulimia.

Depressed girls tend to carry their self-criticism to other

* Daniel Goleman, "Why Girls Are Prone to Depression," *The New York Times,* May 10, 1990, p. B7.

areas—school, home, peer relations. They begin to feel they are unacceptable failures everywhere.

Boys tend to show depression by irritability, withdrawing from friends and losing interest in school. Though depressed boys are more likely to specifically mention suicide than depressed girls, they are less likely to talk about their feelings than girls. Usually, boys don't have the social network or the cultural permission to express self-doubt that girls have. But the fact that they go through puberty later and there is somewhat less emphasis on their appearance seems to make them less prone to depression at this early age.

Those who treat depressed youth report that therapy tied to specific skills helps many young people overcome depression. Teaching them to think constructively and counter self-defeating thoughts, helping them to get along better with parents, friends and teachers and showing them ways to relax and enjoy activities have all proven successful.

SUMMARY

Loss is an experience many children must endure, whether the loss is the result of a divorce or the death of a loved one, or the less serious loss entailed in a move to a new location. Parents carry a double burden when they go through a divorce or a death in the family—trying to cope with their own emotional pain and that of their children. Yet, they must allow their children to go through the grieving process. Unexpressed childhood grief can have severe consequences in adolescence and even into adulthood.

In order not to hold out false hopes, parents must be clear about the finality of a divorce or death, but they must also reassure the child that the loss was not his or her fault. Sensitivity to the child's age should guide parents, helping them to speak appropriately about the loss and offer the kind of comfort the child requires. Parents need to encourage their children to express feelings and ask questions about the loss. The grieving process takes time, between one to two years in the case of a divorce or the loss of a parent. There is also a pattern to the process which includes phases of shock and denial, yearning and searching, disorganization, and finally, reorganization. With the help of parents, most children eventually accommodate their lives to the loss. In the case of divorce, they have grieved over the loss of the family they knew and are now prepared to live with the new family situation. In the case of a death in the family, the child recognizes that the loved one is gone, but the child will survive and return to involvement in life.

Children who either refuse to show their emotions or who display uncontrollable anger or other symptoms of pathological grief require therapy to help them cope with their feelings. A small percentage of children become depressed and require professional help, whether or not a loss is involved. Girls approaching puberty seem particularly vulnerable to depression. If depression afflicts their children, parents can confront it and see that children get the additional help they need to express their feelings and begin to experience more positive, hopeful feelings about themselves and their future.

RESOURCES

The National Institute of Mental Health offers brochures on recognizing and treating depression. Write: NIMH, Depression Awareness, Recognition and Treatment Campaign, Rockville, Md 20857.

Many states have hot lines for those feeling desperate. Some have special hot lines for children and teens. One of these is: (800) 234-TEEN.

Some public schools offer after-school groups for children who have experienced a divorce.

The findings of Judith Wallerstein's study of divorce and children are published in *Second Chances: Men, Women and Children a Decade After Divorce* by Judith Wallerstein and Sandra Blakeslee (New York: Ticknor & Fields, 1989) and in *Surviving the Breakup* by Judith Wallerstein and Joan Kelly (New York: Basic Books, 1980).

John Bowlby's three volumes are *Attachment, Separation,* and *Loss,* all published by Basic Books, Inc., New York.

Claudia L. Jewett's *Helping Children Cope with Separation and Loss* (Harvard Common Press, Boston, 1982) and Jill Krementz's *How It Feels When a Parent Dies* (New York: Alfred A. Knopf, 1988) are useful guides for discussing loss with children.

Divorcing parents may find mediation a means of helping them focus on the needs of their children. A national referral service is available through the Academy of Family Mediators, P.O. Box 10501, Eugene, Oregon, 97440, James Melamed, Executive Director at 503-345-1205.

9

LOOKING AHEAD TO THE TEENAGE YEARS

Adolescence is the path to becoming a person, the road to an identity, the part of life when we begin to answer the question "Who am I?" It's the stretch of time between childhood and adulthood, or at least personhood. It's the period of time between the first signs of puberty and the last physical developments that indicate the girl is now a woman, the boy is now a man. The ages vary but for girls it's roughly between nine and seventeen years, and for boys eleven and nineteen years. It's a normal stage of life, one American parents often await with anxiety and foreboding rather than happy anticipation.

In some countries adolescence is marked by puberty rites, ceremonies that separate the young man or young woman from childhood. Dramatic events such as circumcision or isolation suddenly declare that a new adult has entered the tribe. But in America and many industrialized countries, adolescence is a gradual process. It's a long period of time that includes the physical changes of becoming adult but not necessarily the full independence and responsibilities of adulthood.

In Samoa, a girl of sixteen is expected to be married and having children. "Teenage pregnancy" is not an issue in that culture, because biological capability is synchronized with social and cultural norms. In America, a girl of sixteen is also capable of having a baby, but social and cultural norms are such that she is rarely equipped to handle that responsibility. She lacks the education or training that will enable her to support herself. With a baby she will prolong her dependency and prevent herself from realizing her own possibilities. Having a baby early in life may be the single most significant predictor of poverty for American women.

Similarly in this country, a young man of sixteen may feel restless in school with his increased physical strength and emotional need for challenge and competition. But if he quits school, his chances for jobs and a decent future are very slim. If he becomes a father, he will sense even more limits.

Even in this country, the experience of adolescence has varied from time to time and from one cultural group to another. One of the authors discussed adolescence with her mother, a woman who became a teenager the year the stock market crashed. Instead of completing her high school education, she was forced to get a job. At fifteen she was actually supporting her entire family of six. Responsibility followed hard on the heels of puberty. The search for identity was a luxury in that time of economic need. Undoubtedly, there are still instances in this country where circumstances prevent children from experiencing adolescence as we describe it, but for most parents the period is an extended one divided into different phases.

early adolescence versus late adolescence

We have already looked at the first signs of puberty and the earliest indications of adolescence in our chapter on love and sex. Because adolescence lasts so long, and covers so many changes, it's easier to think of it as two parts, early and late. Early adolescence covers the beginning of puberty—for girls, ages nine through thirteen; for boys, ages eleven through fifteen. This first part of adolescence may be the hardest for parents and children. Late adolescence is a time when the emotional and mental changes catch up with the physical changes—for girls, the years roughly from fourteen to seventeen; for boys, the time from sixteen to nineteen.

In this chapter we are looking ahead to the entire span of adolescence and the many changes that will take place—intellectual and emotional changes as well as the physical transformation.

danger! adolescence ahead

Many parents approach the teenage years as soldiers approaching a minefield. They know the territory is fraught with problems and even some life-threatening dangers. They feel that one false step could result in disaster—for themselves and their children. Before mentioning some of the possible problems you may confront as the parent of a teenager, it's important to remember that most families survive the adolescent years. There are many young people who move from childhood through the teenage years without serious problems; they don't even exhibit much of the rebellious behavior typically associated with this period. If you lay the groundwork for self-esteem, open communication and loving limits, you reduce the chance that the teenage years will be years of distress for you and your child.

Yet there are some difficulties unique to this stage of life. It's helpful for parents to look ahead to the teenage years, try to understand the causes of unrest during this particular stage of development and prepare for some of the likely sources of conflict, as well as some of the satisfactions.

The teenage years are, in many ways, the dangerous years—and they seem to be getting more dangerous. In this age group, mortality has risen since 1960; in other age groups mortality has declined. Most teens die because more are involved in accidents, suicide and homicide.

There are also certain myths about the teenage years that may lead parents to make inappropriate choices, choices that may cause them to remove their support from their children too soon. There is a myth that teenagers don't need their parents. While it's true that most teenagers will indicate that they want us to be less involved in their lives, teens need parents to keep them on course, headed toward the future.

Parents of children on the brink of adolescence know that tomorrow they may be offered a cigarette, a wine cooler, a beer. Somebody may tell them they're not really grown up until they've tried marijuana. And if they try that—why not go on to crack?

How can we shield them from these dangers? What can we give them that will protect them from problems, problems that might someday hurt them, or even kill them?

they continue to need you

Adolescents are still children. Don't expect them to admit that. Don't expect them to welcome your advice and guidance. But as their bodies change, in sometimes awkward and embarrassing ways, they continue to need you. Even as their emotions erupt and they strive to become more independent, they will continue to need you.

Children going through puberty need

- a parent who can hang in but not hang on to the child,
- a parent who will let the adult inside the child come out,
- a parent who will continue to set limits in a firm but loving way,
- a parent who will grow and adapt as his or her children grow and begin moving on a separate path, a path that will inevitably lead them away from home to their own life.

they still need you to build their self-esteem

Remember some of the ingredients of self-esteem and you will realize that teens continue to need the support you can offer, even as they look more to the world of peers. Self-esteem is feeling good about yourself. Self-esteem is believing you can do things. Self-esteem is believing you can make choices.

all parents can become builders of self-esteem

The teenage years tend to be costly years—emotionally and financially. Teenagers become more aware of status symbols. They are more likely to want not just a pair of shoes, but a pair of hundred-dollar Air Jordan high tops, not just a windbreaker but a leather bombadier's jacket, and the list goes on. Clothes, cars and spending money become more important. Parents and single parents who have limited income may feel that they are less able to guide their teenagers, less able to offer them the outward supports they seem to need. But all parents—no matter what they have, where they came from, how much education they have, how much money they make—can build their children's self-esteem.

The basic means of building self-esteem don't vary that much from childhood to adolescence. So it might be well, at this point, to remember what the ways are and remind ourselves that these approaches do not cost money.

Parents build self-esteem in children by:

spending time with their children
talking with their children
listening and watching and finding ways to offer support, information and answers, even when children don't actually ask questions
respecting their children's feelings
and encouraging them to share those feelings
setting clear rules
but not being overly harsh with words or punishments
encouraging achievement
but not constantly pressuring their children
sharing their beliefs and values
and sharing some of what they've learned from their own mistakes and victories
praising their children when they make good choices

self-esteem: a lifesaver and a life-enhancer

It's true that time is money. And if you are a working parent, you may find it difficult to spend time with your teenager, especially if she or he is not inviting this sharing of time—and possibly even discouraging it. Yet remember how vital this time sharing is, the difference it can make for your child. Remember that *self-esteem can save their lives.*

Young people who feel good about themselves, children who have high self-esteem, are less likely to use alcohol and other drugs when they are underage. They are less likely to engage in unprotected and premature sex. They are less likely to feel so down and hopeless that they use drugs or sex as escape from pain, less likely to attempt suicide. They are also better equipped to resist pressures to engage in illegal activities. The use of drugs and sex are connected to AIDS. Because young people with high self-esteem are less likely to use drugs and have unsafe sex, they will have more protection against AIDS and other sexually transmitted diseases.

To express it in positive terms, *self-esteem can make life more satisfying*. Adolescents who have high self-esteem are more likely to enjoy activities and achieve in school, forge friendships and make healthy choices. They tend to feel they control their lives and so they are more likely to feel good about their work and their relationships. Adolescents who have high self-esteem will make mistakes, but they are more likely to learn from their mistakes. They are less likely to die from their mistakes.

encouraging independence while enforcing limits

Teens continue to need your support and discipline. Yet the changes that are taking place in your child's mind and body call for some changes in your manner of offering love and limits. The trickiest challenge for parents of teenagers is fostering independence but still enforcing limits. One of the significant tasks of the adolescent stage of life is achieving independence. Teens have mixed feelings: sometimes yearning for independence and sometimes trying to retain the security and comforts of the dependent childhood days. Parents are ambivalent, too. How can they let the child they have loved and protected go forth alone into an uncertain and possibly dangerous world?

Yet there is a certain style of parenting that can help a teenager achieve independence. A more democratic, egalitarian approach is in order as teenagers demonstrate their emotional and intellectual maturity, as well as their greater height, weight and voice power. Frequent explanations by parents of the reasons for rules of conduct, statements of what they expect and why, will foster responsible independence. During the teenage years parents need to provide opportunities for increased autonomy, while monitoring how their children are using that independence and being clear about what will happen when that independence is abused. Parents can help their children identify with Mom and Dad by showing children love and respect, rather than rejection—or worse—indifference. Parents can provide a model of responsible independence by exhibiting a degree of self-control and reliability in their own activities.

Let's say a father has remarried and is scheduled to pick his son up for the weekend. If he's promised to be there at noon, he shouldn't show up at 3 P.M. If he's taking his teenage son out on the boat for the day, he shouldn't spend the afternoon getting drunk on beer. If he's trying to instill in his son respect for women, he shouldn't dwell on all the mistakes his ex-wife made or is making.

It would be helpful if problems in our own personal lives could wait until our children finish adolescence, but instead, parents of teenagers are often faced with their own mid-life crisis, divorce, or the need to care for their own ailing parents. The best we can do is try to find support for personal self-esteem through a network of friends and relatives, activities that relieve stress, personal satisfaction in new career goals or new avocations and—if we feel overwhelmed or in need of professional advice—therapy. It's unhealthy and unrealistic for parents to seek personal emotional support and solutions to their problems from their own adolescent children.

We're bound to feel a pang or two as we allow our adolescent children to test the waters of reality. It's natural to be concerned about the dangers that are out there, but if the letting-go process is very gradual and if our children are bolstered by internalized self-discipline and self-esteem, they are much more likely to navigate those waters effectively.

tasks of adolescence

There are six tasks or goals of adolescence. In our culture, some of them will not be completed until the teenage years are over and the period of young adulthood has begun.

1. Adjust to physical and physiological changes
2. Relate to opposite sex and same-sex peers
3. Develop a sense of ego identity

4. Establish independence
5. Prepare for a vocation
6. Develop a guiding philosophy of life

After reading this list, you may feel that there are some of those areas you are still struggling with, but adolescence is a time when these tasks are, if not completed, at least undertaken in earnest. Let's concentrate on the first three of these tasks, which are likely to preoccupy teenagers and their parents throughout adolescence.

adjusting to physical and physiological changes

We've already talked about the changes children undergo during puberty. Let's concentrate now on the emotional and social challenges of adjusting to those changes.

"The predictable reliable face, arms, legs, thighs, chest, genitals, hair now alter and become strange and unknown," noted social psychologist Kurt Lewin.* Notice how unsettled we can be if any one part of our bodies is altered, if a haircut is done poorly, if a blemish develops. Multiply all that a hundredfold and you have the dilemma of a child turning into an adolescent. It feels like being a stranger in a strange land, and the alien land is one's own body.

ASYNCHRONY OF ADOLESCENCE

The dramatic physical changes of adolescence don't proceed in an orderly harmonious fashion. Different parts of the body are enlarging or sprouting hair or lengthening at different times. This asynchrony or unevenness in the rates of growth means that feet and hands grow before legs and arms lengthen. The nose assumes its large adult shape and peculiarities before the jaw thickens, so that one's very own reliable face that has stared back from the mirror over twelve or thirteen years suddenly seems to be lopsided and alien.

---

* Kurt Lewin, *Field Theory in Social Science* (New York: Harper & Row, 1951), p. 143.

There is also a disharmony or asynchrony between the relatively early development of adult physical and sexual characteristics and the much later acquisition of adult social skills and psychological traits. Girls, for example, experience the growth spurt in height and weight, the onset of menstruation and the development of breasts usually somewhere between ages nine and thirteen (though much later for some). But it's not until the ages of eighteen to twenty-eight or later that they feel the psychological comfort with their sexuality and social skills that gives them a sense of being ready for the long-term commitment of marriage and parenthood, not until the ages of twenty to thirty that they have completed their education and have the job skills to be self-supporting.

Boys may have the physique of adult men at age sixteen but they may not achieve economic independence for another ten or twelve years. Their genitals have gone through a growth spurt and they have reproductive capabilities, but they probably won't gain the social maturity and emotional stability for marriage and parenthood for another decade or more.

FEELINGS OF PERSONAL DOUBT AND DISSATISFACTION

Considering the apparently chaotic course of physical and internal physiological changes, it's not surprising that many adolescents experience some dissatisfaction with their new bodies. For example one national survey revealed that nearly half of the girls (48.4 percent) wanted to weigh less and nearly half of the boys (49.8 percent) wished they were taller. Teenagers are also unhappy about their skin and their posture.

And most of all they were afraid that the physical characteristics they had developed in a sudden and seemingly uncoordinated fashion, were not normal, not as good as those of other teens. How does a teenage boy know whether his height, strength and muscles are up to par? How does he know if his testes and penis are big enough, especially if those of a teammate seem to be bigger? What about the amount of hair they have on their chests and under their arms—is it enough? Why, one may ask, is my lockermate shaving and I barely have whiskers?

As Thomas Cottle has posed the dilemma, how do teenage boys know "whether others masturbate or have wet dreams or fear the darkness, even at age fifteen, or peek through keyholes at girls?"*

If boys are prone to compare height and strength and hairiness, girls anxiously await breasts and menstruation, then compare breast size and worry about weight.

BODY IMAGE

The emotional reaction a person has to his or her body is called body image. Whether or not a teenager is satisfied with his or her body depends a good deal on—you guessed it—self-esteem. The earlier feelings children have about themselves and their bodies will have a great impact on the way they ultimately feel about the new shape of things as they go through adolescence.

Parents can lay the groundwork for this vulnerable period of body reassessment by encouraging children to have good feelings about their bodies before adolescence, helping them to acquire healthy eating habits and develop patterns of exercise and physical skill that will enhance their chances of looking and feeling healthy. When the teenage years are actually under way, a parent can be there to reassure their children about what is normal, to let them know that everyone feels a certain amount of discomfort with a body that is changing dramatically. It's a time for what can be called "mutual vulnerability"—a time for you as a parent to share some of your fears, to communicate your vulnerability and recall the embarrassing moments you experienced during adolescence.

You can be particularly helpful to your child if he or she has a pattern of development that is different from peers—if your child has matured very early or seems to be a late bloomer. With such a wide range of variation in the process of adolescence, most problems of timing will take care of themselves. But if a girl starts menstruating at age eight, or hasn't menstruated by age nineteen, there is reason to seek professional help. If a boy of seventeen has experienced no growth spurt he should be seen by an endocrinologist.

* Thomas Cottle, "The Connections of Adolescence." In *Sixteen: Early Adolescence,* edited by J. Kagan and R. Coles (New York: Basic Books, 1971), p. 328.

EATING DISORDERS

Another cause to seek professional help involves the issue of weight. Overweight is regarded as a detriment in our society, and the stigma attached to being fat tends to make overweight young people the subject of rejection, which can lead to isolation and emotional upset, which can then lead to overeating and more pounds. A program that combines therapy and manageable dieting can help an overweight child moderate his or her eating.

Some adolescents become so obsessed with being "thin enough" they develop eating disorders. They either fast and binge or binge and induce vomiting in a pattern known as bulimia. They may start to diet and exercise to such an extent that they put their health in danger. Anorexia nervosa, as this severe form of psychological eating disorder is called, can become a life-threatening problem. It tends to affect girls who have generally seemed to be exceptionally "good." They are girls who have been unusually compliant. They get good grades. They strenuously try to please their parents. But inside, they are afraid of growing up, and the onset of adolescence presents a threat. Their unbridled dieting seems to be an effort to reduce their bodies to the size and shape of a child's. Once they have lost 25 percent or more of their body weight, they tend to stop menstruating. In their minds, this makes them little girls again. Anorexics and their families require therapy and young people experiencing the more severe symptoms may require hospitalization.

You may get the feeling as you read that parenting is a no-win situation. Aren't I supposed to encourage my children to get good grades and be able to perfect their skills? Again, it's a question of striking a balance between encouragement and pressure, between guidance and oppressive control.

THE VALUE OF GRADUAL REINFORCEMENT
OF SELF-ESTEEM

The research done on anorexia simply reinforces the notion that children need to be taught gradually, between the ages of five and twelve, before adolescence occurs, that they are capable of making decisions, they are capable of managing areas of their lives. This gradual process of building your child's confidence in making choices will have major benefits in adolescence and will help to avoid such serious problems as anorexia.

Fortunately, most of an adolescent's dissatisfaction with his or her body is a temporary thing. When all the various parts have completed the growth spurt, when the jaw has caught up with the nose and the hands with the feet, when breasts have emerged, genitals have developed and weight has stabilized, teenagers become slightly less self-conscious, slightly more at ease with themselves and less unhappy with their parents.

For no matter how excellent a parent you are, some of that temporary upset is bound to show itself in family squabbles. At least knowing and remembering the cause of the dissension, remembering the anxieties you felt, may make your child's adjustment to these physical changes a little easier and a little more bearable.

A NEW OUTLOOK ON THE WORLD

If the landscape of an adolescent's body is changing, so, too, is the landscape of her mind. Just about the time the first pubic hairs have sprouted, a child begins to develop the mental ability to think about the future. Remember that throughout the grade school years and up to about ages eleven or twelve, children are mastering reasoning about the present and the past—what has been called concrete operations. At age eleven or twelve, according to Jean Piaget, most children can begin to imagine not only what is, but what might be. They can project themselves into the future, talk about ideas, manipulate facts and speculate about different outcomes. Adolescents can think about their own thoughts and evaluate them.

At first, their thinking may be quite egocentric. They may fluctuate between thinking their thoughts and feelings are unique and believing everyone thinks as they do. But their early feelings of egocentrism and unlimited power gradually abate and they gain a more realistic grasp on their thinking. They can debate ideas now. Should a young person be required to remain in high school in order to get a driver's license? Should drug programs concentrate on prevention and education or should they put more money into treatment and punishment?

It may be a time when their dress and taste in music are at their most outrageous, but it is nevertheless a period when a parent can appeal to reason. A person of fourteen can not only understand:

All elephants are mammals.
All mammals give birth to live offspring.
All elephants give birth to live offspring.

They can also understand—whether or not they admit it—

All smokers have a greater risk of lung cancer.
I am smoking a pack of cigarettes a day.
I now have a greater risk of lung cancer.

Chances are, given their concern for their appearance and attractiveness, the argument that

All smokers smell of cigarettes.
I have been sneaking cigarettes.
I smell of cigarettes—

may carry more weight with them. The point is that future consequences can begin to play a greater role in their choices.

Another feature of this new mental landscape is the ability to think logically about symbols, propositions and other abstractions, as well as to mentally manipulate available facts. Teenagers can generate hypotheses. They can ask, What if . . . ? Teenagers can speculate about religion, politics, philosophy. They become more acute critics of the social scene. They can be outraged by injustice. And they may begin to question ideas and beliefs that have been part of your family life for years.

NEW PERSPECTIVES AROUSING NEW
FEELINGS

If these new cognitive abilities lead to periods of brooding introspection, unsettling questions about the differences between how things are and how they ought to be and criticism of certain family beliefs—don't despair. These same sometimes unnerving habits are indicators that your child is acquiring the mental equipment necessary for planning a career, making decisions with long-term consequences, moving toward a meaningful philosophy of life.

Just give your child time to let this brand-new ability to project into the future mature. Intellectually, a thirteen-year-old is light-years away from a seventeen-year-old. National Assessments of Educational Progress reveal that most thirteen-year-olds were unable to answer word problems involving computations, such as how long would it take a car traveling 50 miles per hour to go 275 miles. They were able to make change in a grocery store, but few could figure out which brand of cereal was the best buy. Instead of checking the price per ounce, they tended to choose the biggest box. At seventeen many more teenagers are able to perform tasks that involve manipulating figures and thoughts.

Just as the older adolescent is less likely to be deceived by the size of the cereal box, the older adolescent is also less likely to be deceived by appearances in social situations. As they mature, they become more discerning, recognizing, for example, that "stuck-up" behavior may be a cover-up for shyness, that "macho" attitudes may be a cover-up for guys who feel uncertain or inadequate, that a girl who acts wild at a party might be trying to get attention she lacks at home. The older adolescent is able to discern what people are really like, which of their traits endure.

relate to opposite sex and same-sex peers

Of all the tasks of adolescence, this is the one that probably sticks in our minds as the hallmark. In America, there is often a significant gap between the onset of puberty and the formation of an intimate relationship. In between is a period of learning—through frustration, rejection, trial and error.

The whole situation is complicated by differences between male and female—physiological, cultural and social. At this stage of life, all forms of sexual behavior are more frequent in males than in females. The tenfold increase of the hormone testosterone at puberty impacts male behavior—exactly how may vary from person to person. Adolescent males appear to be more easily aroused than adolescent females, more open about their preoccupation with sex. Whether or not they act on their impulses, they may feel some social pressure to indicate they are sexually active. Hormone levels affect behavior, though it's not known exactly to what extent. Many adolescent males have "raging hormones." Fewer have rampant opportunities.

Interestingly, research indicates that social circumstances influence hormone levels. The top monkey in a colony of rhesus monkeys has higher testosterone levels than the other males. But if this top monkey is taken from his position of dominance and put into a colony where he is unknown, his testosterone level falls dramatically. A male with low status and low levels of testosterone will experience a rise in the level of that hormone if he is put in a cage with a female whom he can dominate and sexually engage. While one can't draw an exact correlation with humans, these experiments show that the interaction between social behavior and physiological states is a two-way street.

Our sexual stereotypes and double standard of morality have undoubtedly exaggerated differences between male and female. Even though some of those stereotypes are fading, behavior differences persist. Adolescent females seem to be more concerned with meaningful interpersonal relationships than adolescent males, more influenced by public standards and somewhat more concerned about personal morality. Adolescent males seem to have a more direct need to express sexual feelings. Though a greater number of girls are becoming sexually active in high school, boys tend to make this choice earlier and in greater numbers than girls. Religious affiliation, however, affects both males and females, tending to increase the likelihood of abstinence.

PARENTAL INFLUENCE ON SEXUAL ATTITUDES

Another factor influencing sexual attitudes and adjustments is the prior parent-child relationship and parental attitudes toward sex. If a girl has received admiration from her father and seen her father loving and admiring her mother, she will anticipate a positive response from the teenage boys she encounters. She is less likely to settle for a negative response or demeaning treatment at the hands of males. Children with rewarding relationships are more likely to have positive attitudes about sex, more likely to feel in control of sexual decision making, less likely to have sex for the sake of acceptance.

DATING

Teenagers typically move from an early stage of same-sex groups, which may interact tentatively with the opposite sex groups, to heterosexual cliques, to cliques of couples and then to separate couples. This process gives males and females the opportunity to learn to interact with peers. They can develop social skills, learn to share problems and feelings and gradually move toward an intimate relationship.

That movement toward an intimate relationship—specifically a sexual relationship—seems to take place more swiftly now and at an earlier age. Dating, in terms of one boy and one girl going someplace together because of mutual interest, can start as early as nine or ten years old, especially in affluent, urban areas. And the distinctions between what is accepted for male and female seem to be blurring. Young teenage girls are as likely to call boys for a date as boys are to call girls. In 1991, over 20 percent of teenage girls under age fifteen were having intercourse and the trend was toward more sexual activity among young teenage girls than in previous years. Teenagers of sixteen who are dating are even more likely to be sexually active. Over a third of the girls this age and nearly half of the boys are sexually active. By age eighteen, seven out of ten teenagers, male and female, are sexually active.

The teenage girl is more likely to consider hers a love relationship. This is not necessarily so with her male counterpart. Judging from a college poll of young men and young women regarding their first sexual intercourse, a quarter of the women said they were in love with their first partner and 60 percent said they were planning to marry that person. Very few (less than 5 percent) reported no emotional involvement with their first sexual partner. Among young men 45 percent reported no emotional involvement with their first sexual partner. It will be interesting to see if these statistics change in this decade, as some of the attitudes about male and female change. Will more men come to associate sex with love and marriage, or will a greater number of women dissociate sex from love and marriage? Some of these attitudes will be influenced by the way today's parents bring up their children.

Dating is an important testing ground for learning how to relate to the opposite sex, but it can also encourage superficiality, since physical attractiveness is a key initial ingredient. The yearning to be considered attractive is obvious when a group of young teens attend a social event—all wearing the same outfits and hairstyles. The emphasis on appearance continues to be a major feature of high school dating, with friendliness, popularity, personality, athletic and academic abilities and shared interests playing less significant roles.

The deepest friendships of adolescence may, in fact, be with a friend of the same sex. At ages eleven to thirteen, girls' friendships tend to center on shared activity, such as being on the soccer team or in the orchestra. But between fourteen and sixteen, girls become capable of deeper friendships with a mutual give and take. As girls venture out into the world of dating, they feel more secure if they have at least one loyal friend who will be there whether or not the new boyfriend works out.

By seventeen or eighteen friendships mature into more relaxed relationships where there is tolerance and sharing. This will be the kind of relationship young women will seek with men as they become young adults. The friendship capabilities of high school boys tend to develop more slowly, with boys of fourteen to sixteen more likely to have the superficial type of relationship that comes of shared activities, which characterize the relationships of younger girls.

DECIDING WHETHER TO BECOME SEXUALLY ACTIVE

The decision to become sexually active is influenced by many factors: parental attitudes, attitudes of peers, use of drugs and drinking. A teenager's particular style of thinking may also influence when sexual activity begins and whether birth control and protection against STD's is used.

Richard and Shirley Jessor conducted a social-psychological

study in which they followed a group of several hundred teenagers during the seventies. Teenagers were more likely to engage in sex if parents, and especially peers, were less controlling and sanctioned sexual exploration. Marijuana was much more common among the sexually active group. Virtually all of the sexually active teenagers—96 percent of the males and 87 percent of the females—were also involved in drinking. These findings and other research suggest significant links between indifferent parents, alcohol and other drug use, and early sexual activity. This dangerous combination is tied to parental concern rather than parental income.

Jody lives in an affluent suburb of a major city. She's a high school junior, the daughter of a business executive father and a gynecologist mother. Despite her above-average intellectual ability, Jody's grades started dropping shortly after the school year began. Jody was asked by her school counselor if anything was wrong at home. She complained that as the oldest of three, she had the least of her parents' limited attention and the greatest amount of responsibility, and was often required to watch or sit for her younger siblings.

Her mother had seen to it that she had adequate knowledge of contraception, STD's and sexuality, but this was conveyed in a hasty, clinical manner. Jody told her school counselor, "Mom only cares that I don't get pregnant and embarrass her. She doesn't care a bit about me. She doesn't even know me."

One evening Jody and her girlfriend left their suburban community to "hang out" in the city. With false ID's they entered several singles bars and became intoxicated. "Just for kicks" Jody accepted a limousine ride with several sailors on leave, even though her friend backed out and went home. In the morning, Jody returned to her girlfriend's home, disheveled, covered with hickeys. She just couldn't remember the sexual events that occurred after entering the limousine. She's hoping that she didn't "pick up anything" or get pregnant. She doesn't want to tell her parents, but she's going to take tests for AIDS, chlamydia and pregnancy, "just in case."

Would Jody have behaved so irresponsibly if she received more attention from her parents, as well as clearer limitations? Parental concern is not the only factor here, but when it's combined with ongoing communication and personalized preparation for the dangers ahead, it may keep people like Jody from becoming statistics on the next AIDS report.

Using the example of Jody, we might imagine the type of communication that would have offered Jody more support.

Let's say her mother arrived home just as she and her friend were leaving for their "evening on the town." The conversation might have gone this way.

MOM: Oh, I see you're all dressed up. Where are you going?
JODY: Just out.
MOM: Well, I need to have an idea of where.
JODY: A party.
MOM: Will there be a parent at this party?
JODY: Oh, Mom. Give me a break.
MOM: You're getting older, but I still need to know. With no parent around, there's likely to be drinking or drugs, maybe much older guys. I love you, Jody, and I love the way you're growing up. But drinking and drugs are off limits.
JODY: Then I'll just stay over at Lila's.
MOM: What's the number there in case I need to reach you?
JODY: Oh, Mom. I'm not a baby.
MOM: You're certainly not. But babies don't run the risk of getting involved with alcohol or coke. Babies don't run the risk of pregnancy or AIDS. You're a beautiful girl, Jody. I want you also to be a careful girl.

One conversation can't possibly make all the difference. Hundreds of expressions of this type are bound to get through, even to a resistant, rebellious teenager.

Over the long span of adolescence, a teenager's intellectual abilities and social understanding gradually catches up with his or her physical maturity. In the early years of adolescence, girls and boys are not well equipped to think about the future. They may be aware of future consequences, but they rarely let that awareness influence the impulse of the moment. In terms of sexual activity, this means that younger adolescents are less likely to use birth control to avoid pregnancy, less likely to allow their knowledge of AIDS and other STD's to cause them to use condoms.

Among older adolescents there are encouraging signs that

precautions are now more likely to be taken. A 1988 survey revealed that sexual activity is more common among seventeen-year-olds than it was a decade ago, but condom use among seventeen- to nineteen-year-olds is increasing. Analyzing the survey results of 1,980 unmarried males, Freya Sonenstein, Joseph Pleck and Leighton Ku found that the number of sexually active teens has been rising, despite the AIDS threat. In 1979, 56 percent of this age group said they had sexual intercourse; in 1988, the number rose to 72 percent. In the earlier survey only 21 percent of the sexually active seventeen- to nineteen-year-olds reported they had used a condom last time they had sex. In 1988, 58 percent reported having used one.

Delaying the onset of sexual activity seems to give teenagers a better chance to avoid pregnancy and sexually transmitted diseases. Helping teenagers to avoid the use of alcohol and other drugs, giving them clear messages that sexual activity at an early age is not sanctioned and continuing to enhance their self-esteem are ways parents can help adolescents make decisions to delay sexual activity until their minds and emotions have caught up with their sexual drive.

develop a sense of ego identity

One of the most complicated jobs of adolescence is to find the answer to the question, "Who am I?" Even before children can speak, they start figuring out from the way they are treated whether or not the world will be a safe place, whether or not they can trust people. At adolescence this issue of trust is raised again, as are many other challenges from the years of childhood. (For example, if a child has been abused or neglected during the first two years of life, adoptive or foster parents are likely to have a difficult time dealing with the child at adolescence—even if their treatment of the child in the intervening years has been exemplary.)

Using his background in psychoanalysis, anthropology and teaching, Erik Erikson modified Freud's views and established the foundation for many of our current beliefs about child development. Erikson saw adolescence as a particularly significant time when the individual must use all past experiences to meet the challenge of establishing an identity. As he explained it, identity was a series of pieces gathered from different stages of life, pieces that come together at adolescence, almost like a patchwork quilt. From the toddler years there would be a piece called self-control, from early childhood a piece called grand dreams: "I can become what I dream of being." From the school years the child would have a piece of identity called industry. "I can make things work."

This question, "Who am I?" has been kicking around for a while, ever since the child recognized "I am a boy" or "I am a girl." The child has been figuring out whether he is smart or stupid, attractive or unattractive, liked by others or disliked, loved and cherished by parents, ignored or abused by them. During the teenage years, with all the physical changes that take place and the emotional ups and downs, a person can become confused about who he is. The confusion may express itself in trying out different identities—strange hairdos, odd clothes. It may bring about a series of experiments with different activities and different groups of friends.

If they can't get into the flow, if they can't find a place for themselves in a group doing something worthwhile, or at least not destructive, teenagers may experiment with a negative identity.

Lots of adolescents experiment with breaking the rules. They might steal something from the store, cheat on an exam, or break the family's rules regarding drinking or driving. If their family and society respond, chances are they will look elsewhere to find themselves.

NEGATIVE IDENTITY VERSUS POSITIVE IDENTITY

Teenagers who can't find positive roles may choose a negative identity. It can be difficult to resist the pressures of gangs, for example, especially in areas where they seem to control the neighborhood. The gang offers young people groping for approval a temporary sense of importance and group status. The gang colors, the gang signs, the sense of belonging to a "special" group are one way of being a part of a kind of substitute "family."

The price teenagers pay for being in a gang is violence, and sometimes death. The link between gangs and drugs pulls members into illegal, unhealthy and possibly fatal activities. Some teenagers want to be part of a gang. Other teenagers are pressured into becoming members of gangs. Some boys in neighborhoods where gangs seem to control the streets become delinquents, yet some boys from the same neighborhoods finish school and become responsible adults. Why? What makes the difference?

People who have compared these kinds of groups find that boys who resist gangs and delinquency have good feelings about themselves, high self-esteem, feelings of self-worth. These are the feelings that parents can help create from the earliest childhood days. These are the feelings that need to be nurtured throughout the teenage years.

GETTING INTO THE FLOW

Adolescents are looking for intense experiences, the kinds of activities that offer challenges and make them strive, the kind of involvement that will help them figure out who they are and what they should do with their lives.

University of Chicago Psychologist Mihalyi Csikzentmihalyi who has conducted extensive studies on both teenagers and creativity, calls these "flow experiences."

Flow is a feeling of such great involvement and concentration that one loses oneself and yet finds something good in oneself. It can happen with sports, art, music, hobbies; it can happen working on a car, rewiring a radio. One loses track of time. There's no boredom, just a sense of moving steadily toward some goal.

Whether the flow is produced by playing in a rock band or on a basketball team, working at the computer or dancing, teenagers find their most enjoyable experiences to have a certain pattern:

1. Concentration based on rules. Music, sports, mechanics—these things all have clear rules that require concentration.

2. Actions that produce feedback—from an audience, or a partner or the faces of the opposite team when the ball is slam-dunked.

3. Involvement that makes one less self-conscious. The

young person kicking with the chorus line, swimming against the clock, trying to figure out how to rebuild a carburetor will be too involved to worry at that moment about his or her complexion or popularity rating.

4. Victory over the self—getting a better score than ever before, mastering a dance step, reaching a high note or low note, giving from the heart, feeling closer to God.

Perhaps your past efforts to get your children interested in various activities have led them to one they particularly enjoy. Sometimes you as the parent can help your teenager find such an activity. More often you can watch for opportunities to encourage your teenager to get involved in an activity that appeals to her and seems to produce some excitement for her.

You can attend your children's game or recital or just watch them practice. Encourage your children to get involved in things that are positive and productive. It's easier to say no to alcohol and other drugs when you are saying yes to life.

Adolescence is not simply a basket of troubles. It's a time when young people discover their talents, develop new skills, plan for the future. Despite the tensions and challenges to parental authority, despite the arguments over who does what and when—most parents will manage to stay in touch with their teenagers. They'll learn to make some changes as their children become more mature, giving them a bit more freedom and responsibility, respecting their individual tastes and wishes. They will realize that they are still needed, to provide love, wisdom and rules, to offer guidance and convey values that will serve young people well as they become adults.

Though the road from childhood to adulthood may be a rocky one, good things can and do happen along the way. You can look for those good things and help to make the most of them.

SUMMARY

Parents may be apprehensive as they look at the adolescent years, imagining these years to be fraught with dangers. To be sure there are reasons for concerns, as the prevalence of drinking and using other drugs and early sexual activity increases. But parents continue to be important to their adolescent children as builders of self-esteem. In these years, feelings of self-worth, bolstered by parental warmth and guidance, may literally be a lifesaver.

Teenagers will want more independence. And a more democratic, egalitarian approach is in order as teenagers demonstrate greater maturity, though rules need to be enforced. In the early adolescent years, young people have several "developmental tasks"—they must adjust to radical physical and physiological changes. They must learn to relate to opposite sex and same-sex peers. And they must develop a sense of their own identity. The uneven pattern of physical change may heighten the teenager's feelings of personal doubt and dissatisfaction. During this vulnerable period, parents can help by sharing their own awkward moments from the past and encouraging their children to develop a positive body image.

Many factors influence a young person's choice to become sexually active, but parental concern plays a role in this choice. A larger number of teenage girls become sexually active at an early age and by the time boys and girls are eighteen, the majority of them have decided to become sexually active. Parental concern, expressed through affection as well as by imparting information and setting rules, may prevent teenage children from engaging in early and unprotected sexual activity.

The most important task for adolescents is to arrive at a sense of identity. Their ability to meet this challenge will depend, to a large extent, on their childhood experiences, whether they have come to trust their caregivers, whether they have developed a sense of industry and accomplishment in grade school, whether they have been made to feel attractive or unattractive, smart or stupid, rejected or loved. Teens may experiment with different identities at this time, possibly even a negative identity through a gang or troublemaking group, but those with a higher sense of self-worth are better able to reject destructive groups such as gangs.

Adolescents can use their greater mental capacities and physical energies in the service of new accomplishments. They relish the feeling of great involvement or so-called "flow experiences." Most adolescents and parents learn to navigate the rough waters of the teenage years and emerge intact, the children now more independent teenagers, the parents wise survivors.

YOU HAVE WHAT IT TAKES

We've spent a good deal of this book talking about children's self-esteem, the importance of helping children to feel good about themselves. We know that parents need encouragement and support. There are many incentives built into various occupations, but few incentives in our society for being a good parent. Yet each of us has what it takes.

We are uniquely equipped to be our children's best guide and support. As parents, we will make mistakes. We won't always be able to follow even the best advice. But we can recognize and overcome our own mistakes and seek information and avail ourselves of support through family, friends and knowledgeable people in the community. We can continue to build our children's self-esteem—by giving them time, encouraging and supporting them, setting clear, consistent and reasonable limits, treating them with respect and gradually encouraging their independence.

We can get help for our own problems so that we will be able to cope with problems that arise with our children. We can give our children the best facts and personal insights about people, sex and dangers, including drugs. We can share with them some of the mistakes and triumphs of our own experience of life. And above all, we can love them.

APPENDIX I

sexually transmitted diseases

Semen and the female body fluids can carry various kinds of microorganisms like bacteria and viruses. These are called sexually transmitted diseases or STD's. These include syphilis, gonorrhea, chlamydia, genital herpes, in addition to HIV that leads to Acquired Immunodeficiency Syndrome or AIDS which has been already discussed in detail. Some of these sexually transmitted diseases are relatively new. These include genital herpes, chlamydia, human papillomavirus and AIDS. Twenty years ago, these STD's were virtually unknown. In 1990, the Center for Disease Control estimated there were 12 million new cases of STD's in the United States.

Syphilis is a long-term infection that may involve any organ in the body. The rates of syphilis in adolescents and young adults (thirteen- to twenty-four-year-olds) has increased since 1977. There are estimated to be approximately 130,000 cases in 1990. People who want to get married have to take a blood test which detects syphilis. It occurs in three stages. In the first stage, there is a painless sore, called a chancre, on the genitals and swollen lymph glands in the genital area. Two weeks to six months later, if untreated, secondary syphilis occurs. At this point the syphilis organisms are circulating in the bloodstream. Ninety percent of people will have a rash which is infectious by non-genital contact. A rash on the palms and soles is particularly suspicious for syphilis. After four to eight weeks the rash goes away and the syphilis is latent. The syphilis, however, can still be transmitted by blood products or across the placenta. The third stage of syphilis shows itself as the slow, progressive deterioration of organ systems in the body which may include skin, liver, bone, the central nervous system or any other organ. Studies have shown mortality rates from untreated syphilis of 15 percent in men and only 8.3 percent in women. Syphilis can be detected by a blood test and treated with penicillin.

Gonorrhea is a common STD—almost as common as the cold. Approximately 1.4 million new cases of gonorrhea are reported each year. Treatment with a drug called ceftriaxone is recommended. The symptoms of gonorrhea are burning on urination, discharge from the penis or vagina, the rectum, or throat. Most women have gonorrhea for some time without knowing. This could cause her to give it to someone, to transmit it to a baby during birth. She might just let it go untreated and then it could cause pelvic inflammatory disease (PID), a painful abdominal infection that could result in damage to Fallopian tubes and ovaries that could prevent her from having a baby. Early treatment of gonorrhea can prevent these complications. The rates of gonorrhea in adolescents and young adults have been decreasing since 1979.

Genital herpes is a virus related to one that causes cold sores. It's very contagious. There are about 200,000–500,000 new cases of genital herpes every year. It is transmitted by skin-to-skin contact with the affected area. Of course, a common way it can be transmitted is during intercourse. It can be passed on to an unborn fetus, causing brain damage and death. Herpes causes small painful sores on the penis in males, in the vagina or cervix in females or the mouth of either sex, along with flu-type symptoms like aches and fever. There is no cure for herpes. The symptoms disappear within a few weeks, but the disease comes back throughout one's life, especially during times when the body is weak from illness or stress. Early treatment of herpes can reduce the frequency and severity of the outbreaks.

Chlamydia is currently one of the most common STD's. There are approximately four million new cases of chlamydia reported in this country each year. Though chlamydia affects men and women, women can carry the organism without knowing it, transmit it and later discover its destructive effects on their own reproductive sysem. The transmission is sexual. Chlamydia can do damage to Fallopian tubes that can prevent women from having babies. (A 1984 study estimated that chlamydia infections were rendering fifty thousand women infertile each year.) Chlamydia can be detected by a penile or vaginal culture test. If treated early with doxycy-cline or tetracycline, it has much less chance of causing severe damage.

Human Papillomavirus, also known as HPV or condyloma, is a skin-to-skin contact and also sexually transmitted virus, some strains of which are associated with cancers of the cervix, vagina and vulva. Some varieties of the virus cause genital warts. Six hundred thousand to two million cases of HPV in women are reported each year. The virus may be present in the body without any visible warts. Without these obvious symptoms, HPV often goes untreated and continues to spread, resulting in more serious consequences.

When there are symptoms males usually show signs of HPV on their penis or scrotum. In females, HPV is detected by a Pap smear. After an abnormal Pap smear suggesting HPV is re-turned, a biopsy may be taken to determine what strain of HPV is present. Early detection and treatment are recommended to stem the virus and prevent life-threatening forms of cancer from developing.

ways to avoid stds

Abstinence
There is only one absolutely sure way to avoid contracting AIDS or any of the sexually transmitted diseases, as there is only one absolutely sure way to avoid pregnancy, and that is abstinence. Informed abstinence is the best advice for young adolescents.

Condoms as a way to avoid STD's
The use of condoms during intercourse significantly reduces the chances of getting the HIV virus and other STD's. However, scientific studies of couples who wished to avoid pregnancy by using condoms showed that there were some failures. That means in some cases, sperm got through the condom barrier. So even with the use of condoms, there is some risk that HIV or another of the STD viruses will go through the condom bar-rier. In addition, condoms vary in their effectiveness. The use

of a latex condom—not animal skin—and the use of a spermicide containing Nonoxynol-9 (at least 5%) that also serves as a lubricant and kills some organisms which cause STDs, provides the best barrier to HIV and other sexually transmitted diseases.

APPENDIX 2

questions and answers about aids for young adolescents

1. What is AIDS?

AIDS is a group of illnesses that happen after a certain kind of virus called HIV gets into the body. The letters A I D S stand for Acquired Immunodeficiency Syndrome. That's a fancy way of saying that the army of cells that fight sicknesses is not working.

The HIV kills the cells that are needed to defend against all kinds of germs and bacteria and other viruses. When that happens, people get very sick. They have AIDS.

2. Why is everybody so worried about AIDS? They're even talking about it at school.

People are worried because there is no cure for AIDS, no vaccine like we have for polio or measles. They're worried because AIDS is usually fatal. People who get it eventually die.

3. How do you get it?

The virus that leads to AIDS is called "HIV," which means "human immunodeficiency virus." The HIV virus is carried in the blood and in body fluids. People can get HIV from the blood of an infected person—through a blood transfusion. People who share the same needle, such as heroin users, can get HIV. People can also give it to each other when they have sexual intercourse.

4. But how?

The HIV virus is carried in the fluids that come out during sex. When a man is infected with HIV, the semen he ejaculates when he has sex contains HIV and can be passed to his partner. When a woman is infected with the HIV virus, the fluid that comes from her vagina when she has sex contains HIV and can be passed along to her sex partner.

5. Is it true that washing after sex cuts down on your chances of getting AIDS?

Washing after sex is like shutting the barn door after the horse has galloped out. Soap and water applied to the outside of the penis or the vagina don't reach the semen inside, which contains the HIV. (However, urinating and washing after sex can lower the risk of other STDs, especially syphilis.) A person must prevent infected semen, vaginal fluids or infected blood from getting inside their bodies. Once it is inside, it can't be killed.

6. Does the AIDS virus come out when you go to the bathroom?

Urine and feces carry only very low concentrations of HIV. The disease has not been known to be transmitted this way. HIV is found in significant amounts only in blood and in body fluids like semen and vaginal fluid and fluids from the mucous membranes of the rectum.

7. Why do children have AIDS? Children don't have semen, and they don't have sex.

Some children have gotten blood from HIV carriers through transfusions. Other children who have a disease called "hemophilia" bleed easily, even from ordinary things like cuts and bruises. Those kids have had to get extra blood through blood transfusions. Some of the blood they got had HIV in it. Lastly, some children have gotten HIV from their mothers, who were infected and passed it on to them when they were in the womb.

8. Can people get AIDS if they give blood?

No. Hospitals use sterile disposable needles when people donate blood. Donating blood cannot give you AIDS.

9. Can I get the AIDS virus? I mean, what if someone in our school has it?

You can't get the AIDS virus from touching a person with AIDS or just being in the same room with him. You're not a person who needs blood transfusions. And now that doctors know about the AIDS virus, they're testing all the blood to make sure it doesn't have that AIDS virus in it. So even children who need blood, and adults who need it, won't have as much risk. There's more testing for AIDS now, so people will know when they have it.

10. Then why do babies have AIDS? Why would a mom give it to her own baby?

Before people get the disease called AIDS, they can carry the virus for it quietly, for a very long time, without even knowing they have it. Remember when you got chicken pox? Someone passed it along to you before he knew he had it, before he broke out with the itchy bumps. Some mothers may not know they have the AIDS virus, because they don't yet have the disease, the part that makes you sick. They become pregnant and they don't know they've got it. Then they find out and then the mother and the baby have the disease.

11. *Did they have the AIDS test when you and Dad had me?*

No. But there wasn't any AIDS virus here when we decided to have you. Now people have to be concerned about it, especially people who have sex with people they don't know. That's why we don't want you to have sex until you find the one person you want to marry, until you really get to know that person.

12. *Why are most of the people who have AIDS gay people?*

In this country, AIDS was introduced into the gay community first. But it's not just gay people who have AIDS. If someone's infected with the AIDS virus, he or she can give it to another person. That could happen with people who have partners of the same sex—homosexuals—but it could also happen with people who have partners of the opposite sex—heterosexuals. It can happen with anyone having sexual intercourse with an infected person or getting the blood of an infected person or sharing a needle with a drug user who has AIDS.

13. *Do you mind if a kid with AIDS goes to our school?*

I've been very concerned about this. I wouldn't want you to be in danger of anything that might make you sick and threaten your life. So I've been finding out about how AIDS is spread. There are only two ways children get AIDS: from an infected mother or from contact with contaminated blood, blood from a person who carries the HIV virus. Children have never gotten AIDS from being with other children who have it. A person in your class who has AIDS should be treated as kindly as any other classmate.

14. *But what if you're in school with an AIDS kid and you accidentally touch him or he gets too close to you?*

AIDS is not carried on the air, like flu or cold viruses. It's the kind of virus that dies right away when it reaches the air. So you can't get it if you touch the clothes of a person with AIDS, or even use his dish or chew on a pencil he's used. I don't recommend using another child's dish, chewing another's pencil, but that's for ordinary reasons of not wanting to get someone else's germs. These are not the ways AIDS is transmitted.

You can't get AIDS from touching the hand of a child infected with the AIDS virus, or from swimming in the same swimming pool they use. Experts know this because they've checked families where there is a child who got AIDS from a transfusion. None of the family members got the virus, even though they played with the brother or sister who had AIDS, or ate or slept or wrestled with the child.

15. Then why have people burned down the houses of AIDS families and refused to let kids with AIDS go to their schools?

People get very frightened when they know there's something around that can cause death. They get very frightened when they see people getting sick and dying. They're like mother lions with their cubs, ready to kill anyone who gets too close. But we're not animals.

We have minds and hearts. We can learn about what we fear. We don't have to be afraid of children in class who have AIDS, or other people who have AIDS. They deserve our kindness and our understanding.

APPENDIX 3

frequently abused drugs and their effects*

alcohol

What to look for:

Cans, bottles, cartons of beer, wine coolers, wine, spirits, smell of alcohol or mouthwash on breath, glassy or red eyes, slurred speech, giddy or confused behavior, hangovers.

Immediate effects:

Slows down the brain and the nervous system. In small amounts reduces anxiety, increases self-confidence and produces euphoria. In larger amounts, the euphoria turns to depression and inebriation. Depresses brain, especially control of thoughts, recognition of space between objects; slurs speech, impairs memory and judgment. Vision blurs, reflexes slow, legs and hands become unsteady, all of which affect driving. Blood vessels enlarge, creating a warm, flushed feeling. Body temperature, however, decreases. Many people combine alcohol with other drugs, which multiplies the effects of each drug. For example, marijuana and alcohol can be a particularly dangerous combination. The active ingredient of marijuana (called THC) turns off the brain's vomit center. Normally, when the stomach becomes irritated by alcohol, the stomach seals off by closing a valve called the pylorus, which causes vomiting. When THC is in the blood, the brain never sends the message to shut off the valve and someone can drink much more than the body can tolerate safely. A thousand people in the United States die of alcohol poisoning every year.

Long-term effects:

Alcohol is psychologically and physically addicting and thereby causes alcoholism. Due to the immaturity of their ner-

---

* Ken Barun and Philip Bashe, *How to Keep Children You Love Off Drugs* (New York: Atlantic Monthly Press, 1988) pp. 119–145.

vous systems, children and teenagers can become addicted faster than adults—even within only six months. Alcohol destroys brain cells and causes liver damage. Scarring of the liver is called cirrhosis. People under twenty-one years old can develop cirrhosis after only twenty months of drinking. Cirrhosis is one of the ten top causes of death in the United States. Alcohol also damages the kidney and the pancreas.

tobacco

What to look for:
Cigarettes, pipe, chewing tobacco, tins of snuff, matches, lighters, morning cough, yellow teeth or fingertips. Cigarettes contain nicotine, tar and carbon monoxide.

Immediate effects:
Nicotine raises the blood pressure and heart rate, and stimulates the brain and nervous system. Carbon monoxide produced while smoking is the same gas that is emitted from auto exhaust. It can reduce the red blood cells' capacity to carry oxygen through the body.

Long-term effects:
Excessive smoking leads to physical and psychological dependence. Tar contains several cancer-causing gases. Lung cancer, jaw and mouth cancer (caused by using smokeless and chewing tobacco) as well as chronic cough, respiratory infections and emphysema can result.

marijuana and hashish

What to look for:
Green or brown dried leaves, stems, oval-shaped small seeds, yellow flowers. Hashish is brown and gummy, or black and hard, balls or cakes. Hashish oil is sticky, viscous; color ranges from black or brown to yellow or red or clear. Sweet smell of marijuana in room, on breath, hair, clothes. In-room deodorizers, mouthwash to cover smell. Bloodshot eyes, cough, yellow fingers or teeth. Marijuana butts called roaches, roach clips, rolling papers, pipes, bongs (water pipes), matches, lighters, small plastic bags, foil-wrapped cakes of hashish.

Immediate effects:
Has sedating, stimulating and hallucinatory effects. There are thousands of chemicals in smoked marijuana, the one most re-

sponsible for the "high" sensation is THC. The amount of THC per marijuana cigarette or hashish dose may vary. Certain strains such as Colombian, Acapulco gold, and sinsemilla contain two to three times more THC than the average marijuana cigarette. The "high" effect of marijuana is euphoric. Immediately, the smokers' inhibitions relax. Some smokers are more sociable, others more withdrawn or confused. Users claim marijuana enhances the senses: music, lights, colors are more vibrant, conversation more intense or witty. However, at times environmental circumstances are not conducive to a euphoric high. Paranoid feelings and anxiety set in. Physical effects include dry mouth, bloodshot eyes, lowering of body temperature, ravenous hunger or "the munchies," increased heart rate and often a sense of panic or loss of control. Marijuana users have reduced attention span; time sense and distance perception are altered; short-term memory and coordination are impaired. Marijuana users tend to underestimate both the intensity and duration of the drug's effect—one marijuana cigarette (joint) reduces driving reaction time by 42 percent for four to six hours; two joints by 63 percent for four to six hours.

Often marijuana is combined with harmful substances such as phencyclidine (PCP-angel dust), insecticides, and formaldehyde. Hashish is the dried resin of the cannabis plant. It is three to ten times stronger than marijuana. It produces a euphoria of one to three hours' duration similar to marijuana but more intense and sometimes including hallucinations.

Long-term effects:

Marijuana, although not physically addictive, creates a tolerance and psychological dependence. Almost one third of occasional smokers will become daily users within three to five years of use. THC remains in the bloodstream and urine as long as thirty days. Habitual use reduces short-term memory and leads to an amotivational syndrome including shortened attention span, lack of interest in activities and lethargy. It can cause brain atrophy. It does not cause mental disorders but it can bring to the surface existing mental problems. Marijuana contains more cancer-causing substances than tobacco smoke and the deep inhalation and retention method of smoking cause more lung damage than cigarette use.

Marijuana reduces normal sex hormone levels and can disrupt the menstrual cycle in young adolescents. Marijuana can also impair the body's white blood cells, which are necessary to fight disease, thereby reducing the body's ability to fight illness.

pcp

PCP (angel dust) was an animal and human anesthetic. It was taken off the market because it caused psychoses in humans. It is now illicitly produced and distributed. It can be taken orally, injected or smoked in cigarettes. Often it is taken unwittingly because unscrupulous drug dealers often substitute less expensive PCP for other drugs.

What to look for:

Liquid, white powder, rock crystal or pills, small plastic bags, foil-wrapped marijuana cigarettes, liquid, syringes.

Immediate effects:

Immediate effects occur within fifteen minutes if swallowed, two to five minutes if smoked. Effects last at least four to six hours and it may take twenty-four hours to return to normal. Effects are unpredictable and vary from person to person. Users may be withdrawn, violent, confused or psychotic. Users can become delusional and feel they are invulnerable, can fly or have superhuman strengths. As a result users can injure themselves without realizing it.

Other symptoms include sweating, nausea, cramps, tearing, drowsiness, convulsions and coma.

Long-term effects:

PCP produces tolerance and psychological dependence. Psychoses can occur three to four days after taking the drug. Mental reactions include violence, suicidal depression, paranoia and auditory hallucinations that can persist up to two years. Other long-term effects include fever, high blood pressure, seizures and kidney failure.

cocaine, crack and ice

Cocaine can be inhaled, injected, swallowed, smoked, inhaled nasally or dissolved in water.

Crack is a freebase variant of cocaine made by mixing cocaine crystals with baking soda, creating a paste that can be cut into light brown pellets or white rocks that resemble soap chips. It is inhaled through a glass pipe. It is ten to twenty times purer than cocaine. Because it enters the bloodsteam through the lungs it enters the brain faster (in fractions of a second). This creates a more intense high, though of short duration, and a greater addictive potential.

Ice, or methamphetamine, is a stimulant often used to replace crack. It costs more than cocaine or crack cocaine, but produces a far longer high, usually eight to thirty hours. A similar dose of crack would last only twenty to thirty minutes. Many users prefer ice since the cost per high is more attractive. Ice can be powder, which is injected, or crystal, which can be smoked. Because of the rapidity and intensity of the high when smoked, ice is very psychologically addicting.

What to look for:

White or yellowish powder, glass vials, straight-edged razor blades, small mirrors, straws or rolled-up bills for inhaling (snorting), small spoons, white glassine paper, chemicals such as ether, potassium carbonate, sodium hydroxide (for freebasing), matches, lighters, weight loss, pallor, running red nose, skin abscesses, needle marks, chest pains, sore throat, hoarseness, singed eyelashes or eyebrows from hot vapors.

Immediate effects:

Users describe feelings of exhilaration and become excitable, talkative and hyperactive. There is a sense of heightened mental acuity. However, as the "rush" of initial euphoria wears off, users experience a "crash" of depression, anxiety, irritability and loss of sense of pleasure and motivation. To avoid the crash, users ingest more drug, often until their supply is exhausted. Crack and ice have similar behavioral and physical effects, only multiplied in intensity. Paranoia and violent behavior are not uncommon behavioral effects of crack and ice.

Long-term effects:

Cocaine produces tolerance and both psychological and physical dependency. The cocaine hot line study at Fair Oaks Hospital in Summit, New Jersey, noted that the average teenaged user progresses from first use to chronic abuse in only fifteen and a half months as compared with over four years for an adult. Crack produces an extreme craving for more stimulation—a craving that cannot be satisfied. Users of cocaine and crack often go on binges, using for a week at a time or longer. There may be other compulsive and eccentric behaviors that occur during a binge—compulsive cleaning, talking, or sexual activity. About half of chronic users suffer depression, panic attacks, low sexual drive and memory impairment. Other symptoms include insomnia, irritability, poor concentration, twitches, hyperactivity, physical neglect, paranoia and hallucinations (imagining bugs crawling beneath their skin). To stop the itching, users often pick their skin or use needles to try and extract these imaginary bugs.

Physical symptoms include nausea, fatigue, headaches, respiratory infections, dry throat, perforated nasal septum, and when used intravenously, skin abscesses, hepatitis and AIDS.

Continued methamphetamine use may cause heart and respiratory problems, kidney damage, insomnia and weight loss.

stimulants

(amphetamines, methamphetamines, dextroamphetamines)
What to look for:
Pills, capsules, tablets. Methamphetamine is a pill, a yellow or white crystal, a waxy rock or powder and is lately called ice (the effects of methamphetamine were discussed with crack and cocaine); vials, plastic bags, syringes, rolled-up dollars, spoons, bottle caps and other drug cooking implements, matches, lighters.

Immediate effects:
The high lasts one half to two hours (ice eight to thirty hours) and is characterized by increased heart rate, blood pressure and respiratory rate. Pupils dilate, mouth is dry, appetite is curbed; headaches, sweating, dizziness, blurred vision, insomnia and anxiety may occur. Excessive doses produce fever, chest pains, loss of coordination, tremors, heart failure, strokes.

Users talk incessantly and feel indestructible. Violence and paranoia are common with stimulant users. As with cocaine, the high is followed by a crash of depression, which is particularly unpleasant and the avoidance of which leads to a psychological dependence.

Long-term effects:
Amphetamines create a quickly developed tolerance, a psychological dependence and possibly a physical dependence. Ha-

bitual users compensate for their crash and insomnia by using other drugs like "downers." This cross-addiction is common. Habitual users deteriorate physically and develop other disorders like skin conditions, ulcers, malnutrition and vitamin deficiencies. Psychosis with hallucinations, delusions and paranoia also occur. These are similar to cocaine psychoses but longer lasting. Violent behavior is not uncommon. Users who inject the drug are susceptible to skin abscesses, hepatitis, AIDS, lung disease, kidney disease.

sedative-hypnotics

Barbiturates, methaqualone, tranquilizers and others. Downers are taken orally, crushed and dissolved in liquid and injected.
What to look for:
Capsules (white, red, blue, yellow or red and blue), suppositories, liquid, powder, pill bottles, syringes, bottle caps or other cooking implements, matches, lighters.
Immediate effects:
Within twenty to forty minutes after swallowing barbiturates, the user feels high, dreamy and tranquil, experiencing contentment and a lack of inhibitions. Most downers' effects last four to six hours, although some last twice that long. Effects include slurred speech, poor reflexes, slow and unsteady walking, drunken-like behavior, tremors and mental impairment. The drugs also suppress breathing, heart rate and blood pressure so that users can overdose, become comatose, stop breathing and die.
Long-term effects:
Regular use of barbiturates creates a physical dependency. Tolerance also develops, so more drug is needed to produce the same effect. Chronic use leads to more bizarre and at times violent behavior. When the usual intake is reduced or diminished, physical withdrawal occurs. The withdrawal is more severe than heroin and can be lethal.

inhalants

Nitrous oxide, amyl and butyl nitrite, hydrocarbons, chlorocarbons

What to look for:

Solvents, glue, gasoline, Whiteout™, aerosol cans; clear, yellow liquid in ampules (amyl nitrite); butyl nitrite—a liquid sold in bottles; aerosol paint, handkerchiefs or plastic bags used for smelling of inhalants; small metal cylinders with attached balloon or pipe. Alcohol-like intoxicated behavior, impaired coordination and slurred speech, smell of solvents.

Immediate effects:

Use of inhalants is most common among seven to seventeen-year-olds. Vapors can come from everyday substances like whipped cream cans, airplane glue, cleaning fluids, gasoline and others. The high varies from product to product. Effects are similar: reduced blood pressure, heart rate and breathing rate. Amyl and butyl nitrite produce three to five minutes of confusion, dizziness and a weightless feeling. Coughing, nosebleeds, sneezing, hallucinations, loss of appetite and occasionally violent behaviors occur.

Inhalation of high concentration can lead to unconsciousness and choking on their own vomit, which can cause death.

Long-term effects:

Permanent brain damage. Kidney and bone marrow and liver damage can occur with even occasional use. Parents should watch for mental and muscle fatigue, and serious weight loss.

heroin and narcotics

What to look for:

Pills, white or light brown powder, tar-like substance, syringes, burned spoons, razor blades, bottles, aluminum foil packets, dollar bills or straws, pipes, matches, lighters, glassine envelopes, tourniquets, eyedroppers. Constricted pupils, slow breathing, lethargy, nodding, impaired judgment and coordination.

Immediate effects:

Heroin is ingested orally, smoked, mixed in water, heated and injected into flesh (skin popping) or a vein (mainlining). Heroin is considered among drug users as the ultimate high. After venous injection there is an initial feeling of nausea, followed by a warm rush that lasts less than a minute. The high lasts three to six hours and is characterized by a sense of calm and well-being. Pupils constrict, breathing is shallow, nodding alternating with excessive talking are present. Reduced sensitivity to pain, general body slowdown and sleep.

Long-term effects:
Narcotics are physically addicting and chronic users inject the drugs not to feel the rush but to avoid withdrawal symptoms of restlessness, cramps, tremors, sweating and chills, nausea, diarrhea, body pain, runny nose and gooseflesh. Withdrawal occurs four to six hours after the last dose. Chronic heroin use also causes reduced sex drive, lethargy and mood changes.

Overdose, seizures, coma and death can occur because of impurities in the drug, contaminated needles or taking too much drug. AIDS is a serious risk for those who use intravenous injections of heroin or other narcotics.

l s d

What to look for:
Powder, blotter paper, pills, clear liquid, gelatin squares, dilated pupils, bizarre behavior, rapidly changing moods.

Immediate effects:
Hallucinations, elevated blood pressure, and heart rate, dilated pupils, euphoria (good trip); or fear, agitation and paranoia (bad trip); experience of time distortion and sensory distortions (users claim to see sounds, or to taste colors). Immediate effects begin within ninety minutes and continue for nine to twelve hours.

Long-term effects:
Memory impairment, confusion, shortened attention span, which may or may not be permanent, occurs after extensive use. "Flashbacks" of a few seconds or a few hours may occur up to two years after use. No addiction.

anabolic steroids

What to look for:
Because of the life-threatening, adverse effects of steroids, few doctors prescribe them. Most steroid use among adoles-

cents and athletes is illicit. Pills, vials for liquid, needles, acne, needle marks in the muscles, rapid weight gain with maintenance or increase in lean-muscle mass, male-pattern baldness; increased hairiness, atrophied breasts, and, or deepened voice in females; breast development in males.

Immediate and short-term effects:
Alleged by athletes to increase aerobic capacity and to enhance endurance. Believed to increase lean-body mass while decreasing the percentage of body fat. May experience headaches, dizziness, muscle spasms and aches, urinary frequency, menstrual abnormalities, mood swings, irritability, aggressiveness, depression, increased or decreased energy levels, disturbances in appetite, changes in level of sexual interest, reduced attention span. Hallucinations and suicidal feelings may occur during use and withdrawal.

Long-term effects:
Most effects are reversible after stopping steroid use, however long-term effects of steroid drugs as they are used by illicit drug users have not as yet been scientifically studied. Addiction and withdrawal do occur.

INDEX

self-esteem, child's (*cont.*)
  expectations and, 68–69
  high, 16–17, 57–58, 236
  high-risk behavior and, 16–17,
    57, 219–20
  low, 16, 29, 208
  mirror and lamp and, 28, 29–30,
    55, 56
  parents as builders of, 17–18,
    20–21, 35–36, 40–41, 44, 47,
    51–52, 55, 56–57, 218–20,
    221
  praise and, 69–70, 127
  protectiveness vs. independence
    and, 37, 72–73
  setting limits and, 40–41, 70–71,
    76, 219
  sexual activity and, 16, 57,
    219–20
  social skills and, 16–17, 57
self-esteem, of parents:
  enhancing of, 33, 67, 76, 221
  importance of, 67
self-help groups, *see* support
    groups
self-reliance, 17, 37
sensory motor experiences, 62
separation, *see* loss and separation
seven-year-olds, 34, 59, 60, 64–66,
    84, 193
sex, 93–155
  age-appropriate attitudes about,
    104–6
  as basic need, 95–97
  boys' embarrassment about,
    112–13
  curiosity about, 101
  ethnic values and, 95, 98
  family values and, 95, 98, 109,
    111–12
  five- to twelve-year-olds'
    awareness of, 94
  jokes about, 137
  linking love with, 96–97, 99,
    106, 109, 111, 114, 123, 131,
    230–31
  in media, 15, 84, 94, 97, 123–24
  overemphasis on, 93

  privacy, personal rights and,
    102
  religious beliefs and, 95, 98
sex education, 93–129
  age-appropriate facts of, 102–4,
    105–6
  birth control and, 98–99, 131,
    233–34
  children's embarrassment about,
    108
  connecting menstruation with
    pregnancy in, 122–23
  describing intercourse in, 103–4,
    105, 110, 111, 113
  discussing feelings in, 120–23
  for eight- to ten-year-olds, 108–
    114, 130, 134–37
  for eleven-year-olds and up,
    114–27, 131, 151–53
  female anatomy and, 105, 110,
    113–14, 115, 117, 120–23
  for five- to seven-year-olds,
    100–108, 130, 131–34
  gender identity and, 100–101
  health professionals and, 136–37
  home-based, 19, 26, 97–99,
    128–29
  linking love with sex in, 96–97,
    99, 106, 109, 111, 114, 123,
    131
  making opportunities for,
    109–11
  male anatomy and, 105–6, 110,
    112, 113
  menstruation and, 113–14, 115,
    117, 121–23
  naming body parts in, 101, 107,
    110
  parents' discomfort with, 94,
    99, 104, 107
  parents' sexual history and,
    107–8, 118–20, 128
  parents' support system for,
    21–22
  role of media in, 15, 84, 94, 97,
    123–24
  in school, limitations of, 19, 26,
    98–99

ABOUT THE AUTHORS

Joanne Barbara Koch is an author, playwright and script-writer specializing in writing about human behavior. She is the author of the six books in the *Families In Touch Series,* federally endorsed books used in schools, prevention programs and homes to strengthen family bonds and prevent alcohol and other drug use and sexually transmitted diseases including AIDS. Over one million InTouch books are currently in use. Joanne also wrote the six-part children's television series "High Top Tower," which received awards from the U.S. Department of Education, the Office of Substance Abuse Prevention and an Emmy Award as the best children's television series broadcast in 1990. Joanne is coauthor of three college textbooks, one on child development and one on marriage and family, author of many magazine articles on family relationships and parenting, coauthor of a book on marriage counseling and sex therapy *The Marriage Savers,* and she has been coauthor with her husband Lew of a syndicated column on coping with family challenges. She has also written plays and teleplays on child abuse, domestic violence, and teenage pregnancy. She lives in Evanston, Illinois with her husband, Lewis. They have three grown children: Lisa, Rachel and Josh.

Linda Nancy Freeman, M.D., holds the Marion E. Kenworthy Chair in Psychiatry and is Assistant Professor at the Columbia University School of Social Work in New York City. She was the Training Director in Child Psychiatry and the Medical Director of the Children's Inpatient Psychiatry Unit at Rush Presbyterian St. Luke's Medical Center in Chicago. She is supervising editor of the *Families In Touch Series.* In addition to her practice, which has consisted of treating troubled children and youth and their families, she consults with and lectures to staffs of agencies providing services for families and children in communities with high rates of substance abuse, teenage pregnancy and AIDS. She has conducted research, lectured and written professional articles on the subjects of childhood depression, adolescent suicide and the effects of community violence on children. Currently, she is engaged in research to design effective models for the prevention of high-risk behaviors of children and youth such as smoking and drug abuse. She lives in New York City with her husband Carl Thompson.